Piaget – Vygotsky
The Social Genesis
of Thought

Edited by

Anastasia Tryphon
and Jacques Vonèche
Jean Piaget Archives
University of Geneva

Psychology Press
An imprint of Erlbaum (UK) Taylor & Francis

Psychology Press
27 Church Road
Hove
East Sussex, BN3 2FA
UK

British Library Cataloguing in Publication Data

A catalogue record for this book is available from the British Library

    ISBN 0-86377-413-X (Hbk)
    ISBN 0-86377-414-8 (Pbk)

Cover illustrations by Maia Geheb
Cover design by Joyce Chester
Printed and bound by Redwood Books, Trowbridge, Wilts.

Contents

List of contributors

Ioanna Berthoud-Papandropoulou, Université de Genève, Faculté de Psychologie et des Sciences de l'Education, 9 route de Drize, 1227 Carouge, Switzerland

Jean-Paul Bronckart, Université de Genève, Faculté de Psychologie et des Sciences de l'Education, 9 route de Drize, 1227 Carouge, Switzerland

Jens Brockmeier, University of Innsbruck/Linacre College, Oxford. Address for correspondence: Nassauische Str. 21, 10717 Berlin, Germany

Ann L. Brown, University of California at Berkeley, School of Education, Berkeley, CA 94720-1670, USA

Joseph C. Campione, University of California at Berkeley, School of Education, Berkeley, CA 94720-1670, USA

Helga Kilcher, Université de Genève, Faculté de Psychologie et des Sciences de l'Education, 9 route de Drize, 1227 Carouge, Switzerland

Eduardo Martí, Universitat de Barcelona, Departament de Psicologia Evolutiva i de la Educació, Passeig de la Vall d'Hebron 171, 08035 Barcelona, Spain

Kathleen E. Metz, University of California at Riverside, School of Education, Riverside, CA 92521, USA

Leslie Smith, Lancaster University, Department of Educational Research, Lancaster LA1 4YL, UK

Anastasia Tryphon, Université de Genève, Archives Jean Piaget, 18, route des Acacias, 1227 Acacias-Genève, Switzerland

René van der Veer, Rijks Universiteit Leiden, Faculty of Social and Behavioral Sciences, Department of Education, Pieter de la Court Bldg, Wassenaarseweg, 52, B.P. 9555, 2300 R.B. Leiden, The Netherlands

Ignasi Vila, Universitat de Girona, Departament de Psicologia, Plaça Santa Domènec, 9, 17071 Girona, Spain

Jacques Vonèche, Université de Genève, Archives Jean Piaget, 18, route des Acacias, 1227 Acacias-Genève, Switzerland

James V. Wertsch, Washington University, Department of Education, One Brookings Drive, St. Louis, MO 63130-4899, USA

Robert H. Wozniak, Bryn Mawr College, Dept. of Psychology, 101 North Merion Avenue, Bryn Mawr, PA 19010-2899, USA

CHAPTER ONE

Introduction

Anastasia Tryphon & Jacques Vonèche
Jean Piaget Archives, University of Geneva,
Switzerland

Leading up to the common centenary of the birth of Piaget and Vygotsky in 1996, the *Jean Piaget Archives Foundation* decided to devote its 14th advanced course to a comparison of Piaget's and Vygotsky's theories. The aim of the course was essentially to evaluate the state of the art in both schools at a peak moment for both of them and, by the same token, to tackle some basic oppositions between the two systems. The organisers wondered whether such oppositions were not superficial, and wanted to measure the depth and the width of the gap, if any, between them, to check whether such oppositions were not mainly due to over-orthodox and dogmatic followers eager to promote themselves by setting up easy targets that could be described as "men of straw". In other words, our epistemological problem was: are we faced here with two radically different world hypotheses, or are Piaget and Vygotsky comrades-in-arms against a common enemy, the old associationism, which is still a live issue for many psychologists today?

In order to answer this central question, this book will place the two thinkers and researchers in their common historical and critical context, especially in their common struggle to overcome the dichotomy between behaviourism and the psychologies of consciousness by constructing developmental views, designed to transcend the opposition without falling into the old pitfalls of nativism or empiricism—which would have meant replacing recent mistakes with errors that originated some 200–300 years ago. This book will thus review their common fascination and opposition (for obvious reasons) to Gestalt psychology, and their relationship to construction and interpretation, as well as the determinant role played by their selection of different units for the analysis of development in the type of theories they created. Their common claim to Rationality as a *telos* for development will be questioned, as well as their construction of social understanding and the mechanisms by which they explain the double character of any knowledge as being, at the same time, internal and external. In particular, the simple opposition between a Piagetian inside-out construction and a Vygotskyan outside-in one will be discussed. In the second part of this volume, several applications of Vygotsky's and Piaget's theories, especially in the classroom, will be discussed.

Our intention, in this introduction, is not to review or summarise all these important contributions but rather to limit ourselves to a brief comparison of Vygotsky and Piaget during the short period (1920–1934) in which they were contemporary in the scientific community. This was the time when Vygotsky was elaborating his historical-critical theory while Piaget's earlier publications in psychology were already widely read and his experiments replicated. Piaget's books, such as *Language and thought* (1923), *Judgement and reasoning* (1924), and *Physical causality* (1927) were being translated into several languages. No wonder, then, that Vygotsky read them and commented on them. It is also not surprising, given the originality of Piaget's books at the time, that Vygotsky was durably influenced by them in his own research and theorising. In their book, *Understanding Vygotsky*, René van der Veer and Jan Valsiner (1993) estimate that several hundred children were tested using Piagetian tasks in the then Soviet Union.

This interest in Piaget can be explained in two main ways: (1) the very process of constructing a new society and a new conception of human beings prompted Communist thinkers to look for alternative views of humanity; (2) the necessity for a revolutionary country to fight bourgeois science, represented in psychology by various forms of associationism. Piaget was one of the few possible choices. His book *Language and thought* was not a study of the acquisition of language by associating a word to a thing. It was not even a cognitive or an emotional approach to language acquisition. It was a study in communication among children interacting freely in the non-oppressive environment of *l'Ecole active*. In addition, this was also the time when Henri Wallon[1] advised Piaget to reverse his perspective on development by no longer explaining cognition by social factors, but socialisation by cognitive mental structuring:

> Instead of making sociability the agent ... of relational thought, I would rather reverse perspectives and say that, when, because of his/her mental development which is conditioned by organic development, the child becomes capable of holding simultaneously in mind two different viewpoints ... then sociability will be translated into relational thought.

Beside offering a theoretical alternative to Soviet psychologists, Piaget also presented a methodological one, because, if Anna O. (Freud & Breuer, 1895/1991) allegedly described psychoanalysis as the "talking-cure", Piaget's method could also be defined as a talking approach very similar in many respects to the psychoanalytic method. Piaget's "free conversations" (a term so important to him that he requested it as the French title of his interviews with the television journalist J.C. Bringuier, 1977) require a free-wheeling, relaxed attitude from children and a definite absence of prejudice from the adult interviewers. So the two dimensions so essential in Vygotsky's thinking, the historical-social and the language-grounded, were already present in Piaget's writings. Apparently the two men were ready for a dialogue.

This fact is especially obvious in Piaget's preface to the Russian edition of *Language and thought* (1932, pp.55–56, our translation) in which he wrote:

> Thanks to this preface, I have the great pleasure to express publicly my gratitude to the Soviet psychologists for their choice to undertake the translation of my work into Russian and especially for the organisation of the series of researches they are currently continuing. The goal of these researches is to complement and correct the work done in Geneva. I wish to disclose here in a few words the immense meaning for me of this beginning collaboration.
>
> In the work published here, the dominant idea is, so it seems to me, that children's thinking cannot be defined only by innate psycho-biological factors cum influences from the physical environment. One must also and most probably above all take into account the relationships between the child and the social milieu. I do not mean to say that the child reflects thoughts and opinions expressed around him; this would be banal. The very structure of individual thought depends on the social surroundings. Whenever one thinks for oneself alone in an egocentric way (so typical of childhood) one is subjected to one's own fancies, desires and personal

inclinations, and, as such, this sort of thinking is totally different from rational thought. Whenever one is under the systematic influence of a determined social milieu (like a child subjected to adult authority) one comes to think according to determined external rules. These rules generate verbalism and verbal syncretism in one's thinking or what is called legalism in one's own moral judgement. Conversely, the more individuals collaborate with one another, the more the rules of that collaboration develop and give a discipline to their thinking that shapes reason theoretically and practically. Egocentrism, constraint and collaboration are the three tendencies among which the child's developing thought oscillates and to which adult thinking is linked differently if it remains autistic or if it is integrated into one or another type of social organisation.

This is just an outline. In real life, social influences and individual organic aptitudes of thought are interwoven in a most subtle fashion. An important methodological problem necessarily arises here in the case of child psychology. If children's thinking depends on the relation between the individual and the social environment, how can we determine exactly what belongs to each of these two factors? When one works within one single social milieu (such as that of Genevan children) as I was forced to do, this determination is impossible. One has to study children in a totally different and very diversified social environment to make this determination.

This is the reason why I take great pleasure in having such qualified collaborators as some Soviet psychologists. They study children in a very different milieu from that I observed myself. Nothing is more useful to science than this confrontation of researches by Russian psychologists and by other psychologists in other countries.

As far as the specific results of the researches described in this volume are concerned, I should add so much to what was written in 1922 that I could not possibly do it in a short preface. I am well aware that my results are only fragmentary and questionable. But this does not distress me, because I know that others go on with such researches.

The sad reality seems to be that Piaget and Vygotsky never met, in spite of this preface. There are some speculations about a possible encounter in Moscow at a conference on Pedology, but here is no evidence of such a meeting between the two men, neither in Piaget's letters, nor in the recollections of Vygotsky's daughter. What seems more likely is that Piaget met Luria in 1929 at Yale University, New Haven, for the Congress of Psychology (a proven fact according to a letter from Piaget to I. Meyerson; see Fonds Meyerson, Paris: Université de Paris) and that both decided to collaborate in one form or another in a triangle: Luria, Vygotsky, Piaget.

So we are reduced to restating in this introduction what each of them wrote about the other.

VYGOTSKY ON PIAGET

In Chapter 2 of his own book *Thought and language* (1934/1962), Vygotsky criticised the concept of egocentrism as presented by Piaget. In Chapter 6 of the same book, Vygotsky discussed critically Piaget's distinction between spontaneous and "scientific" or learned concepts.

Vygotsky considers egocentrism as the cornerstone of Piaget's theoretical system. Indeed, there is no doubt that, for Piaget, mental development goes from the solipsism of the baby to the egocentrism of the child and from there to the decentration of the adult. But what Vygotsky regrets in this view is the linearity of such a conception of mental development. For Vygotsky, there is no such thing as a linear movement from egocentric to socialised language. On the contrary, his own observations, in Russia, show that egocentric language is much more than a mere companion to action to be disposed of at the right time. Egocentric language is, in addition, more than an emotional discharge of tension within the child or a simple means of expression. Egocentric language should be considered as an instrument of thinking adapted to all sorts of problem-solving situations, because it helps the child define a problem and build up plans for a possible solution.

Clearly, Vygotsky was fusing into one concept the notion of egocentric language *à la Piaget* and that of internal, private language. Therefore, Vygotsky could not accept Piaget's idea that egocentric language disappears with age. On the contrary, he maintained that school-aged children continue to use egocentric language as a means to a cognitive end, the only difference being that egocentric language, having been internalised, is less and less observable, although the mental processes at stake remain the same.

Thus, if for Piaget the developmental movement goes from the individual to the social, for Vygotsky language is originally and primarily social. Development goes from a lack of differentiation of the various functions of language towards a progressive differentiation and an hierarchisation of the initially fused functions. Egocentric language becomes a way for the child to transfer external social behaviour into intra-psychic functions.

At the very end of Chapter 2 of *Thought and language*, Vygotsky points out some conceptual "errors" made by Piaget. The first one bears on the notion of syncretism. Vygotsky feels that the child tends to think syncretically about unfamiliar situations or objects but not about familiar ones. Familiarity depends on the education received by the child. The role of educational methods is crucial here for Vygotsky.

Vygotsky's second criticism has to do with the degree of universality of the developmental trends observed by Piaget. Obviously, Piaget's discoveries are not universal but historically and socially grounded.

In Chapter 6 "The development of scientific concepts in childhood", Vygotsky deals with the distinction Piaget makes between spontaneous and non-spontaneous or scientific concepts that are learned in schools. Piaget considers spontaneous concepts as more revealing of the inner structure of children's thinking processes than learned ones. Vygotsky thinks that spontaneous and scientific concepts are intertwined in their development in a highly complex relationship that makes teaching effective only when it points to the road for development.

He takes the example of two concepts: exploitation, which is taught in school as a scientific concept, and the notion of brother, which is spontaneous. He shows that exploitation develops before brotherhood (as concepts not as behaviours!). In general, in Soviet Russian children, scientific concepts anticipate spontaneous ones. This demonstrates, according to Vygotsky, the structuring and generalising effects of schooling on children's awareness about their own mental processes. As he says, reflective consciousness comes about through the door of scientific concepts.

This discovery is, for Vygotsky, a specific instance of a more general problem: the relationship between development and learning. Vygotsky is opposed to Piaget's spontaneism in those matters; he thinks that formal education in one specific domain definitely influences development in other domains of knowledge by a sort of generalisation process that is essential for him.

PIAGET ON VYGOTSKY

Piaget's comments on Vygotsky are known mainly through his preface to the English translation of Vygotsky's *Thought and language* (Piaget, 1962, p.1): "It is not without sadness that an author discovers, twenty-five years after its publication, the work of a colleague who has died in the meantime, when that work contains so many points of immediate interest to him which should have been discussed personally and in detail."

But this statement does not mean that Piaget had no knowledge of Vygotsky's work. As a matter of fact, the preface to Kostyleff's book *La réflexologie et les essais d'une psychologie structurale*, published in 1947, shows that Piaget was not unaware of the various trends of Soviet psychology. Piaget was also a rather frequent visitor to the Soviet Union as evidenced by his short paper (re-published in this book) *Some impressions of a visit to soviet psychologists* (1956). He met with Luria and Leont'ev and evidently discussed Vygotskyan and post-Vygotskyan psychology.

Although he is in general agreement with Vygotsky, Piaget points out some differences. On egocentrism and egocentric language, Piaget acknowledges Vygotsky's criticisms but makes his own position more explicit using more recent studies carried out by him and his collaborators. However, he disagrees with Vygotsky's assumption that egocentric and communicative languages are both socialised but differ only by their functions. To illustrate the opposition between his and Vygotsky's positions, he gives the following example (Piaget, 1962, p.8):

> ... if an individual A mistakenly believes that an individual B thinks the way A does, and if he does not manage to understand the difference between the two points of view, this is, to be sure social behaviour in the sense that there is contact between the two, but I call such behaviour unadapted from the point of view of intellectual co-operation.

The writing of the word cooperation as co-operation indicates Piaget's will to appeal to mental operations in the structuring of social relations, which is the stand that Henri Wallon wanted him to take back in 1928 showing that logical operations are as important as social relations in the shaping of decentration in the child's mind.

This is followed by a detailed discussion by Piaget of the general agreement between Vygotsky and himself about spontaneous and scientific concepts and especially about the necessity to study carefully the origins and development of scientific concepts in the child, which Piaget had considered as his personal research programme since the 1930s. Piaget agrees with Vygotsky on the statement that "scientific and spontaneous concepts start from different points but eventually meet" (Piaget, 1962, p.11) and interjects the fact as a meeting point between the sociogenesis of scientific concepts and the psychogenesis of spontaneous structures. Piaget does not deny the influence of the environment on psychogenesis but raises the question of its part in development.

Once again, here, the differences are apparent. For Piaget development is a stage-like biological evolution, a succession of "events" to use Bronckart's apt phrase, whereas, for Vygotsky, development is a meaningful human generalisation. Piaget cannot accept such a concept as an adequate explanation of development. To him, generalisation is purely descriptive and not explanatory. Piaget (1962, p.12) is strongly convinced that development "consists in interiorised actions becoming reversible and coordinating themselves into patterns of structures subject to well-defined laws".

This process of development is necessarily socialised, as every logical operation entails communication under the form of co-operation. But this does mean for Piaget that there should be a difference between intra-individual and inter-individual operations. On the contrary, they must necessarily be identical in order to be truly operatory, as they both result from the same general explanatory mechanism of equilibration. As a corollary of this position, society is merely an addition of individuals. Therefore, in Piaget's own words (1960, p.234, our trans-lation) "asking whether intra-individual operations generate inter-individual operations or the reverse amounts to asking which is first from the hen or the egg".

This is Piaget's way of thinking in the 1960s and after. But as we have just seen, in his preface to the Russian translation of *Language and thought* (1932), Piaget thinks that "the very structure of individual thought depends on the social surroundings" (p.55).

Such a statement might seem surprising from Piaget's pen. But it is contemporary to the period during which Piaget was more concerned with the influence of social factors on development than he would be later on, especially when he commented, years later, on Vygotsky's book mainly at the personal request of Jerome Bruner and for an Anglo-Saxon audience considered by him, rightly or wrongly, as too sensitive to the role of the environment. Of course, Piaget could not anticipate then the present wave of nativism, not to mention "geneticism" (meaning here the role of genes) in the United States. He would most probably have reacted to it by putting the emphasis back onto the environment, so natural and spontaneous to him was the process of equilibration.

CONCLUSION

This debate has had the great merit of showing that there is some significant overlapping between Vygotsky's and Piaget's ideas. For instance, contrary to the generally held view, facile oppositions between the two thinkers are pointless: learning is not a solo performance for

Piaget, the development of knowledge is not simply inside/out for Piaget and outside/in for Vygotsky. Both views combine intrapsychical and interpsychical mechanisms. They both share actions as the starting block for further development. But they understand it differently. For Piaget, action is a natural event taking place in a natural environment. For Vygotsky it is a rich and meaningful human act constructed by history and society. The Kantian nature of Piaget's investigations contrasts with the cultural-historical approach of Vygotsky's researches. Piaget is more concerned with the development of universal processes for the validation of knowledge, and Vygotsky is more focused on psycho–socio-historical genesis and its interpretation. One is more devoted to the discussion of the constructive character of interpretation and the other more to the interpretive dimension of construction. As such they complement each other well, and they close the door to the strictly physicalistic structuralistic model of Gestalt with the "interpretative turn" of meaning-making conceived in complementary turns of logic, on the one hand, and rhetoric, on the other. But for one, logic means the logic of meanings and for the other, rhetoric means the rhetoric of thought and action, because both were very committed to the same sort of rationality grounded in the philosophy of the Enlightenment. Both viewed progress of the human mind as the conquest of the universal over the particular, the general over the local, and the timeless over the timely.

Therefore, at this time of their common centenary, it is not untimely, especially under the present social and historical circumstances, to think that the real heritage left for us by both Piaget and Vygotsky is the return to those domains of the human psyche that were neglected by both and the exploration of them, even-handedly, without any rationalistic prejudice, to rediscover in the so-called more primitive forms of behaviour their unavoidable value for ever and everyone. This, we think, is the most general conclusion to be drawn from this discussion of the genesis of thought according to Piaget and Vygotsky.

REFERENCES

Bringuier, J.-C. (1977). *Conversations libres avec Jean Piaget* [Conversations with Jean Piaget]. Paris: Robert Lafont.

Freud, S., & Breuer, J. (1991). Studien über Hysterie [Studies on hysteria]. Frankfurt: Fischer Verlag. [Original work published 1895.]

Maury, L. (1984). *Piaget et l'enfant* [Piaget and the child]. Paris: PUF.

Piaget, J. (1923). *Le langage et la pensée chez l'enfant* [Language and thought in the child]. Neuchâtel, Paris: Delachaux et Niestlé.

Piaget, J. (1924). *Le jugement et le raisonnement chez l'enfant* [Judgement and reasoning in the child]. Neuchâtel, Paris: Delachaux et Niestlé.

Piaget, J. (1927). *La causalité physique chez l'enfant* [The child's conception of physical causality]. Paris: Alcan.

Piaget, J. (1932). Predeslovie k rouskomou izdanio [Preface to the Russian edition]. In J. Piaget, *Rietch i michlenie ribienka*. Moscow and Leningrad: Itchliedgiz.

Piaget, J. (1960). Problèmes de la psychosociologie de l'enfance [Psycho-sociological problems in infancy]. In. G. Gurvitch (Ed.), *Traité de sociologie*, Tome 2 (pp. 229–254). Paris: PUF.

Piaget, J. (1962). Comments. In L. Vygotsky, *Thought and language* (pp.1–14). Cambridge MA: MIT Press.

Van der Veer, R., & Valsiner, J. (1993). *Understanding Vygotsky*. Oxford: Blackwell

Vygotsky, L. (1962). *Thought and language*. Cambridge, MA: MIT Press. [Original work published 1934.]

NOTE

1. Bulletin de la Société Française de Philosophie T. XXVIII, 1928, quoted by Liliane Maury in *Piaget et l'enfant*, 1984, p.39).

CHAPTER TWO

Qu'est-ce que l'intelligence? Piaget, Vygotsky, and the 1920s crisis in psychology

Robert H. Wozniak   *Bryn Mawr College, USA*

In the epilogue to their book, *Understanding Vygotsky*, Van der Veer and Valsiner (1991) point to the static, taxonomic contrasts of Piaget versus Vygotsky that litter the intellectual landscape and suggest, provocatively, (p.392) that "it is difficult for many psychologists to understand how Vygotsky could be 'a Piagetian' in much of his thinking (whilst being highly critical of Piaget in some areas) ...". They then discuss Vygotsky's dialectical use of criticism in the synthesis of ideas, the importance of his interdependence with the body of concepts embedded in the social discourse of the times, and the polysemantic nature of such discourse as a vehicle for continuity and change in thought and culture.

In the spirit of this epilogue, this chapter is organised around four themes. First, I characterise a persistent feature of social/intellectual discourse in the psychology of the 1920s—the so-called "crisis in psychology"—and suggest that the need to transcend age-old dichotomies at the heart of this crisis provided both the young Piaget and the young Vygotsky with a guiding and shared problematic.

Second, I argue that, in articulating conceptions of human psychological structure and process designed to transcend these dichotomies, Piaget and Vygotsky constructed developmental conceptions of mind/environment transaction exhibiting converging homologies that are numerous and striking, and I briefly document this claim by listing some of the more significant convergences.

Third, I suggest that despite a shared problematic and frequent convergence, the ideas of Piaget and Vygotsky were in fundamental opposition on at least two grounds—one having to do with normative criteria for development (equilibration vs. acculturation); the second with the assumed relationship between action and thought (continuity vs. discontinuity).

Finally, I outline a few highly tentative and preliminary suggestions about possible ways in which these oppositions might be synthesised developmentally.

CRISIS IN PSYCHOLOGY

Engendered by conflict between experimental psychology in the tradition of Wundt and Titchener—focused on the introspective, elementalistic analysis of consciousness without behaviour or development—and analytic objective psychology in the tradition of Pavlov, Bekhterev, and Watson—focused on behaviour and learning without consciousness—and intensified by the emergence of the holistic, structural critiques of the gestaltists, the 1920s were witness to an extraordinary proliferation of schools and views (see, for example, Murchison, 1926, 1930).

Among the perspectives prominent in the 1920s were traditional structuralism (still represented by Titchener and his many students, including Chelpanov in the USSR); pragmatic functionalism (with its roots in James, Baldwin, Dewey, and Angell, represented in Europe by Claparède among others); several distinct forms of behaviourism (Watson's, of course, but also the more theoretically sophisticated and ultimately more influential views of E.B. Holt and A.P. Weiss); reflexologies (most notably those of Pavlov and Bekhterev); the reactology of Kornilov; gestalt psychology (Wertheimer, Köhler, and Koffka); the early topological conceptions of Lewin; the personalism of Stern; the semiotic psychology of Karl Bühler; and the comparative genetic approach of Werner.

It would be hard to imagine a richer, more challenging body of social/intellectual discourse; but it was also discourse riddled with age-old dichotomies—rationalism and empiricism, subjectivity and objectivity, analysis and synthesis (including the systemic relation of part to whole and whole to part), invariance and transformation. The problem of the nature and relationship of thought to things—temporarily submerged in the first wave of enthusiasm for the new scientific psychology—had resurfaced with a vengeance.

Traditional psychology was *subjective* in its insistence on introspective method and *adevelopmental* in its emphasis on universal attributes of conscious mind; reflexology and behaviourism were *objective* in their rejection of introspection in favour of external observation but *equally adevelopmental* in ascribing change to universal laws of learning. Furthermore, both the traditional view and objectivism were *empiricist* in their insistence on the primacy of experience and *analytic* in their approach.

In contrast to these views, on the other hand, gestalt psychologists were arguing both that the events of mental life are, as a rule, *coherent wholes* whose properties—form, sense, and value—are not discoverable in their isolated parts, and that such mental structures exist prior to experience and serve to organise it. In other words, where traditional psychology and objectivism were empiricist and analytic, the gestalt view was *rationalistic* and *synthetic*. However it too was largely adevelopmental in that structures were viewed as a priori constituents of mind.

That this situation served as a framework for the young Piaget's defence of his own distinctive perspective is well known. In the final chapter of the *Child's conception of physical causality* (Piaget, 1927/1966) and then again, in *Origins of intelligence in children* (Piaget, 1936/1963), for example, Piaget faults empiricism for failure to recognise the active principle in mind, and gestalt psychology for failure to understand the principles of structural transformation inherent in development.

It is undoubtedly less well known that Vygotsky also articulated many of his views in criticism and synthesis of these perspectives. In a manuscript, entitled *Istoricheskii smysl psikhologicheskogo krizisa* [The historical meaning of the crisis in psychology], written in 1926, but only first published in the *Collected works*, Vygotsky (1982) developed what was, for the period, a sophisticated critique of the naive empiricism implicit in both the traditional subjective introspectionism of consciousness (especially as elaborated in the USSR by Chelpanov) and the objective psychologies of behaviour (especially as exemplified in the reflexologies of Pavlov and Bekhterev).

Arguing that facts are method-sensitive and theory-laden, Vygotsky attacked the empiricist belief that valid knowledge must or even can be grounded in direct observation (whether introspective or external) and empiricism's consequent failure to recognise the indirect, interpretive, inferential nature of scientific knowledge construction and validation. Empiricism, in other words, tended to construe experience as imposing itself on the subject and failed to recognise the subject's own, active organising activity.

In 1930, as his own dialectically reconstructed notion of structure began to emerge, Vygotsky also became quite critical of the adevelopmental conception of gestalts as universal a priori forms. For Vygotsky, the emphasis was on the constant process of transformation and reorganisation, the formation of novel structures and the functioning of such structures in the further synthesis of even newer forms. The similarity of this analysis to that of Piaget is evident.

What is even more interesting is that in articulating conceptions of human psychological structure and process designed to transcend the dichotomies inherent in the crisis in psychology, Piaget and Vygotsky also took somewhat parallel routes—constructing developmental conceptions of mind/environment transaction in which the intent was to retain the empiricist emphasis on adaptive function and the introspectionist concern with mind and consciousness, while avoiding extremes of both objectivism and subjectivism. It is little wonder that their views converged in numerous ways.

CONVERGING HOMOLOGIES

Thus, for example, Piaget and Vygotsky both emphasised interaction—mind as an active, organising principle, collaborating with the environment in transforming thought towards an increasingly delicate adaptation of thought to things and things to thought. Inherent in this view for both were principles of assimilation—the notion that active selective and co-ordinating mechanisms give action and thought stability and coherence and relieve the organism from direct dependence on external stimuli—and environmental relativity—the idea that to be psychologically effective, the environment must be appropriate to the psychological organisation of the developing child—the "assimilable" (Piaget) or "relational" (Vygotsky) environment.

Piaget and Vygotsky both adopted dialectical conceptions of development as proceeding from opposition between interdependent contraries and progressing by transcending opposition in a transformation and hierarchical integration of structures. Both focused on issues of structure defined in terms of relational totalities arising from interaction among component parts. In this regard, both took the view that structure and function are interdependent and that organisation is hierarchical and systemic—with qualitative features varying with level, and higher levels integrating and therefore retaining lower levels. Piaget and Vygotsky also shared a concern with the construction of meaning, recognising that cognising the environment is an act of sense-making.

Lastly, both employed a clinical research method that was fundamentally intersubjective—involving the co-construction of knowledge between the psychologist-as-subject and the subject-as-subject and departing in at least three ways from the canons by which experimental method is supposed to guarantee objectivity—(a) the independent variable cannot be set at predefined levels independent of the subject, but depends on the subject's initial level of development; (b) manipulation of the independent variable is quasi-systematic— questions, prompts, and actions-on-objects are organised to take advantage of the subject's and the experimenter's changing levels of understanding; (c) dependent variables are not, as a rule, quantified observations, but statement-action-object-complexes—protocols that stand in need of interpretation. These and other points of convergence stand as testimony to a shared problematic.

OPPOSITIONS

At the same time, however, there were also many substantive ways in which the young Vygotsky's views differed from those of the young Piaget. Among these differences, there were, I think, two that involved contradictory oppositions of particular importance. To clarify the nature of these oppositions, the essence of Vygotsky's cultural-historical theory must be briefly described.

Starting from the assumption that psychological function in the acculturated adult human being must be understood in relation to its phylogenetic, socio-historical, and ontogenetic origins, Vygotsky adopted a *comparative developmental method*, that is, he proceeded from the additional assumption that the study of the respective psychological processes of animals, preliterate peoples, and children can shed light on these origins (see, especially, Vygotsky & Luria, 1930/1993). From work with animals, especially Köhler's (1925) *The mentality of apes*, Vygotsky characterised the nature and biological function of primate intelligence as invention leading to tool use. When habitual reactions fail, immediate action is inhibited in favour of mental invention of new means–ends relationships permitting the creation of tools. Tool use marks a critical turning point in the course of phylogenesis.

Borrowing from Lévy-Bruhl's (1925) *How natives think* and Thurnwald's (1922) *Psychologie des primitiven Menschen* [Psychology of primitive man]—work premised on the notion (Vygotsky & Luria, 1933, p.82) that "the comparison of different social institutions of different societies ... [can] establish sequences of historical development and differences in *functional* social structures that foster higher mental processes"— Vygotsky (1930/1993) argued that "primitive" psycho-logical processes are natural, direct, and concrete. With socio-historical evolution, tool use in communal labour leads to increasingly complex cultural forms of behaviour—mnemonic devices, gestures, forms of enumeration, and especially language and writing. While these cultural means function initially as external signs for others, over time and by their very nature, such signs reflect back on and gradually reorganise the mental operations that they externalise. Acculturated psychological functions, in other words, become mediated and indirect—social and cultural not only in their content, but in their mechanism.

Finally, drawing from the early work of Piaget (1923, 1924, 1926, 1927/1966), Stern (1927), Bühler (1919) and others, but most especially from the highly innovative studies of children's acquisition of artificial means in the control of memory, attention, and abstraction carried out with his co-workers (e.g. Leont'ev, 1931/1983, 1932; Vygotsky, 1929; Vygotsky & Luria, 1930/1993), Vygotsky offered a theory of the ontogenetic reorganisation of psychological function through increasing literacy. The course of ontogenesis, like that of cultural history, consists of a series of transitions.

The child's starting state is one of *precultural, primitive functioning that is immediate, direct, and natural.* The primary system of inter-relations among psychological functions such as attention, perception, memory, and thought—which Vygotsky called "the systemic structure of consciousness"—is given biologically. In the course of the child's development, however, the primary, biologically given system becomes radically reorganised (i.e. consciousness becomes restructured) in a process that consists first of the child's mastery of the use of external objects as semiotic tools to gain mediated, indirect control of internal processes, then to acquisition of the more abstract and conventionalised semiotic tools of literacy, and finally to the internalisation of such semiotic systems with consequent reorganisation of function—attention, perception, memory, thought now take on a mediated, self-regulated (and hence "specifically human") form.

Finally, and particularly in the last years of his life, Vygotsky stressed the fact that the semiotic tools that the child masters are transpersonal in two different but related ways. First, they are acquired by the child in the context of hierarchical social interactions—interactions (especially those involving communicative speech) with more experienced others (Vygotsky, 1935). Second, human beings are born into a sociocultural world already defined in large part by systems of historically derived social meanings embedded in already existing forms of symbolic discourse (Vygotsky, 1934/1987). Although at the time of his premature death, Vygotsky had not, as far as I know, articulated the implications of this last point in any detail, the general implication that he did draw, and to which I will return in the final section of this chapter, is that sociality and historicity are embedded at the core of human meaning-making.

Cultural-historical theory is a powerful and provocative account, manifesting both strengths and weaknesses. Probably its greatest strength is its view of acculturation as a developmental transformation of mind through the internalisation of systems of signs that reflect the social history of the child's culture. Although this idea is far from theoretically well defined in Vygotsky's writings, the basic point is clear. In development, human nature is not simply socialised, it is *transformed* by society and history embedded in the very system of meanings by which humans make sense of their experience and action. Such a view carries implications for problems as diverse as the structure and development of mind, the nature of meaning, the nature and psychological function of semiotic systems, and the role of history, culture, and literacy in psychological process.

The greatest weaknesses of cultural historical theory, in my view—aside from or perhaps because of the fact that Vygotsky's premature death and subsequent political events in the Soviet Union left the theory in an almost embryonic state—involve its failure to address the issue of a normative criterion for development and its overemphasis on discontinuity between the primary, biological and the secondary, socially derived systems of functions, between the so-called "pre-cultural, primitive" state of mind in the young child and the acculturated mind of the adult—in effect, between practical and reflective intelligence. In clarifying the nature of these weaknesses, it is useful to oppose them to Piaget's rather different views.

Normative criteria for development
The first opposition has to do with specification of normative criteria for development. What constitutes development? How can we determine that X is more developed than Y? How do we know, for example, that human reflective intelligence is of a higher order than the practical intelligence of the ape? How do we know that the technologically acculturated intellect of 20th-century Western "man" is more developed than that of our stone-age ancestors—not that of contemporary pre-literate peoples, another problem and one to which I will return shortly—and how do we know that the mind of the adult is more developed than that of the child? If development is viewed as normative—and both Vygotsky and Piaget so viewed it—then development must be distinguished from mere change.

As far as I can see, there are at least two general approaches that can be taken to this problem. One is universalist; the other historical. *Universalism* involves specification of domain-general developmental criteria. This is clearly the path that was taken by Piaget. Relative equilibrium (in terms of the joint co-ordination of parts and whole, in the early theory, or the number and scope of the compensations, in the mature theory) served Piaget as a domain-independent criterion of development. With this criterion, development was simply defined as change leading from lower to higher forms of equilibrium.

An historical approach is one based solely on temporal order of emergence. That which is developmentally later is developmentally more advanced. Although, as far as I know, Vygotsky never explicitly addressed the criterion issue (and would quite probably have eschewed an historical criterion if he had—for reasons shortly to be addressed), an historical criterion is nevertheless implied in the comparative developmental method. Psychological function in the technologically acculturated adult human being is taken as normative with regard to children, preliterate peoples, and animals. Developments presumed to be evolutionarily later are presumed to be evolutionarily higher.

Needless to say, this is a problematic position. In addition to its obviously questionable socio-political overtones, it is logically flawed in at least two ways. First, it makes no provision for regression. Dissolution of a hierarchical system only makes sense in the context of independent criteria for hierarchical level. To the best of my knowledge, Vygotsky never specified such criteria—indeed, the whole concept of the systemic structure of consciousness in Vygotsky was vague at best—and, as Van der Veer and Valsiner (1991) have correctly pointed out, Vygotsky was quite inconsistent in his handling of the concept of regression.

Second, and more seriously, the comparative developmental method, both in its cross-species and its cross-historical aspects is founded on quicksand. The issue is simple—there is no way to know in what way or to what extent modern sub-human primates, *evolved for specialised niches over the same millennial course required for human evolution*, are similar psychologically to any ancestor we might share in common. Nor, on similar grounds, is there reason to believe that adults grown to maturity in modern preliterate societies somehow provide a window into the human cultural past. Data on primate intelligence and cultural variation in psychological function may be of interest in their own right. Employed comparatively, they may even serve a valuable heuristic function for studies of cognition wherever it is found, but it is highly questionable to use such data in the service of developmental analysis.

Continuity/discontinuity between action and thought

The second opposition has to do with the question of continuity or discontinuity between practical intelligence—intelligence in action—and reflective, symbolic (or, for Vygotsky, mediated) intelligence. Piaget founded his entire enterprise on the assumption of continuity between action and thought—the inventions of the sixth stage of sensorimotor development involve the mental combination of schemes of action and make use of symbolic representations directly derived from action via imitation. Indeed, the very operations utilised by logical and mathematical thought (e.g. posing, adding, or subtracting classes), develop, for Piaget, from the interiorisation of action (e.g. joining or separating objects in space).

Vygotsky, as we have already seen, took a very different perspective. Although there is always an element of continuity in any dialectical change and on this, as on many other issues, Vygotsky was occasionally ambivalent, the general sense of his view was that the inventive and ultimately internal use of tools is what makes humans human. Reorganisations in the systemic structure of consciousness that occur through the internalisation of social semiotic systems raise the child from a "pre-cultural, primitive" state to one that is "truly human".

In a paper written in 1928 on development and education of atypical children, for example, Vygotsky (1983) argued for "deep conflict" (p.169) between natural and cultural lines of development. The mastery of cultural tools has a profound effect, he argued, on the natural, biological functions of the child. Children's old, natural ways of thinking are pushed aside and destroyed. This too is a problematic position; and to clarify the nature of the problem inherent in this view, I conclude by discussing two possible extensions of Vygotsky suggested by these contradictions with Piaget.

TOWARDS THE FUTURE

Internalisation of social semiotic systems

As I read Vygotsky, there is something seriously wrong with his developmental juxtaposition of the acquisition of tools of literacy (reading, writing, arithmetic, strategic memory) and the internalisation of a speech system. Infants use symbolic gestures at 10 months, possibly earlier (Bates, 1979). First symbolic use of words emerges at the end of the first year, mental inventions and two-word grammar by or before the middle of the second year; and by 3, children are making very effective use of communicative speech. That the use of speech for thinking awaits the ultimate fate of egocentric ("private") speech at ages 5, 6, 7, or later seems, on the face of it and for a variety of reasons having to do with what we now know about frequency and form in private speech (Berk, 1992), to be highly implausible.

It is similarly implausible that the participation of speech in the process of concept formation requires anything like the slow, elaborate, process outlined in either of Vygotsky's major series of concept formation studies (see, especially, Vygotsky, 1934/1987). This is not to argue against the notion that the semantic system forms slowly—that goes without saying—but rather to suggest that a consistent Vygotskian perspective demands participation of speech at a much earlier point in development than that at which Vygotsky typically focused his attention.

As Vygotsky frequently emphasised, the child (and to this I would add "from early infancy") experiences the world in the context of communicative speech/action transactions. Encountering cups in a variety of contexts, a 12-month-old, for example, may be told: "Hold the cup", "Let's put milk in the cup", "Don't drop the cup", "The cup will break if you do that", "The cup is empty", or "Give me the cup" as the cup is handed back and forth, filled by one and emptied by the other, turned upside-down by one, righted by the other, dropped by one, retrieved by the other and so on. It would be fully consistent with the general tenor of Vygotsky's views if, even at 12 months, the common lexical item "cup" were to serve as a nexus around which the child begins to abstract and generalise experience, not only with sets of objects in the world, but with other people, and even with the relationships between objects and others. It is in the spirit of Vygotsky to suggest that the development of abstract, categorical concepts—in other words the very transition from sensorimotor thought of the infant to the symbolic thought of even the youngest pre-schooler—occurs in and through the internalisation of speech.

Furthermore, as Vygotsky constantly stressed, words are embedded in discourse that conveys cultural meaning. This discourse, in turn, depends on the fact that lexical items—lexical items that, on this account, participate in the child's earliest conceptualisations of experience—pre-exist the child in socially developed systems of meanings and articulated beliefs. These meaning systems, sociocultural ideologies, exist in social structures at all levels of complexity (friendship pairs, families, peer groups, schools, religious groups, subcultures, and societies).

This, it seems to me, has an extraordinary implication for theory of mind—one that Vygotsky clearly saw but did not articulate in any detail.

In a patriarchal society, for example, the sentences a child hears and the books a child reads will reflect and foster gender distinctions. Relative to female nouns and pronouns, male nouns and pronouns might, for instance, be paired more frequently with action and mastery verbs (running, jumping, exploring, fixing). A child growing up in such a society and developing concepts of "male" and "female" through experience with men and women synthesised in the context of gendered discourse will automatically come to possess a meaning system that reflects the cultural values implied in this discourse. If the elaboration of social meaning begins with the transition from sensorimotor to abstract thought, this transition, occurring through the internalisation of a social semiotic system, is truly a process of acculturation. Sociality and historicity are embedded in the very core of human conceptualisation.

Action and interaction

For all of Piaget's reasons, I am persuaded by the argument for continuity of action and logic (see Chapman, 1988, for an excellent discussion of this issue). The distinction and developmental relationship between reversibility of mental action and revertibility of physical action makes excellent and intuitive sense. Furthermore, it seems to me highly implausible that development, at any point, is other than fundamentally continuous, the emergence of new forms notwithstanding, and anyone who has read *Origins of intelligence* (Piaget 1936/1952) with care cannot help but recognise this view in Piaget. On the other hand, I find myself equally persuaded, as I have just suggested, that social meaning as content (e.g. "that's grandmother's cup and we have to be *very* careful of it"—which says far more about the child's social relationship to his grandmother than it does about the cup) is abstracted and generalised from experience in the context of and through social discourse.

Is it possible to bring these ideas together into a unified conception? Let me suggest a possible route to such a view. In Piaget's concept of sensorimotor action and his distinction between real and ideal totalities, one can, I think, find implicit the notion that schemes underlying action and goals towards which action is organised furnish hierarchical systems of expectations against which the success of an action is evaluated. The meaning of any action therefore includes the specification of end states and expectations, knowledge of the general structure or scheme for that action, and some specification of the range of variation in action necessary and permissible under different environmental conditions.

Within the broad category of action, one particular class of actions stands out as unique: the category of *inter*actions—actions with people rather than on objects. Interactions, I would argue, differ from other actions in the nature of the expectational control that the cognitive system exerts as action unfolds. When a 12-month-old reaches out to pick up a cup, she must feed forward expectations about how long it will take her hand to make contact with the cup, the relative weight and solidity of the cup, the relative lack of attraction between cup and table, and so forth. These expectations, which are part of the normal function of the sensorimotor scheme and are therefore not in awareness, serve to regulate her reaching action, to serve as parameters against which the results of action will be evaluated.

When that same infant reaches up to her mother to indicate that she wishes to be picked up, it can no longer be a case of acting only in terms of her own expectations. Her action must now take into account her knowledge of the expectations that the other has concerning her action and quite possibly and certainly eventually her knowledge of her mother's expectations concerning her own expectations about the results of her action. Successful interaction, in other words, depends on mutuality of expectation—on what is, fundamentally, intersubjectivity.

By intersubjectivity, I mean the reciprocity of intention between knowing subject and known object that obtains when the known object happens itself to be a knowing, thinking, feeling subject. This is, it seems to me, the very essence of human sociality and as such it appears to have important consequences for any theory of human cognition. As the past 20 years of infancy research have persuasively documented, babies appear to be born into the world with a cognitive system preadapted to developing mutuality of expectation, intersubjectivity, and interaction (Brazelton, Koslowski, & Main, 1974; Gianino & Tronick, 1988; Stern, 1977; Trevarthen & Hubley, 1978). The development of practical reciprocity, in other words, antedates the development of reflective reciprocity.

If so, this suggests that the typical assumption that babies are born preadapted for acting on objects and become socialised by learning how to interact with that special category of strangely variable and unpredictable objects called people, must be modified in favour of the premise that babies are preadapted to the mutuality of expectation that defines intersubjectivity. Indeed, it might very well be that what infants must learn is that actions on objects are a special case—one in which you don't have to concern yourself with what the objects think you happen to be doing.

Human intelligence, in other words, especially as it is biologically motivated, must be organised from the outset in its function and development not only towards the construction of logic and the elaboration of the physical world but towards the acquisition of cultural meanings and the elaboration with others of shared reality in conjoint activity around objects. The child, I would suggest, develops not only through constant striving to understand but through determined effort to become a person, like-minded and companionate with other people.

REFERENCES

Bates, E. (1979). *The emergence of symbols: Cognition and communication in infancy*. New York: Academic Press.

Berk, L.E. (1992). Children's private speech: An overview of theory and the status of research. In R.M. Diaz & L.E. Berk (Eds.), *Private speech: From social interaction to self-regulation* (pp.17–53). Hillsdale, NJ: Lawrence Erlbaum Associates Inc.

Brazelton, T.B., Koslowski, B., & Main, M. (1974). The origins of reciprocity: The early mother–infant interaction. In M. Lewis & L.A. Rosenblum (Eds.), *The effect of the infant on its caregiver* (pp.49–76). New York: Wiley.

Bühler, K. (1919). *Abriss der geistigen Entwicklung des Kindes* [Overview of child's mental development]. Leipzig: Quelle und Meyer.

Chapman, M. (1988). *Constructive evolution: Origins and development of Piaget's thought*. Cambridge: Cambridge University Press.

Gianino A., & Tronick, E. Z. (1988). The mutual regulation model: The infant's self and interactive regulation and coping and defensive capacities. In T.M. Field, P.M. McCabe, & N. Schneiderman (Eds.), *Stress and coping across development* (pp.47–68). Hillsdale, NJ: Lawrence Erlbaum Associates Inc.

Köhler, W. (1925). *The mentality of apes*. New York: Harcourt, Brace.

Leont'ev, A.N. (1932). The development of voluntary attention in the child. *Journal of Genetic Psychology, 40*, 52–81.

Leont'ev, A.N. (1983). Razvitie vysshikh form zapominaniia [Development of a higher form of memory]. In A.N. Leont'ev, *Izbrannye psikhologicheskie proizvedeniia, Tom. 1* [Selected psychological works, Vol 1] (pp.31–64). Moskva: Pedagogika. [Original work published 1931.]

Lévy-Bruhl, L. (1925). *How natives think (Les fonctions mentales dans les sociétés inférieures)*. New York: Knopf.

Murchison, C. (Ed.). (1926). *Psychologies of 1925*. Worcester, MA: Clark University.

Murchison, C. (Ed.). (1930). *Psychologies of 1930*. Worcester, MA: Clark University Press.

Piaget, J. (1923). *Le langage et la pensée chez l'enfant* [The language and thought of the child]. Neuchâtel: Delachaux et Niestlé.

Piaget, J. (1924). *Le jugement et le raisonnement chez l'enfant* [Judgment and reasoning in the child]. Neuchâtel: Delachaux et Niestlé.

Piaget, J. (1926). *La représentation du monde chez l'enfant* [The child's conception of the world]. Paris: Alcan.

Piaget J. (1952). *The origins of intelligence in children*. New York: International Universities Press. [Original work published 1936.]

Piaget, J. (1966). *The child's conception of physical causality*. London: Routledge & Kegan Paul. [Original work published 1927.]

Stern, D. (1977). *The first relationship: Infant and mother*. Cambridge, MA: Harvard University Press.

Stern, W. (1927). *Psychologie der frühen Kindheit bis zum sechsten Lebensjahre* [Early childhood psychology, up to 6 years]. Leipzig: Quelle und Meyer,

Thurnwald, R. (1922). Psychologie des primitiven Menschen [The psychology of primitive man]. In G. Kafka (Ed.), *Handbuch der vergleichenden Psychologie* [Handbook of comparative psychology] (Band I, pp.145–320). München: Reinhardt.

Trevarthen, C., & Hubley, P. (1978). Secondary intersubjectivity: Confidence, confiding and acts of meaning in the first year. In A. Lock (Ed.), *Action, gesture and symbol. The emergence of language* (pp.183–229). London: Academic Press.

Van der Veer, R. & Valsiner, J. (1991). *Understanding Vygotsky. A quest for synthesis*. Oxford: Blackwell.

Vygotsky, L.S. (1929). The problem of the cultural development of the child. *Journal of Genetic Psychology, 36*, 415–434.

Vygotsky, L.S. (1935). *Umstvennoe razvitie detei v protsesse obucheniia* [Mental development of children during education]. Moskva-Leningrad: Gosudarstvennoe uchebno-pedagogicheskoe izdatel'stvo.

Vygotsky, L.S. (1982). *Sobranie sochinenii. Tom. 1. Voprosy teorii i istorii psikhologii* [Collected works. Vol. 1 Questions of theory and history of psychology]. Moskva: Pedagogika.

Vygotsky, L.S. (1983). Defektologiia i uchenie o razvitii i vospitanii nenormal'nogo rebenka [Defectology and the study of the development and education of abnormal children]. In L. S. Vygotsky, *Sobranie sochinenii. Tom. 5. Osnovy defektologii* (pp.166–173). [Collected works, Vol. 5. Fundamentals of defectology]. Moskva: Pedagogika. [Original work written 1928.]

Vygotsky, L.S. (1987). Thinking and speech. In L.S. Vygotsky, *The collected works. Volume 1. Problems of general psychology* (pp.39–285). New York: Plenum Press. [Original work published 1934.]

Vygotsky, L.S. & Luria, A.R. (1993). *Studies on the history of behavior: Ape, primitive, and child*. (Edited and translated by V.I. Golod & J.E. Knox). Hillsdale, NJ: Lawrence Erlbaum Associates Inc. [Original work published 1930.]

CHAPTER THREE

The role of abstract rationality in Vygotsky's image of mind[1]

James V. Wertsch *Washington University, USA*

For somewhat different reasons and in somewhat different ways both Jean Piaget and Lev Semenovich Vygotsky were committed Enlightenment rationalists. As part of his general philosophical orientation Piaget embraced universal human rationality as the *telos* (Kaplan, 1983) of human development. Vygotsky took a similar position, but as a Marxist he also viewed rationality as an essential tool for constructing a centrally planned economy and state. Piaget's commitment to such rationality was manifested in his claim that the development of intelligence is a matter of increasing equilibrium defined in terms of logico-mathematical structures. For Vygotsky, it was reflected in his claims about how increasing levels of abstraction and generalisation attach to "genuine" and "scientific" concepts.

My purpose here will not be to make a full-fledged comparison of these two "titans of developmental theory" (Bruner, 1986, p.136). Each produced such a rich and extensive body of ideas that this task is far beyond what it is possible to accomplish in one chapter. Instead, I shall focus on Vygotsky's ideas and argue that although many of his theoretical pronouncements and empirical analyses situate him clearly in the camp of Enlightenment rationality, the picture of human mental life he envisioned was actually somewhat more complex and even ambivalent. Specifically, I shall argue that there are some major inconsistencies in his writings, in that he sometimes strongly espoused abstract rationality as the *telos* of development but on other occasions assumed that other forms of mental functioning occupy that role. I shall also argue that such inconsistency reflects a struggle between basic philosophical commitments, on the one hand, and the results of analysing the complexities of human speech, on the other.

VYGOTSKY THE ENLIGHTENMENT RATIONALIST

As dedicated participants in the effort to carry out the first grand socialist experiment in the form of the Soviet Union, Vygotsky and his students and colleagues in the 1920s and 1930s were committed to formulating a psychology grounded in Marxism. To be sure, major divisions emerged over the years among the various parties involved in this effort (see Zinchenko, 1985). However, the fundamental tenets accepted by all included a belief in some form of universal human rationality and a belief in the evolution or progress of such rationality. The rationality involved was viewed as being accessible to all humans, although some groups and individuals were viewed as lagging behind others in their mastery of it.

Based on this assumption Vygotsky and his colleagues made several distinctions within the "genetic domains" (Wertsch, 1985) of sociocultural history and ontogenesis between "higher" and "lower" forms of mental functioning. For example, with regard to sociocultural history, Vygotsky and Luria argued in *Studies on the history of behaviour: Ape, primitive, and child* (1930/1993) that "cultural" peoples are distinct from "primitive" peoples in the forms of language and thinking they employ. Specifically, "primitives" were viewed as not having the requisite "psychological tools," or "mediational means" (Wertsch, 1985) for higher mental functioning. According to Vygotsky & Luria (1930/1993, pp.118–121):

> The primitive man does not have concepts; abstract, generic names are completely alien to him. He uses the word differently than we do ... All the characteristics of primitive thinking can be reduced to this main fact, that is, to the fact that instead of [conceptual] notions, it operates with complexes ... The main progress in thought development affects a shift from the first mode of using a word as a proper name to the second mode, where the word is a sign of a complex, and finally to the third mode, where a word is a tool or means for developing the concept ... [T]he cultural development of thinking is found to have [a] close connection with the history of the development of human language.

In making such claims about thinking and language, Vygotsky was making strong assumptions about universal human rationality and progress. "Primitive thinking" in general differs from modern forms in that the former does not rely on abstract concepts. Such abstract concepts are viewed as emerging at a later historical point. One of the results of this formulation is that what we would today call cross-cultural differences were for Vygotsky and his colleagues "cross-historical" in nature (see Wertsch, 1985).

The tendency to view history as universal human progress reflects what Shweder (1991, pp.117–118)) terms "evolutionism", a view in which "diverse beliefs and understandings" are taken to be "steps on an ideational Jacob's ladder moving progressively in the direction of the normative endpoint". Such a critique of evolutionism is at the foundation of much of the thinking in contemporary cultural anthropology and cultural psychology. In contrast to grounding cultural and psychological analyses in assumptions about "psychic unity" (Jahoda, 1993) and the evolution thereof, figures such as Boas (1911, 1920) focused on the qualitative differences among cultures and argued that each has its own historical, psychological, and social configuration and must be understood in its own terms (see Lucy & Wertsch, 1987). This critique and the ensuing theoretical framework outlined by Boas and his students such as Sapir (1931) and Whorf (1956) are what provide the basic framework for much of today's cultural anthropology in the West.

In addition to playing a role in his account of sociocultural history, Vygotsky's evolutionism appears at several points in his writings about other genetic domains. In particular, it plays an important role in his account of the ontogenesis of concepts. Chapters 5 and 6 of *Thinking and speech* (1934/1987) are very instructive in this regard and hence bear close analysis. Chapter 5 is titled "An experimental study of concept development" and is primarily concerned with the transitions Vygotsky saw from "heaps" to "complexes" to "pseudoconcepts" to "true concepts" as manifested in subjects' performances in a task involving what came to be known as "Vygotsky blocks". This chapter, which was probably written sometime during the early 1930s, is based on research Vygotsky conducted with Sakharov (1930) in the late 1920s.

Chapter 6, "The development of scientific concepts in childhood," was written somewhat later. Specifically, it was written for *Thinking and speech*, which was published in 1934, the year of Vygotsky's death. In this chapter, Vygotsky focused on "scientific" concepts and contrasted them with "everyday" or "spontaneous" concepts. The Russian adjective "*nauchnyi*", which has been translated as "scientific" could also be translated as "academic" or "scholarly," reflecting the fact that Vygotsky saw scientific concepts ("*nauchnye ponyatiya*") as being tied to the discourse of formal instruction. Indeed, at one point he went so far as to write (1934/1987, p.214) that "the basic characteristic of [the] development [of scientific concepts] is that they have their source in school instruction".

As I have noted elsewhere (Wertsch, 1991), there are some important differences between Vygotsky's notions of true or genuine concepts, on the one hand, and scientific concepts, on the other. For my present purposes, however, I shall focus on an underlying similarity in outlook which characterises his account of both types of concepts. Specifically, I want to examine how he viewed them as reflecting a kind of universal *telos* of abstract rationality.

When outlining his notions of complexes and concepts in Chapter 5, Vygotsky (1934/1987, p.137) wrote:

> The foundation of the complex lies in empirical connections that emerge in the individual's immediate experience. A complex is first and foremost a concrete unification of a group of objects based on the empirical similarity of separate objects to one another ... The most important characteristic of complexive thinking is that it occurs on the plane of concrete-empirical thinking rather than on the plane of abstract-logical thinking ...

In Chapter 6 (1934/1987, p.168), a similar orientation is reflected in connection with scientific concepts:

> As part of an organized system [of scientific concepts], this verbal definition descends to the concrete; it descends to the phenomena which the concept represents. In contrast, the everyday concept tends to develop outside any definitional system; it tends to move upwards toward abstraction and generalization.

As I have argued elsewhere (Wertsch, 1985), the nature of everyday and scientific concepts was envisioned by Vygotsky in terms of one of the semiotic potentials of human language, namely "decontextualization". The potential for decontextualisation, which is inherent in any human language, is the potential to consider words in terms of sign-types and to formulate what Vygotsky termed *meaning* ("*znachenie*"), as opposed to *sense* ("*smysl*"), in terms of relationships among sign-types.

In addition to similarities between Vygotsky's account of true and scientific concepts, on the one hand, as opposed to complexes and everyday concepts, on the other, there are important parallels in how he viewed the relationship between the two contrasting elements in the each case. In accordance with his evolutionist leanings, he viewed true concepts as being more developed than complexes, and scientific concepts as being more developed than everyday concepts.

At several points, Vygotsky went even further in his evolutionist claims and argued that mastery of the more highly evolved forms of concepts results in a transformation of the less-developed forms. He followed this path in particular in Chapter 6 of *Thinking and speech* where he argued (1934/1987, pp.216–217):

> The possibility that the mastery of scientific concepts influences this development in the child's spontaneous concepts is obvious. Everyday concepts are restructured under the influence of the child's mastery of scientific concepts ... when the child masters the structure that is associated with conscious awareness and mastery in one domain of concepts [i.e. scientific concepts], his efforts will not have to be carried out anew with each of the spontaneous concepts that were formed prior to the development of this structure. Rather, in accordance with basic structural laws, the structure is transferred to the concepts which developed earlier.

In this view, there is a strong homogenising force in concept development which would presumably result in *all* concepts taking the form of scientific concepts.

The key to understanding the homogenising forces Vygotsky saw as being set in motion with the appearance of scientific concepts has to do with the "mastery" associated with "conscious awareness", "intellectualisation", and "volition". Everyday concepts are defined by the fact "that they lack conscious awareness" (1934/1987, p.191), whereas a hallmark of scientific concepts is precisely such awareness. Furthermore, Vygotsky saw the key to the conscious awareness, intellectualisation, and volition associated with scientific concepts as being their organisation into a system (1934/1987, pp.191–192):

> *Only within a system can the concept acquire consciousness, awareness and a voluntary nature. Conscious awareness and the presence of a system are synonyms when we are speaking of concepts, just as spontaneity, lack of conscious awareness, and the absence of a system are three different words for designating the nature of the child's concept.*

Carried to its logical extreme, this principle of systematicity suggests that mathematics would provide an ideal case, and indeed Vygotsky (1934/1987) did turn to mathematics in the course of making his argument. He did so in the context of a discussion of the claim (1934/1987, p.224) that "by its very nature, each concept presupposes the presence of a certain system of concepts. Outside such a system, it cannot exist". One of the implications of this systematic property is that concepts can be defined in accordance with "the law of concept equivalence" (1934/1987, p.226), which, in principle, means that "any concept can be represented through other concepts in an infinite number of ways" (1934/1987, p.226). In applying this to numbers as concepts, Vygotsky wrote (1934/1987, p.227):

> Thus, the number one can be expressed as 1,000,000 minus 999,999 or, more generally, as the difference between any two adjacent numbers. It can also be expressed as any number divided by itself or in an infinite number of other ways. This is a pure example of the law of concept equivalence.

This example of arithmetic provides what is perhaps the closest approximation possible to abstract rationality as a *telos* of development. By taking maximal advantage of the semiotic potential of decontextualisation, it is possible to operate strictly within an abstract system, with all the attributes of mastery, conscious awareness, intellectualisation, and volition that Vygotsky associated with scientific concepts. Furthermore, the decontextualisaton and abstraction involved strongly suggest that the kind of rationality involved is universal. It is a kind of rationality accessible to all individuals and groups.

To say that the systematisation and conscious awareness associated with scientific concepts reflects a semiotic potential is of course not to say that this potential is always fulfilled. Indeed, the studies that Luria and Vygotsky conducted in Central Asia in the 1930s (Luria, 1976) concerned cases in which this potential for the decontextualisation of mediational means was not attained. A further question that arises here is whether scientific concepts and other forms of rationality are invoked in all contexts by individuals or groups who have demonstrated a capacity for using them in at least one context. That is, can one assume a kind of homogeneity of the rational mind across contexts?

At several points in his writings about concept development Vygotsky indicated that he did not assume such homogeneity of abstract rationality. His doubts on this score seemed to stem from two basic sources. First, he argued that even though humans may have access to highly evolved and hence more powerful forms of conceptual functioning, they sometimes fail to use them. Almost all of his comments on this issue can be found in Chapter 5 of *Thinking and speech*, comments such as (1934/1987, p.155):

> Although adult thinking has achieved the formation of concepts and generally operates on that foundation, not all the adult's thinking is based on these operations. In dreams, for example, one can observe the ancient primitive mechanism of complexive thinking, the concrete fusion, condensation, and shifting of images ... In our [i.e. adults'] everyday lives, our thinking frequently occurs in pseudoconcepts. From the perspective of dialectical logic, the concepts that we find in our living speech are not concepts in the true sense of the word. They are actually general representations of things. There is no doubt, however, that these representations are a transitional stage between complexes or pseudoconcepts and true concepts.

When considering these issues Vygotsky made it clear that he interpreted different forms of conceptual functioning (i.e. complexes versus true concepts) in terms of different levels in an evolutionary hierarchy (1934/1987, p.160):

> *The various genetic forms co-exist*, just as strata representing different geological epochs coexist in the earth's crust. This is more the rule than the exception for the development of behavior more generally. Human behaviour is not consistently characterized by a single higher level of development. Forms of behavior that have emerged very recently in human history dwell alongside the most ancient ... The adult's thinking is often carried out at the level of complexes, and sometimes sinks to even more primitive levels.

All these comments from Chapter 5 of *Thinking and speech* indicate that Vygotsky did not assume that human mental functioning can always be characterised in some homogeneous way, specifically in terms of abstract rationality. Instead, he saw clear evidence for a kind of "heterogeneity" (Tulviste, 1991; Wertsch, 1991) of mental functioning. Specifically, his comments in this chapter comprise a statement about "heterogeneity as genetic hierarchy" (Wertsch, 1991). As characterised by Tulviste (1986, p.19), this view asserts that "having attained higher stages in the development of thinking, humans sometimes nonetheless drop to lower levels, to already completed stages of ontogenesis or sociogenesis [i.e. sociocultural history] ... It is held that the completed stages in the development of thinking are not lost without a trace, but are preserved, and the return to them is viewed as regression".

Heterogeneity as genetic hierarchy has played a role in the ideas of several major developmental psychologists. For example, it was much in evidence in the reasoning of Werner (1948) who wrote (p.38) that "the normal adult, even at our own cultural level, does not always act on the higher levels of behavior. His mental structure is marked by not one but many functional patterns, one lying above the other. Because of this the isolated individual, genetically considered, must occasionally exhibit in his varying behavior different phases of development".

As noted by Tulviste (1986) and Wertsch (1991) perhaps the most problematic aspect of claims about heterogeneity as genetic hierarchy is why lower forms of functioning would continue to exist and be used when higher, and presumably more powerful ones are available. It is a problem that Vygotsky himself did not address. Indeed, certain passages from his later writings suggest that, if anything, he was moving towards a position that strongly posited homogeneity. As noted earlier for example, he argued in Chapter 6 of *Thinking and speech* that the mastery of scientific concepts results in the transformation of everyday concepts into a like form. The key to this transformation is the systemic organisation of scientific concepts outlined earlier (1934/1987, p.223): "it is this new system that transforms the child's everyday concepts".

Even in Chapter 6 of *Thinking and speech*, however, Vygotsky gave at least some indication that heterogeneity was still a possibility. For example, he noted (1934/1987, p.222) in passing that "scientific concepts are as inadequate in some contexts as everyday concepts are in scientific contexts", a comment that suggests that he did not envision a *telos* in which all mental representation was of one homogeneous sort.

There are other passages of his later writings, however, that suggest that Vygotsky was moving towards a position grounded in assumptions about heterogeneity. These passages concern his analysis of "egocentric" and inner speech. As I have outlined elsewhere (Wertsch, 1985), Vygotsky's account of egocentric and inner speech relies on a quite different semiotic potential in language than that which lies at the foundation of true or scientific concepts. Specifically, he was interested in a kind of inherent contextualisation that exists in human speech. Instead of focusing on abstract meaning and the definitions that can be generated out of a timeless system of meanings, he focused on ways in which unique speech events are situated with regard to "extralinguistic" and "linguistic" context.

Vygotsky's most extended analysis of these and other issues surrounding inner speech appears in Chapter 7 of *Thinking and speech*. For example, it is there that he outlined the properties of inner speech, relying on the distinction between "meaning" (*znachenie*) and "sense" (*smysl*) to develop his claims about its "semantic" properties. According to him (Vygotsky, 1934, p.305, our translation):

> The sense of a word ... is the aggregate of all the psychological facts emerging in our consciousness because of this word. Therefore, the sense of a word always turns out to be a dynamic, flowing, complex formation which has several zones of differential stability .... As we know, a word readily changes its sense in various contexts. Conversely, its meaning is that fixed, unchanging point which remains stable during all the changes of sense in various contexts ... The real meaning [i.e. sense] of a word is not constant. In one operation a word emerges in one meaning and in another it takes on another meaning.

There is of course much more to be said about Vygotsky's notions of concepts and inner speech. My point at present, however, is to consider how they fit into an account of mind that is grounded in assumptions of homogeneity or heterogeneity, an issue on which Vygotsky was largely silent. If one focuses on Chapters 5 and 6 (especially the latter) of *Thinking and speech*, a clear orientation towards abstract rationality as *the telos* of development and a commitment to homogeneity on this basis seems to emerge. In contrast, in Chapter 7 one finds Vygotsky focusing on a quite different form of mental functioning, one that stands in contrast to the kind of abstract, decontextualised, system-bound rationality that lies at the foundation of his notion of conceptual thinking. Furthermore, there is nothing to suggest that Vygotsky attempted to relate these two forms of mental functioning in some kind of genetic hierarchy.

Based on this overview of Vygotsky's writings, it would seem that he was unclear or ambivalent about whether human mental functioning is fundamentally characterised by a kind of homogeneity grounded in abstract rationality or by a form of heterogeneity that recognises other forms of contextualised functioning as well. Correspondingly, it reflects an ambivalence about what Vygotsky envisioned as the ideal outcome, or *telos* of human mental development. At several points in his writings he committed himself to abstract rationality as the ideal and as the highest stage of development, but a combination of empirical observations and semiotic analyses of a phenomenon such as

contextualised sense led him to recognise the possibility of
heterogeneity as well.

How can Vygotsky's commitment to the ideal of abstract rationality
as the highest point of development be reconciled with his recognition
that various forms of contextualised functioning co-exist with it? I shall
address this question in two steps. First, I shall examine why Vygotsky
attributed such an idealised status to abstract rationality. Again, the
idealised status is not simply a matter of taking it to be higher. It is a
matter of assuming that abstract rationality is so obviously superior to
other forms of contextualised functioning that it naturally leads to the
transformation of the latter into a like form. And second, I shall address
the issue of why it was that, in the context of this argument, Vygotsky
also recognised the power of the kind of contextualised thinking found
in inner speech.

VYGOTSKY'S AMBIVALENCE ABOUT ABSTRACT RATIONALITY

In my view Vygotsky's commitment to an ideal of homogeneity based on
abstract rationality is best understood as part of the general
philosophical perspective that he brought to his work. As noted earlier,
the basic philosophical perspective at issue was that of an
Enlightenment rationalist, and this orientation took a particular, and
perhaps a particularly strong, form in the context of Soviet discussions
on how to build the first centrally planned socialist society. It seems to
me, however, that philosophical commitments of the Enlightenment
more generally considered are at the heart of the matter; something that
is suggested by the similar commitments to Enlightenment rationality
that seem to underlie theories in developmental psychology from other
parts of the world.

In his volume *Cosmopolis: The hidden agenda of modernity* Toulmin
(1992) has outlined some of these philosophical commitments in a way
that is quite relevant for understanding Vygotsky's predilection for
assuming that abstract rationality is the *telos* of homogeneous mental
functioning. In this volume (p.13) Toulmin outlines a challenge to the
"*standard account* or *received view* of Modernity", a view that provides
many of the implicit assumptions underlying today's debates between
moderns and post-moderns. As outlined by Toulmin the received view
generally takes two statements about the origins of Modernity as given,
namely (1992, p.13):

> ... that the modern age began in the 17th century, and that
> the transition from medieval to modern modes of thought
> and practice rested on the adoption of rational methods in
> all serious fields of intellectual inquiry—by Galileo Galilei
> in physics, by René Descartes in epistemology—with their
> soon being followed in political theory by Thomas Hobbes.

These two widely accepted claims are precisely what Toulmin wishes to bring into question. Instead of accurately reflecting the emergence of Modernity, he views them as reflecting some very questionable historical interpretations. In particular, he questions the widespread assumption that the developments of the modern age neatly superseded the accomplishments and concerns of Renaissance humanism and that the latter simply died away as a result of their obvious inadequacy in the face of abstract rationality. Although the founders of Modern Philosophy generally rejected or disparaged the concerns of Renaissance humanists, Toulmin argues that the insights of these humanists had a powerful impact on what immediately followed as well as on today's philosophical debates.

Toulmin (1992, p.30) analyses the relationship between humanist insights and the concerns of the founders of the modern age in terms of how the latter "disclaimed any interest in four different kinds of practical knowledge". His summary of these four issues is very useful for reconsidering the nature of Modernity in general as well as for understanding Vygotsky's tendencies to privilege abstract rationality in particular.

In Toulmin's account the first issue has to do with a move "from the oral to the written" (p.30). What he has in mind here concerns "the right of rhetoric [associated with the oral] to stand alongside logic [associated with the written] in the canon of philosophy" (p.30). In the context of outlining developments in the history of philosophy during the 17th century, Toulmin argues (1992, p.31) that:

> The research program of modern philosophy thus set aside
> all questions about *argumentation*—among particular
> people in specific situations, dealing with concrete cases,
> where varied things were at stake—in favour of *proofs* that
> could be set down in writing, and judged as written.

The result of this historical development was that it "reinstated Plato's libel against rhetoric so successfully that colloquial uses of the word 'rhetoric' have ever since been insulting, hinting that rhetorical issues have to do only with using dishonest tricks in oral debate" (p.30).

In Toulmin's revised historical account the point is that "the tradition of Modern Philosophy in Western Europe concentrated on formal analysis of chains of written statements, rather than on the circumstantial merits and defects of persuasive utterances" (p.31). In short, "formal logic was in, rhetoric was out" (p.31).

The second issue Toulmin addresses in his revisionist account of how Modern Philosophy arose is the move "from the particular to the universal" (p.31). He goes on to say (1992, p.32):

> Within the practice of medicine and law, the pragmatic demands of daily practice still carried weight, and the analysis of particular cases retained intellectual respectability. But, from now on, casuistry met the same comprehensive scorn from moral philosophers as rhetoric did from the logicians ... [Modern philosophers] view as unphilosophical or dishonest those writers who focus on particular cases, or on types of cases limited by specific conditions.

This focus on the abstract and general principles of ethical theory meant that "*general principles were in, particular cases were out*" (p.32).

The third point Toulmin raises is the tendency for Modern Philosophy to insist on a move "from the local to the general" (p.32). In this connection he writes (p.33):

> Descartes saw the curiosity that inspires historians and ethnographers as a pardonable human trait; but he taught that philosophical understanding never comes from accumulating experience of particular individuals and specific cases. The demands of rationality impose on philosophy a need to seek out abstract, general ideas and principles, by which particulars can be connected together.

This attitude among the founders of Modern Philosophy was summarised by Toulmin as "*abstract axioms were in, concrete diversity was out*" (p.33).

The final issue that Toulmin raises in his review of the relationship between humanist insights and the concerns of the founders of the modern age has to do with the move "from the timely to the timeless" (p.33). Here again he formulates his comments in terms of the contrast between the practical concerns of law and medicine with the theoretical and abstract concerns of philosophy, and he uses this point to summarise parts of the other three as well (1992, p.34):

Questions about the timeliness of decisions and actions, utterances and arguments, had been staple topics for earlier philosophy. For 16th-century scholars, the very model of a "rational enterprise" was not Science but Law. Jurisprudence brings to light, not merely the link between "practical rationality" and "timeliness", but the significance of local diversity, the relevance of particularity, and the rhetorical power of oral reasoning: By comparison, all projects for a universal natural philosophy struck the humanists as problematic. A hundred years later, the shoe was on the other foot. For Descartes and his successors, timely questions were no concern of philosophy: instead, their aim was to bring to light permanent structures underlying all the changeable phenomena of Nature.

From the start, then, transient human affairs took second place for modern philosophers, and they sidelined matters of practical relevance and timeliness, as not being genuinely "philosophical".

In short, *"the permanent was in, the transitory was out"* (p.34).

Toulmin's review of the four fundamental ways in which there was a "retreat from the Renaissance" (p.30) in the 17th century puts a quite different slant on the relationship between Modern Philosophy and Renaissance humanism than can be found in the "received view" of Modernity. Instead of viewing the emergence of Enlightenment rationality, which can to a large extent be characterised in terms of the four tendencies he outlines, as a kind of victory of reason over irrational dogma, he portrays the relationship as being much more complex. Specifically, he views the history of philosophy over the past several centuries as a kind of complex dialogue between these two tendencies, with all the attendant disputes and rediscoveries one might expect.

The implications of Toulmin's analysis for understanding Vygotsky's writings are profound. On the one hand there are many points in Vygotsky's writings where he made explicit statements supporting the views of Enlightenment rationality as outlined in what Toulmin terms the "received view". Time and again he revealed a strong tendency to value and focus on logic, the universal, the general, and the timeless. His account of higher mental functioning, especially "advanced higher mental functioning" (Wertsch, 1985, p.33), was formulated largely in terms of the four tendencies outlined by Toulmin, and this orientation is particularly pronounced in his analysis of scientific concepts.

At the same time, however, Vygotsky seemed to recognise that human mental functioning could not be adequately characterised in terms of the ideals of Enlightenment rationality alone. As noted earlier, he sprinkled his writings on concept development with caveats to this effect, and a concern with issues that fall outside the realm of abstract rationality altogether is particularly evident, indeed pervasive in his analyses of inner speech. Problems of rhetoric and argumentation involving "particular people in specific situations, dealing with concrete cases" were clearly at the core of dealing with this latter form of semiotic mediation, and in this context consideration of the particular, the local, and the timely "were in". In short, Vygotsky's analyses of inner speech relied heavily on the very kinds of issues Toulmin associates with Renaissance humanism.

Taken as a whole, then, Vygotsky's writings reflect a kind of ambivalence with regard to where he stood on the ideals of Enlightenment rationality. Instead of focusing consistently on what Toulmin calls the logical, the universal, the general, and the timeless, he was often apparently tempted to consider the rhetorical, the particular, the local, and the timely. In a sense, this is precisely what Toulmin's account of the dialogue between Modern Philosophy and the Renaissance humanism would predict. Instead of being a totally consistent follower of the tenets of Enlightenment rationality, Vygotsky, or anyone else in the 20th century for that matter, had to operate in an intellectual setting that reflects a complex relationship between these two world views. The fact that he was thus situated made it extremely difficult for him to be a monolithic follower of the dreams of Enlightenment rationalists.

SEMIOTIC MEDIATION AND VYGOTSKY'S AMBIVALENCE ABOUT ABSTRACT RATIONALITY

Along with the philosophical conflicts outlined by Toulmin, there were other factors in Vygotsky's concrete research agenda that militated against his formulating an account of human mental functioning based solely on abstract rationality. The most important of these derives from his claims about how "mediational means", or cultural tools fundamentally shape communicative and mental processes. The importance of this claim is clear in any analysis of his writings (cf Van der Veer & Valsiner, 1991; Wertsch, 1985), and Vygotsky himself was quite adamant about it in statements such as "the central fact about our psychology is the fact of mediation" (Vygotsky, 1982, p.166).

Given the centrality of mediation, especially semiotic mediation, in Vygotsky's analyses, it is important to consider how it may have influenced what I have called his ambivalence towards abstract rationality. One of the hallmarks of his analyses of semiotic mediation was a recognition of the *multifunctionality* of signs, especially those found in natural language. In contrast to accounts of language that explicitly or implicitly, and often somewhat naively, assume that language functions in a single way, Vygotsky's line of argument was centrally concerned with multifunctionality and associated issues such as functional differentiation (see Silverstein, 1985; Wertsch, 1985). For example, he distinguished between "social" and "individual" functions, "communicative" and "intellectual" functions, and "indicative" and "symbolic" functions of speech, and his point in many cases was that language simultaneously serves more than one functional role. Furthermore, Vygotsky relied heavily on a general functional differentiation between two "semiotic potentials" of human language— the potentials for "decontextualization" and "contextualization" (Wertsch, 1985).

Vygotsky's ambivalence about abstract rationality can be seen in passages where he struggled to deal with this general functional differentiation between contextualisation and decontextualisation while at the same time trying to hew to the commitments of Modern Philosophy as outlined by Toulmin. For example, as noted earlier he argued in Chapter 5 of *Thinking and speech* that alongside the use of genuine concepts human mental functioning continues to be characterised by less abstract and more primitive forms of thought.

Such passages differ from those in Chapter 6 where Vygotsky claimed that mental development tends towards homogeneity modelled around scientific concepts. However, even at the points in his writings where he explicitly recognised heterogeneity he seems to have been struggling to retain a commitment to abstract rationality in that such heterogeneity was interpreted primarily as a failure to reach full-fledged homogeneity. This heterogeneity consists of "strata", many of which remain from earlier, primitive forms of mental functioning. In such a view their continued existence reflects the fact that they have not been fully transformed and integrated into an all-encompassing system as envisioned in the case of scientific concepts. This latter outcome is a version of what Toulmin (1992, p.104) sees as the dream of the Rationalists, namely "to 'purify' the operations of human reason, by decontextualising them".

In my view the key to understanding Vygotsky's position on these issues and the ambivalence that resulted is his analysis of semiotic mediation. The whole notion of scientific concepts is grounded in his analysis of the systemic properties of sets of meanings that derive from treating words as decontextualised semantic entities. In this case the semiotic potential associated with the "decontextualisation of mediational means" (Wertsch, 1985) is foregrounded, and the properties associated with contextualisation are backgrounded, if not ignored.

Although there are limits to the powers of decontextualisation (cf Linell, 1988; Rommetveit, 1988; Saljo, 1988), there is no doubt that words can be treated as "sign types" (Wertsch, 1985) with all the ensuing possibilities for generating definitions and definitional systems. This is precisely the functional approach to words emphasised in formal instructional contexts (cf Scribner & Cole, 1981), and it is why Vygotsky used the term *nauchnyi*, which can be translated as "academic" (e.g. see the translation in Luria, 1976) as well as "scientific." The extreme case of this foregrounding can be seen in cases such as Vygotsky's account of the potentially infinite number of ways in which it is possible to define the number 1.

The problem for Vygotsky that derived from his semiotic analysis, however, was that words and other linguistic signs typically fulfil more than one functional role. In contrast to decontextualised sign use, he also recognised the potential for contextualisation. Furthermore, he did not always view contextual uses as failures at decontextualisation. Instead, he turned specifically and at length to cases where this potential was foregrounded.

The best example of this is probably in his analyses of inner speech with all the associated issues of "sense", "predicativity", "psychological subject", "psychological predicate", the "infusion of sense into a word", and so forth. In no way does he suggest in such analyses that these phenomena are associated with "lower" or "rudimentary" forms of mental functioning. Indeed, his account of inner speech in Chapter 7 of *Thinking and speech* deals with what might be viewed as some of the most highly developed human capacities for reasoning and understanding.

In short, Vygotsky's appreciation of multifunctionality led him to resist, at least implicitly, any simple tendency to treat a single semiotic potential and its associated form of mental functioning as a *telos* and others as failures to reach this *telos*. This is not to say that Vygotsky brought the various semiotic potentials together into a coherent explicit treatment in his analyses. He did not. Indeed, he addressed different potentials in different chapters.

The fact that Vygotsky did not manage to integrate his treatments of the two general semiotic potentials he identified is reflected in his failure to specify in any concrete way how the use of scientific concepts is tied to the use of inner speech. Surely one would not want to claim that during certain circumscribed periods of activity human mental functioning can be characterised solely in terms of scientific conceptual reasoning, with all its attendant tendencies towards decontextualisation, and no involvement of the highly contextualised sense associated with inner speech, whereas in other activity periods the reverse is true. The point of course is that *both* semiotic potentials are always simultaneously employed.

The fact that Vygotsky fundamentally grounded his account of human mental functioning in semiotic mediation, coupled with the fact that mediational means are inherently multifunctional, implies that this multifunctionality must somehow be reflected in mental processes. This is precisely what seems to me to be missing in Vygotsky's writings on issues such as scientific conceptual thinking and inner speech. Again, the building blocks are there, but they were not put together to build an integrated framework.

Of course this is hardly a problem that Vygotsky alone encountered. There is a strong tendency even today to focus on one or another potential of language in isolation and take it as *the* basis of human communicative or mental functioning. Such attempts do not even attain the point Vygotsky reached by recognising more than one semiotic function. And it is perhaps fair to say that no one has managed to integrate the various functional orientations of language recognised by Vygotsky into an overarching framework.

The upshot of all this for Vygotsky's views on abstract rationality and the associated account of homogeneous human mental functioning that he at least sometimes envisioned is that he was almost forced into a position of ambivalence. The claims made by the founders of Modern Philosophy and historical interpretations of them outlined by Toulmin were undoubtedly quite powerful influences in the formation of Vygotsky's commitment to abstract rationality. But at the same time, the level of sophistication in semiotic analysis he brought to his concrete research agenda served to "keep him honest" with regard to the limits of such rationality. In my view, he did not satisfactorily resolve this issue, but the ambivalence I have outlined that is reflected in his writings suggests that he was very much in the process of struggling with it. I would maintain that it is an issue that continues to be at the centre of debates today about what would constitute an adequate account of the human mind.

ACKNOWLEDGEMENT

[1]The writing of this chapter was assisted by a grant from the Spencer Foundation to the author. The statements made and the views expressed are solely the responsibility of the author.

REFERENCES

Boas, F. (1911). Introduction. In F. Boas (Ed.), *Handbook of American Indian languages* (Bureau of American Ethnology Bulletin 40, Part I, pp.1–83). Washington, DC: Smithsonian Institution.

Boas, F. (1920). The methods of ethnology. *American Anthropologist, 22*, 311–321.

Bruner, J. (1986). *Actual minds, possible worlds*. Cambridge, MA: Harvard University Press.

Jahoda, G. (1993). *Crossroads between culture and mind: Continuities and change in theories of human nature*. Cambridge, MA: Harvard University Press.

Kaplan, B. (1983). Genetic-dramatism: Old wine in new bottles. In S. Wapner & B. Kaplan (Eds.), *Toward a holistic developmental psychology* (pp.53–74). Hillsdale, NJ: Lawrence Erlbaum Associates Inc.

Linell, P. (1988). The impact of literacy on the conception of language: The case of linguistics. In R. Saljo (Ed.), *The written word: Studies in literate thought and action* (pp.41–58). Berlin: Springer-Verlag.

Lucy, J.A., & Wertsch, J.V. (1987). Vygotsky and Whorf: A comparative analysis. In M.A. Hickmann (Ed.), *Social and functional approaches to language and thought* (pp.67–86). Orlando: Academic Press.

Luria, A.R. (1976). *Cognitive development: Its cultural and social foundations*. Cambridge, MA: Harvard University Press.

Rommetveit, R. (1988). On literacy and the myth of literal meaning. In R. Saljo (Ed.), *The written word: Studies in literate thought and action* (pp.13–40). Berlin: Springer-Verlag.

Sakharov, L.S. (1930). O metodakh issledovaniya ponyatii [Methods for the investigation of concepts]. *Psikhologiya, 3* (1).

Saljo, R. (1988). A text and its meanings: Observations on how readers construe what is meant from what is written. In R. Saljo (Ed.), *The written word: Studies in literate thought and action* (pp.178–194). Berlin: Springer-Verlag.

Sapir, E. (1931). Conceptual categories in primitive languages. *Science, 74*, 578.

Scribner, S., & Cole, M. (1981). *The psychological consequences of literacy*. Cambridge, MA: Harvard University Press.

Shweder, R.A. (1991). *Thinking through cultures: Expeditions in cultural psychology*. Cambridge, MA: Harvard University Press.

Silverstein, M. (1985). The functional stratification of language and ontogenesis. In J.V. Wertsch (Ed.), *Culture, communication, and cognition: Vygotskyian perspectives* (pp. 205–235). New York: Cambridge University Press.

Toulmin, S. (1992). *Cosmopolis: The hidden agenda of modernity*. Chicago: University of Chicago Press.

Tulviste, P. (1986). Ob istoricheskoi geterogennosti verbal'nogo myshleniya [The historical heterogeneity of verbal thinking]. In Ya. A. Ponomarev (Ed.), *Myshlenie, obshchenie, praktika: Sbornik nauchnykh trudov* (pp.19–29) [Thinking, society, practice: A collection of scientific works]. Yaroslavl': Yaroslavskii Gosudarstvennyi Pedagogicheskii Institut im. K.D. Ushinskii.

Tulviste, P. (1991). *Cultural-historical development of verbal thinking: A psychological study*. Commack, NY: Nova Science Publishers.

Van der Veer, R., & Valsiner, J. (1991). *Understanding Vygotsky: A quest for synthesis*. Oxford: Basil Blackwell.

Vygotsky, L.S. (1934). *Myshlenie i rech': Psikhologicheskie issledovaniya* [Thinking and speech: Psychological investigations]. Moscow and Leningrad: Gosudarstvennoe Sotsial'no-Ekonomicheskoe Izdatel'stvo.

Vygotsky, L.S. (1982). *Sobranie sochinenii, Tom pervyi: Voprosy teorii i istorii psikhologii* [Collected works, vol. 1: Problems in the theory and history of psychology]. Moscow: Izdatel'stvo Pedagogika.

Vygotsky, L.S. (1987). *The collected works of L.S. Vygotsky. Volume 1. Problems of general psychology. Including the volume Thinking and speech* [N. Minick Trans.]. New York: Plenum. [Original work published 1934.]

Vygotsky, L.S., & Luria, A.R. (1993). *Studies on the history of behavior: Ape, primitive, and child* [Edited and translated by V.I. Golod & J.E. Knox]. Hillsdale, NJ: Lawrence Erlbaum Associates Inc. [Original work published 1930.]

Werner, H. (1948). *Comparative psychology of mental development*. New York: International Universities Press.

Wertsch, J.V. (1985). *Vygotsky and the social formation of the mind*. Cambridge, MA: Harvard University Press.

Wertsch, J.V. (1991). *Voices of the mind: A sociocultural approach to mediated action*. Cambridge, MA: Harvard University Press.

Whorf, B.L. (1956). *Language, throught, and reality: Selected writings of Benjamin Lee Whorf* [edited by J. Carroll]. Cambridge, MA: MIT Press.

Zinchenko, V.P. (1985) Vygotsky's ideas about units of analysis for the analysis of mind. In J.V. Wertsch (Ed.), *Culture, communication, and cognition: Vygotskian perspectives* (pp.94–118). New York: Cambridge University Press.

CHAPTER FOUR

Structure and development. Reflections by Vygotsky

René van der Veer
Leiden University, The Netherlands

INTRODUCTION

From a formal point of view the work of all truly important scientists can be analysed at several interconnected levels which somewhat arbitrarily can be distinguished as follows. First, we can examine the epistemological level. In that case we are interested in the question of what particular researchers consider to be proper (scientific) knowledge and how in their view this kind of knowledge can be acquired. Questions such as the relation between theory and fact, the legitimacy of induction and deduction, the relation between scientific development and historical society, and between empirism and nativism are of concern at this level. Second, we can discuss what might be called the level of methodology. We then examine the advantages and disadvantages of different research approaches and strategies such as the longitudinal and cross-sectional method, the use of formalisation and quantification, or the experimental and correlational approach, and establish what particular views researchers hold as to these issues. Third, we may discuss the advantages and disadvantages of particular methods, instruments, and techniques such as the clinical interview, the intelligence test, the survey etc. Again, we may ask what particular researchers thought about these respective methods. Finally, we can examine to what extent researchers live up to their own standards and viewpoints at these three interconnected levels, and investigate how they conduct their empirical research themselves.

The work of Vygotsky and Piaget is particularly suited for this kind of analysis. Both investigators were highly conscious of the methods they used and often explicitly discussed the advantages and disadvantages of various epistemological views, methodologies, and research methods. Indeed, about both researchers it has been claimed that the field in which they excelled was not so much developmental psychology but epistemology—in the case of Piaget (e.g. Ducret, 1984; Kitchener, 1986; Seltman & Seltman, 1985)—and theoretical psychology—in the case of Vygotsky (Leont'ev, in press). Interestingly enough, about both researchers it has also been said that their empirical investigations, although highly interesting and a rich source for hypotheses, were somewhat crude and inadequate according to contemporary standards of scientific rigour (cf Van der Veer, Van IJzendoorn & Valsiner, 1994). One is reminded of Flavell's remark (1963, p.431) that Piaget "tendered a series of pilot studies in the guise of a formal and finished experiment", of Vidal's observation (1994, p.233) that Piaget's "empirical results often seem to illustrate his hypotheses rather than test them", and of Luria's confession (1979, p.51) that the individual studies that Vygotsky and his associates carried out at the time "must be considered banal in and of themselves. Today we would consider them nothing more than student projects. And this is exactly what they were".

Vygotsky's general epistemological views

Vygotsky's essay *The historical meaning of the crisis in psychology*, written in 1926 and soon to be published in English (Vygotsky, 1926/in press, a), contains by far the most explicit and elaborate presentation of his epistemological and methodological views. In this essay Vygotsky made it quite clear that there can be no such thing as an atheoretical psychology (or science at large) as the behaviourists seemed to advocate. There is no such thing as objective registration of facts (this he regarded as a sensualistic prejudice) because our epistemological principles always co-determine our scientific facts. The positivistic idea that we merely have to register the objective facts and then through induction and mathematical elaboration can arrive at genuine scientific theories was very foreign to Vygotsky. Just like Piaget he strongly condemned such an approach and he argued that we need interpretation, abstraction, and analysis as the "*salto vitale*" for psychology. The psychologist can and must interpret his findings and then act as "a detective who brings to light a crime he never witnessed" (Vygotsky, 1926/in press, b).

In Vygotsky's view the influence of theory or interpretation begins with the words we use to designate the facts or phenomena discovered in our research, and it is for this reason that he attached such tremendous importance to the choice of proper terminology in scientific research.

Historically, it may be noted that here there are quite strong links between Vygotsky's early interests in linguistic thinkers such as Potebnya and Shpet (and, through them, Von Humboldt) and his emphasis on the importance of words as proto-theories. Similarly, it is quite interesting to see how his analysis of the role that words play in the production of scientific facts (i.e. at the level of methodology) is transposed to the domain of ontogeny in the early 1930s, when he gradually seems to realise that words or word meanings can be viewed as the vehicle of mental development.

CRITICISING OPPOSING VIEWS

These rather general epistemological views served Vygotsky well in his critical analyses of the writings of his colleagues. It is now becoming increasingly appreciated (e.g. Van der Veer & Valsiner, 1991, 1994) that his writings did not develop in a theoretical vacuum, so to speak, but emerged in a constant struggle with the writings of contemporaries whose theoretical work he both valued and resisted. It was part of his dialectical approach to actively promote the work of foreign theorists such as Köhler, Koffka, Bühler, and Piaget in the Soviet Union of that time (for example, by encouraging and making possible the translation into Russian of their major works) while at the same time writing very critical reviews of these same writings (which were often published as prefaces to the translations). He repeatedly argued that we must retain the positive points of certain theories but only as points of departure for a future psychology yet to be developed.

It must be said that Vygotsky showed particular skill in analysing the conceptual systems of his theoretical adversaries. He painstakingly dissected the principal arguments of his colleagues and reached conclusions that have been vindicated by later researchers or even were partially acknowledged by the "victims" (e.g. Piaget) of his analyses. Vygotsky's principal aim was to get as quickly as possible to the heart of the matter, at the fundamental concepts ("germ cells") of the theoretical system of his contemporaries. He himself argued that his goal was made considerably easier by the fact that psychology lacked a unified system of concepts and terms in which to describe and analyse psychological phenomena. Because of this lack of a theoretical system (called "general psychology" by Vygotsky and his contemporaries), each and every psychological discovery and the concepts that went with it quickly spread to adjacent areas and disciplines. The new concepts, explanatory principles, or ideas rapidly conquered the field and grew into general philosophical world views. Thus, the concept of the unconscious first served to explain certain neuroses, then became essential to explain personality in general, and finally was used to explain the origin of war and works of art. Vygotsky (1926/in press, a) argued that as world views stretch, so to speak, the original concept to an impossible degree, they display their true face and are easily recognised as the ideological agents they really were from the very beginning:

> It is only now, when the idea has entirely separated itself from the facts that engendered it, developed to its logical extremes, carried to its ultimate conclusions, generalised as far as possible, that it finally displays what it really is, shows its real face ... it reveals its social nature, which was of course present all the time, but was hidden under the mask of the neutral scientific fact it impersonated ... it is unmasked as a hidden ideological agent dressed up as a scientific fact and begins to participate in the general open struggle of ideas. But exactly here, as a small item of an enormous sum, it vanishes like a drop of rain in the ocean and ceases to exist independently.

Vygotsky added that after an idea has been unmasked as a world view (i.e. an idea or explanatory principle that has transcended its own area and is unjustifiably applied in various sciences or disciplines) the critics will go on to contest its applicability in the field in which it originally emerged. To illustrate this model for the development of general ideas in psychology, Vygotsky examined the fate of four ideas that were influential in his time. These were psychoanalysis, reflexology, Stern's personalism, and Gestalt psychology. Of these currents it was undoubtedly Gestalt psychology that was most important for the development of his own views. Throughout his career Vygotsky attentively followed the theoretical developments within the Gestalt movement and he and his colleagues entertained close personal contacts with both Köhler and Koffka. His critical (and laudatory) analyses of the Gestalt ideas cover a period of about 10 years and ranged from prefaces in Russian editions of books by the major Gestalt psychologists to descriptive overviews.

VYGOTSKY AND GESTALT THEORY

For Vygotsky the crucial issue in the assessment of Gestalt theory was the way this theory deals with the theme of structure and development or, in other words, the theme of continuity and change. The key question can be formulated as follows: How is it possible that continuous development results in intermediate products or stages which are fundamentally distinct? This question recurs time and again in developmental psychology and in Vygotsky's writings and takes various forms; for example, how can we explain continuity in phylogenetic development without taking the viewpoint of either mechanicism (which reduces all qualitatively distinct forms to the workings of some primordial mechanism) or vitalism (which creates a gap between lower and higher forms of development by introducing a mysterious principle that is only applicable to the latter)? How can we explain that the immediate evolutionary predecessors of humans, the anthropoid apes, seemingly have almost all of the prerequisites necessary for intelligent behaviour (such as tool use and tool manufacture) but nevertheless seem fundamentally less intelligent (by human definition) than humans? How can we explain the phylogenetic development from instinct to intellect without either creating an unbridgeable gap between the two forms of behaviour or, alternatively, invoking some mysterious purely mental acts? These are questions that have a long tradition in Western philosophical thought and one will no doubt remember that basically similar questions were already posed in ancient Greek philosophy by such philosophers as Heraclitus, Parmenides, and later by Plato and Aristotle (cf Mourelatos, 1974; Valsiner, 1987). They are also questions that are still—or perhaps I should say, again—very much on the agenda of contemporary developmental psychology (as witnessed by the talks delivered at the 12th advanced course of the Jean Piaget Archives dedicated to this topic—cf Beilin, 1993; Eldredge, 1993; Overton, 1993; Vonèche, 1993) and which one cannot avoid dealing with, for example, the concept of stage.

What initially attracted Vygotsky in Gestalt theory was that it seemed to provide an explanation for qualitatively distinct stages in development without taking one of the extreme positions sketched earlier; Gestalt theorists did not accept fundamental gaps between qualitatively distinct stages of development but neither did they take recourse to irrational (non-biological) principles to explain the very real differences that exist between species and between various stages of ontogenetic development. However, there is a clear evolution in Vygotsky's evaluation of Gestalt theory's contribution to the solution of this problem. At first he believed that the principle of Gestalt was able to struggle at "two fronts" (i.e. to avoid both extremes in the explanation of continuity and change) and thus to perform the magical trick of explaining one of the fundamental paradoxes of Western thought. Thus, in his discussions of Koffka (1924), Köhler (1921) and in his discussion of Gestalt psychology as a whole (Vygotsky, 1930; 1926/in press, c; 1930/in press, d) he was inclined to regard the Gestalt concept as a major contribution to psychological thought because it was a form of monistic materialism, as we find *Gestalten* both in perception, cognitive development, and in inorganic nature. One and the same principle seemed thus capable of explaining different levels of development. But towards 1930 Vygotsky also began to emphasise another theme that had already surfaced in his analysis of the crisis of psychology written some years earlier: the primordial, universal, and therefore metaphysical character of the Gestalt concept. He now argued that it is not enough to posit the existence of *Gestalten* because their existence itself should be explained. Behind this was his growing conviction that it will not do to explain development with the help of a single principle, as development results from the contribution of fundamentally different factors: biology and history (in phylogeny) or maturation and culture (in ontogeny). In his discussion (Vygotsky, 1930/in press, e) of Bühler's (1919) great little book *Abriss der geistigen Entwicklung des Kindes* [Précis of child's mental development], for example, Vygotsky made it quite clear that he believed that the denial of this fact is equal to defending an anti-dialectical viewpoint. In his opinion Bühler was mistaken in attributing paramount importance to biological factors and in claiming that nature makes no leaps. The cognitive development from animal to human being cannot be viewed as ascending a "single biological ladder".

The same kind of reasoning was, of course, applicable to the writings of the various Gestalt theorists and Vygotsky's (1934/in press, f) later discussion of Koffka's (1925) *Die Grundlagen der psychischen Entwicklung* [The foundations of mental development] illustrates this very well. In fighting both Thorndike and Bühler (who in this context play the role of representatives of, respectively, the mechanistic and vitalistic conceptions) Koffka had argued that the Gestalt criterion for intelligent action (i.e. the development of a solution to the task which is in accord with the structure of the field) is equally applicable to both lower and higher forms of mental actions. But according to Vygotsky in so doing he refuted his own criterion because it now lost all its discriminative power. Whereas the criterion was originally introduced by Köhler to designate the intelligent behaviour of anthropoid apes, it subsequently became a characteristic of virtually all mental processes regardless of their complexity. In Vygotsky's view a criterion thus conceived became useless for explaining specifically human capacities. He now argued that the so-called intelligent behaviour of chimpanzees (by which he had earlier been much impressed) is in actual fact much closer to instinct than it is to human intellect. In his view Koffka's main mistake was that he attempted to understand animals and humans by means of a single principle and thereby reduced human behaviour to animal behaviour. He thus managed to "overcome vitalism by making concessions to mechanicism" and failed to solve the "most difficult task that research psychologists ever faced", that is, to explain the origin and development of intelligence (Vygotsky, 1934/in press, f).

Vygotsky went on to criticise Gestalt theory for its view of human perception and in so doing admirably demonstrated the regularity he discussed in his analysis of the crisis in psychology mentioned earlier: that explanatory principles tend to be extended beyond the original area in which they were first formulated and then become vulnerable to critique. In the continuation they are not just contested as general principles or "world views" but also become the subject of criticism in the restricted domain in which they first originated. Similarly, Vygotsky first criticised the Gestalt principle as a general principle to be found in both inorganic nature and child development, and then switched to the field of perception in which the Gestalt principle originally emerged. He now contested Köhler's (1933) discussion of the role that knowledge and *Gestalten* play in perception. Köhler had argued that perception was indisputably often co-determined by previous knowledge but that there is also something like a primitive organisation of the visual field into figure–background, good forms etc. which seems innate and independent of any knowledge the person may have acquired. This amounts to saying that these primitive forms or *Gestalten* are prior to any experience and that knowledge (or "meaning" in Vygotsky's terms) becomes fused with these primordial forms only at a later stage. Against this Vygotsky (1934/in press, f) argued that there is no such thing as primitive or pure perception independent of any knowledge or experience, and that "the child begins to perceive the things with meaning and introduces elements of thinking into his immediate perceptions". His example of chess players of different levels of ability who perceive different things while looking at the same stimulus configuration (the chessboard with pieces) was meant to illustrate this point. The knowledge of each of these chess players fundamentally determines their perception of the situation on the board.

Although the example of the chess players seems debatable (one might argue that all of the chess players, regardless of playing strength, see the chess pieces against the background of the chessboard) Vygotsky was probably right in arguing that Gestalt theorists played down the factor of experience and in so doing "biologised", so to speak, perception. Similar criticisms have been voiced much later by experts such as Hamlyn (1969) who argued that the general theory of *Gestalt* does not allow for the effect of experience as it ultimately regards perception as a purely physiological process. In his view (1969, p.74) it is also a "conceptual mistake to think that it is possible to isolate a pure perceptual experience which is the end-product of a process of stimulation, albeit modified by autonomous neural processes".

The fundamental role of word meaning (experience or knowledge) in all higher mental processes had now become a major theme in Vygotsky's thinking and he went on to demonstrate that word meaning fundamentally determines children's perception. In his view this does not mean that the structural or Gestalt principle is invalid but that it needs to be complemented by other more specific principles. The major shortcoming of Gestalt theory is that it lacks an adequate principle to explain development; that is, it cannot explain why simple structures or *Gestalten* develop into complex structures. In other writings he explained that for him a major factor in human mental development is the introduction of word meanings or concepts in instruction. It is instruction in the school setting that propels child development along lines that are each time specific for a certain culture or society. In other words, the "biological" conception of Gestalt theory must be complemented by a sociocultural or sociohistorical view to get a complete view of human mental development. No single factor and corresponding set of explanatory principles can alone provide a complete account because a new set of explanatory principles is required when the child enters into certain levels of social life in a culture (Wertsch, 1985). Incidentally, it is here that Wertsch sees a difference with Piaget's theory. He says (1985, pp.42–43) that "rather than assuming that a single set of explanatory principles, such as adaptation and equilibration, can account for all aspects of cognitive development, Vygotsky argued that such principles need to be incorporated into a larger explanatory framework that deals with sociocultural phenomena as well".

PIAGET AND GESTALT THEORY

Vygotsky's appreciation and analysis of Gestalt theory show surprising similarity to Piaget's later assessment of the same theory. I will very briefly recapitulate Piaget's attitude towards Gestalt theory as it is probably relatively well known. We know that Piaget, like Vygotsky, highly valued the writings by the Gestalt psychologists and that he attributed his not becoming a Gestalt psychologist in a very early stage of his career to his own ignorance. Or, to put it in his own words: "Si j'avais connu à cette époque (1913–1915) les travaux de Wertheimer et de Köhler, je serais devenu Gestaltiste" (quoted on p.389 of Ducret, 1984). But just like Vygotsky, Piaget later developed one central criticism of Gestalt theory: its lack of concern for the genesis of structures under discussion. Piaget became interested in the way in which structures are transformed from stage to stage and, in fact, this is why we may call his own theory a brand of developmental or genetic structuralism (Gruber & Vonèche, 1977, p.xxxi). He now claimed that *Gestalten* (as opposed to his own schemas) are basically ahistorical; they are not thought of as the product of past interactions whereas Piaget's schemas come about by the organism's efforts to accommodate for new experiences. This led Piaget to say that "the schema is therefore a Gestalt which has a history" (quoted in Flavell, 1963, p.73).

The mature Piaget developed yet another criticism of the Gestalt notion which is perhaps not very relevant here but which I would just like to note in passing. He now argued that Gestalt structures are non-additive whereas his own operatory structures are additive. The difference is that between perceptual structures (*Gestalten*) which are temporal and irreversible and the structures of higher intelligence which are in Piaget's view atemporal and reversible. In Piaget's own additive system the sum of the parts of the elementary operations is equal to the totality of the system (cf Flavell, 1963, p.5; Kitchener, 1986, pp.44–45). Piaget claims that he avoids both elementarism and holism, as in his view the units of behaviour, or schemes of action, are always seen as evolving structures. Thus complex behaviour is not built up out of simple elements that retain their identity; instead, structures grow and change. Insofar as they are hierarchically organised, lower structures are governed and regulated by higher ones (see Gruber & Vonèche, 1977, p.xxxii).

Despite all this Piaget did not regard Gestalt theory as being totally inadequate. With respect to the issue of Gestalt theory's failure to deal with the genesis of structures he said, for example, that "to criticise Gestalt psychology is not to reject it but to make it more mobile and consequently to replace its apriority with a genetic relativity" (quoted in Flavell, 1963, p.75). In this respect as well, his views fully concurred with those of Vygotsky.

CONCLUSIONS

Let me briefly summarise what I have said and what I have not said. I first distinguished several levels at which one can describe or analyse the work of scientists. I then claimed that both Piaget and Vygotsky excelled at the epistemological and/or methodological level and went on to present some of Vygotsky's views in this domain. Having covered Vygotsky's theoretical approach I then switched to his analysis of Gestalt theory and showed how the latter was influenced by the former. I explained that for Vygotsky the core problem was that of structure and development, and showed how his views changed in the course of several years and ended up in a very explicit criticism of Gestalt theory both as applied to child development and in its original area of human perception. I added that for Vygotsky no single factor could ever explain human mental development. I then went on recapitulate Piaget's attitude towards Gestalt theory and noted some strong similarities.

I have not tried, of course, to provide an exhaustive list of the similarities between Piaget's and Vygotsky's thinking (cf Kozulin, 1994; Tudge & Winterhoff, 1993) nor did I attempt to spell out the obvious differences that exist between their views. But I did show that both were genuinely developmental theorists (rather than child psychologists; for the distinction see Valsiner, 1987) who focused on the issue of structure and development and arrived at their own original solution to this problem.

There remains one problem to be addressed: whether Vygotsky's criticism of Gestalt theory is in any sense applicable to other structuralist approaches such as Piaget's genetic structuralism. Earlier I quoted Wertsch who suggested that Piaget's single set of explanatory principles—adaptation and equilibration—would not have satisfied Vygotsky's criteria for a genuinely developmental theory. It is difficult to predict what Vygotsky would have said of Piaget's equilibration theory, of course, but I do not believe he would have been greatly displeased with it. What I do believe is that Vygotsky in the end would have criticised the one-sidedness of any formal or structural theory as he did not believe in strong boundaries between the structure and content of knowledge, a content that is strongly culture-bound and therefore infinitely varied. But this is, perhaps, a topic for another paper.

REFERENCES

Beilin, H. (1993). Mechanisms in the explanation of cognitive development. In J. Montangero, A. Cornu-Wells, A. Tryphon, & J. Vonèche (Eds.), *Conceptions of change over time* (pp.137–157). Genève: Fondation Archives Jean Piaget.

Bühler, K. (1919). *Abriss der geistigen Entwicklung des Kindes* [Précis of child's mental development]. Leipzig: Quelle & Meyer. [Russian translation 1930.]

Ducret, J.J. (1984). *Jean Piaget. Savant et philosophe* (2 Vol.). Genève: Droz.

Eldredge, N. (1993). Stability and change in biological systems. In J. Montangero, A. Cornu-Wells, A. Tryphon, & J. Vonèche (Eds.), *Conceptions of change over time* (pp.33–43). Genève: Fondation Archives Jean Piaget.

Flavell, J.H. (1963). *The developmental psychology of Jean Piaget*. New York: D. van Nostrand Company.

Gruber, H.E., & Vonèche, J.J. (Eds.) (1977). *The essential Piaget*. New York: Basic Books.

Hamlyn, D.W. (1969). *The psychology of perception. A philosophical examination of Gestalt theory and derivative theories of perception*. London: Routledge & Kegan Paul.

Kitchener, R. F. (1986). *Piaget's theory of knowledge*. New Haven: Yale University Press.

Koffka, K. (1924). Introspection and the method of psychology. *British Journal of Psychology, 15*, 149-161. [Russian translation 1926.]

Koffka, K. (1925). *Die Grundlagen der psychischen Entwicklung* [Foundations of mental development]. Osterwieck am Harz: A.W. Zickfeldt. [Russian translation 1934.]

Köhler, W. (1921). *Intelligenzprüfungen an Menschenaffen* [The mentality of great apes]. Berlin: Julius Springer. [Russian translation 1930.]

Köhler, W. (1933). *Psychologische Probleme* [Psychological problems]. Berlin: Verlag von Julius Springer.

Kozulin, A. (1994). The cognitive revolution in learning. Piaget and Vygotsky. In J.N. Mangieri & C. Collins Block (Eds.), *Creating powerful thinking in teachers and students. Diverse perspectives* (pp.269–287). Fort Worth: Harcourt Brace College Publishers.

Leont'ev, A. N. (in press). On Vygotsky's creative development. In R. Rieber (Ed.), R. van der Veer (Transl.), *The collected works of L.S. Vygotsky. Vol. 3. Problems of the theory and history of psychology*. New York, London: Plenum Press.

Luria, A.R. (1979). *The making of mind*. Cambridge, MA: Harvard University Press.

Mourelatos, A.P.D. (Ed.) (1974). *The pre-Socratics. A collection of critical essays*. Gardin City, NY: Anchor Books.

Overton, W.F. (1993). The arrow of time and cycles of time: Implications for change in cognitive development. In J. Montangero, A. Cornu-Wells, A. Tryphon, & J. Vonèche (Eds.), *Conceptions of change over time* (pp.159–180). Genève: Fondation Archives Jean Piaget.

Seltman, M., & Seltman, P. (1985). *Piaget's logic. A critique of genetic epistemology*. London: George Allen & Unwin.

Tudge, J.R.H., & Winterhoff, P.A. (1993). Vygotsky, Piaget, and Bandura: Perspectives on the relations between the social world and cognitive development. *Human Development, 36*, 61–81.

Valsiner, J. (1987). *Culture and the development of children's action*. Chichester: Wiley.

Van der Veer, R., & Valsiner, J. (1991). *Understanding Vygotsky. A quest for synthesis*. Oxford: Blackwell.
Van der Veer, R., & Valsiner, J. (Eds.) (1994). *The Vygotsky reader*. Oxford: Blackwell.
Van der Veer, R., Van IJzendoorn, M.H., & Valsiner, J. (Eds.) (1994). *Reconstructing the mind. Replicability in research on human development*. Norwood, NJ: Ablex Publishing Corporation.
Vidal, F. (1994). *Piaget before Piaget*. Cambridge, MA: Harvard University Press.
Vonèche, J. (1993). The mirror and the lamp: The opposition between mechanical and organismic explanations in developmental psychology. A response to Harry Beilin and Willis Overton. In J. Montangero, A. Cornu-Wells, A. Tryphon, & J. Vonèche (Eds.), *Conceptions of change over time* (pp.181–194). Genève: Fondation Archives Jean Piaget.
Vygotsky, L.S. (1930). Strukturnaja psikhologija [Structural psychology]. In L. Vygotsky, S. Gellershtejn, B. Fingert, & M. Shirvindt (Eds.), *Osnovnye techenija sovremennoj psikhologii* (pp.84–125). [Main currents of contemporary psychology]. Moscow: Gosudarstvennoe Izdatel'stvo.
Vygotsky, L.S. (in press, a). The historical meaning of the psychological crisis. A methodological investigation. In R. Rieber (Ed.), R. van der Veer (Trans.), *The collected works of L.S. Vygotsky. Vol. 3. Problems of the theory and history of psychology*. New York, London: Plenum Press. [Original work published 1926.]
Vygotsky, L.S. (in press, b). The methods of reflexological and psychological investigation. In R. Rieber (Ed.), R. van der Veer (Trans.), *The collected works of L.S. Vygotsky. Vol. 3. Problems of the theory and history of psychology*. New York, London: Plenum Press. [Original work published 1926.]
Vygotsky, L.S. (in press, c). A propos Koffka's article on self-observation. In R. Rieber (Ed.), R. van der Veer (Trans.), *The collected works of L.S. Vygotsky. Vol. 3. Problems of the theory and history of psychology*. New York, London: Plenum Press. [Original work published 1926.]
Vygotsky, L.S. (in press, d). Preface to Köhler. In R. Rieber (Ed.), R. van der Veer (Trans.), *The collected works of L.S. Vygotsky. Vol. 3. Problems of the theory and history of psychology*. New York, London: Plenum Press. [Original work published 1930.]
Vygotsky, L.S. (in press, e). Preface to Bühler. In R. Rieber (Ed.), R. van der Veer (Trans.), *The collected works of L.S. Vygotsky. Vol. 3. Problems of the theory and history of psychology*. New York, London: Plenum Press. [Original work published 1930.]
Vygotsky, L.S. (in press, f). The problem of development in structural psychology. A critical investigation. In R. Rieber (Ed.), R. van der Veer (Trans.), *The collected works of L.S. Vygotsky. Vol. 3. Problems of the theory and history of psychology*. New York, London: Plenum Press. [Original work published 1934.]
Wertsch, J.V. (1985). *Vygotsky and the social formation of mind*. Cambridge, MA: Harvard University Press.

CHAPTER FIVE

Mechanisms of internalisation and externalisation of knowledge in Piaget's and Vygotsky's theories[1]

Eduardo Martí *University of Barcelona, Spain*

INTRODUCTION

When comparing the works of Piaget and Vygotsky, one is at first tempted to point out the differences, which very quickly become incompatibilities. Thus, the individual, endogenous, operatory, universal constructivism, which accounts for the progress of the Piagetian subject, is opposed to the social, exogenous, semiotic, and contextual development inherent in the Vygotskian subject. In a certain way, the rational and individualistic optimism of Piaget (whose motto could be "rationality is constructed despite other people") is set against Vygotsky's social optimism ("it's thanks to others that we become conscious"). Without wishing to deny the important differences between the two authors, which will be apparent throughout this chapter, it would seem more interesting to try see in which ways their views can be brought together rather than demonstrating the irreconcilability of their theses. However, this rapprochement needs to set out from one of the paradigms (in this case, Piagetian constructivism), and show how it could be extended in ways that are indicated by the other paradigm (that of Vygotsky's theory). No attempt will be made at a synthesis of the two theories, for this would be a daunting task. On the other hand, re-examining Piaget's theses in the light of some of Vygotsky's postulates would seem a feasible undertaking, as there exists an important set of epistemological and methodological principles common to the two authors (genetic perspective, dialectic approach, anti-reductionism, anti-dualism, importance of action, primacy of processes, qualitative changes). However, it is beyond the scope of this chapter to compare the two works in their entirety. I have chosen rather to start from the analysis of the concept of *internalisation*, which is found in the writings of both authors, and which is a key concept for understanding both Piagetian constructivism and the social origin of thought in Vygotsky's theory. Owing to the epistemological limitations of taking a single concept to illustrate my point, I have preferred to examine the couple *internalisation / externalisation*, and to analyse its importance in the works of Piaget and Vygotsky. The lacunae in Piaget's explanations of how the internalisation/externalisation mechanisms actually work will be illustrated by reference to certain Vygotskian postulates, which in turn will enable me to outline what could be a Piagetian-based constructivism open to semiotic mediation.

THE DIALECTICS BETWEEN INTERNALISATION AND EXTERNALISATION

The opposition between Piaget and Vygotsky is frequently summed up in two precepts which show the direction of development in each theory. Piaget's conception is thus described as *"inside-out"* which means that, for this author, cognitive processes are constructed internally and it is only subsequently and secondarily that this construction has external repercussions which modify the child's relationship with his or her familiars and environment. Vygotsky's conception, on the other hand, is described as being *"outside-in"*, that is, the child first establishes relationships with others and these relationships, once they are internalised, constitute the basis of the child's cognitive processes (Kaye, 1982). In both cases, development is uni-directional: for Piaget, it corresponds to a process of externalisation, for Vygotsky to one of internalisation.

This view is over-simplistic, because it does not take into account the complexity that both theories attribute to the relationship between the internal and external aspects of knowledge, and to the bi-directional relationship between the two. For both authors, the relationship between the internal (internalised actions for Piaget, intrapsychological functions for Vygotsky) and the external (manifest actions for Piaget, interpsychological functions for Vygotsky) is in constant mutation throughout development[2]. For both authors, internal reality and external reality are not two different, static entities, defined once and for all: they are constructed throughout development and the frontiers between them are mobile. They are opposite aspects and, as such, inherent in all cognitive processes. Piaget accustomed us to this dialectic, explanatory approach which consisted of describing the changing relationships between bipolar properties that present antithetical but, nevertheless, interdependent aspects (Bidell, 1988; Inhelder & Piaget, 1979/1980). The internal/external couple is one of a long list of oppositions, along with "assimilation/accommodation", "structures/procedures", "action/meaning", "finality/causality", "transformation/comparison", etc. As Inhelder and Piaget (1979/1980, p.21) pointed out when speaking of internal and external finalities:

> No matter how antithetical these two types of goals may appear, they are as interdependent as the other pairs described above. On the one hand, logico-mathematical instruments, previously constructed according to internal goals, are needed for fulfilling external goals. On the other hand, internal goals lead to the construction of new mental constructs (classes, numbers, morphisms, etc) that will sooner or later serve for generating problems in physics that imply external goals.

Thus, for Piaget, development is far from being a unique tendency going from the inside to the outside; it is rather a conquest involving the simultaneous organisation of internal mental space and external reality. The whole of Piagetian constructivism is founded on the dialectical nature of knowledge, which arises neither in the subject nor in the object but from the interaction between the two, and progresses in two directions: internalisation and externalisation (Martí 1990; Piaget, 1980a).

Despite the importance accorded by Vygotsky in his research to the passage from the outside to the inside (internalisation process), he defends the notion of a close connection between interpsychological functioning and intrapsychological functioning and talks of an isomorphism between the organisation of the two planes (Wertsch, 1985). Far from supposing a simple transposition of the properties of interpsychological functioning onto the internal plane, the internalisation process supposes, for Vygotsky, an internal reconstruction which, in turn, modifies the interpsychological function. Thus Vygotsky believed, as did Piaget, that the plane of internal functioning is not a given; it is constructed. This idea is well-expressed by Leont'ev (1981, cited in Wertsch, 1985, p.64), who links it to the problem of consciousness:

Thus the process of internalization in not *transferral* of an external activity to a preexisting internal "plane of consciousness": it is the process in which this internal plane is formed.

This first glimpse at Piaget's and Vygotsky's theories shows the similarity of their overall approach as regards the relationship between the inside and the outside. Indeed, both Piaget and Vygotsky were particularly aware of the dangers of reductionism, the former formulating this in terms of nativism vs. empiricism, the latter in terms of individual vs. social origin of mind. Despite these differences, which will be dealt with more fully later in this chapter, both authors diverge from reductionist solutions in their acceptance of the internal/external duality[3]. They reformulate the problem of the construction of knowledge no longer in antagonistic terms of "organism vs. environment", but in terms where the tension between these two entities and the resolution of this tension are at the basis of the construction of knowledge.

FROM METAPHOR TO EXPLANATORY MECHANISMS

The terms *internalisation* and *externalisation* are, in fact, no more than descriptive processes; they relate to a spatial metaphor and indicate the main features of a very general characteristic of the development of knowledge. We must go beyond this purely descriptive stage to see what this twofold process of internalisation/externalisation consists of in Piaget's and Vygotsky's theories, in terms of more explanatory, psychological models. Paradoxically, both authors focused their explicit analyses on the concept of *internalisation*[4]. Our study will show that the externalisation mechanisms are implicit in the explanations of the two authors, but that they can also be made manifest.

Internalisation according to Piaget
The process of internalisation is central to Piagetian constructivism. Throughout his life-work, Piaget bore in mind this developmental tendency which makes it possible to construct an increasingly autonomous internal plane of functioning from an external reality. The crucial point of this tendency is the passage from sensorimotor intelligence to representative intelligence, which Piaget described as follows (1947/1972, pp.105–106):

When the subject no longer acts when confronted with the
data of a problem, and appears to be thinking instead ...
everything seems to indicate that he continues his attempts,
but with implicit trials or internalised actions ...

Piaget put the problem this way (pp.105–106):

The main problem, then, is to understand the mechanism of
these internal co-ordinations, which imply both invention
without trial-and-error and a mental anticipation closely
related to representation.
    ... In fact, it is clear that once he becomes used to tertiary
circular reactions and to the intelligent trial-and-error that
constitutes true active experimentation the child sooner or
later becomes capable of internalising this behaviour ...
Sensorimotor schemata that have become sufficiently
mobile and amenable to co-ordination among themselves
give rise to mutual assimilations, spontaneous enough for
there to be no further need for actual trial-and-error and
rapid enough to give an impression of immediate
restructuring. Internal co-ordination of schemata will, then,
bear the same relation to the external co-ordination of the
earlier levels, as inner speech, a simple rapid, internalised
rough draft of overt language, bears to outer speech.

The interest of Piaget's explanation lies in the fact that internal
psychological reality, far from being considered as a simple product of
the transposition of external knowledge, is conceived of as a new level
of functioning. This new functioning results essentially from an increase
in the structuring activity of assimilation which operates step-by-step
in experimental trial-and-error behaviour, but which is so rapid in
invention that the assimilatory activity is dissimulated and becomes
sudden (Piaget, 1936/1952). This increase in speed changes the mode of
functioning: "At first cut up and visible from the outside, it becomes
regularised and seems to be internalised by becoming rapid" (1936/1952,
p.342). Piaget thus solves the problem of the passage from discovery,
belonging to sub-stage V of the sensorimotor stage, to invention, which
appears at sub-stage VI; in a similar way, he explains the passage from
sensorimotor intelligence to representative intelligence (1936/1952,
p.341):

The two essential questions raised by such behaviour patterns in relation to the preceding ones are those of *invention* and *representation*. Henceforth there exists invention and no longer only discovery; there is, moreover, representation and no longer only sensori motor groping. These two aspects of systematic intelligence are interdependent. To invent is to combine mental, that is to say, representative, schemata and, in order to become mental the sensorimotor schemata must be capable of intercombining in every way, that is to say, of being able to give rise to true invention.

Thus, the creation of a new, internal plane of functioning results from a new property—the combination of schemes (freer, faster). What is important in this new mode of functioning is that the structuring activity no longer needs to rely on actual, successive perceptual data, nor on a continuous, external control. One of the consequences of this freer, more sudden, more rapid functioning is that it is less visible and frequently escapes the eye of the observer. But the most important part of this internal functioning is not so much the fact that it is "not visible", but that intellectual functioning is less dependent on external data; in other words, there is a increase in the subject's autonomy and control.

Now, if we go deeper into the Piagetian explanation, we realise that this release from actual data, inherent in invention, (as opposed to the dependency on external data, typical of sensorimotor trial-and-error explorations) is closely linked to representation (1936/1952, p.343):

> ... the structuring activity no longer needs always to depend on the actual data of perception and, ... can make a complex system of simply evoked schemata converge.

Or yet again (p.351):

> It is ... due to representation that ... assimilatory activity can be pursued and purified on a new plane, separate from that of immediate perception or action properly so called.

These representations or "evocations of absent objects" (p.351) thus allow sensorimotor intelligence to be realised on a new plane. But if, for Piaget, invention necessitates representation, representation in turn depends on invention; indeed, it is the dynamic process inherent in the functioning of the assimilation schemes that creates the necessary conditions for representation to occur. It is thanks to the differentiation between *signifier* and *significate* inherent in the symbolic (or semiotic) function, that Piaget succeeds in specifying the interaction between invention (process resulting from the activity of the schemes) and representation (1936/1952, p.352):

> Things are clarified as soon as, with the theory of signs, one makes of the visual imagery peculiar to representation, a simple symbolism serving as "signifier", and of the dynamic process peculiar to invention the signification itself, in other words, the signified. Representation would thus serve as symbol to inventive activity …

In addition, Piaget explains the origin of symbols by genetic filiation of perceptual mechanisms; deferred imitation is the essential mechanism that enables the subject to evoke physical and human models in their absence (we find this evocation in symbolic play and in drawing; see Piaget, 1945/1962). These imitations are gradually internalised as schemes, which make mental imagery possible. Piaget also explains language development within this context of imitation where the symbolic function becomes possible (Piaget & Inhelder, 1966/1969, p.87):

> Language plays a particularly important role in this formative process. Unlike images and other semiotic instruments, which are created by the individual as the need arises, language has already been elaborated socially and contains a notation for an entire system of cognitive instruments (relationships, classifications, etc.) for use in the service of thought. The individual learns this system and then proceeds to enrich it.

So, for Piaget, the process of internalisation has two components: on the one hand, it requires a more rapid and more mobile composition of action schemes; on the other hand, it has to rely on internal symbols which constitute the necessary tools for representation. Symbols, far from being considered as pre-existing data, are explained, in turn, by imitative activity and are closely linked to the autonomous dynamics of action, even though, once constituted, they favour the development and fixing of the information required by thought (Inhelder, 1976). Piaget adds a third mechanism to these first two mechanisms inherent in internalisation: " … an *awareness*[5] not … of the desired results of actions, but its actual mechanisms, thus enabling the search for the solution to be combined with a consciousness of its nature." (Piaget, 1947/1972, p.121, emphasis added.)

Although Piaget gave special importance to this passage from sensorimotor intelligence to representative intelligence, which is essential if we wish to understand the process of internalisation and the constitution of internal thought[6], he considered the tendency to the internalisation of thought to be present throughout development: When representative intelligence becomes possible, cognitive development is characterised once again by the victory of internal autonomy—arising from a continual coordination of actions—over the dependency on external data, close to perception and direct action. In this sense, development is characterised by Piaget as a recurrent passage from exogenous knowledge (linked to observables, to perception, and to the more external aspects of action) to more endogenous knowledge. This tendency was clearly demonstrated by Piaget during his epistemological studies on the functional mechanisms of the construction of knowledge (Piaget, 1980c). The relationship between empirical abstraction and reflective abstraction and between inductive generalisation and constructive generalisation, or yet again between correspondences and transformations, clearly shows this tendency to go from the exogenous to the endogenous (Piaget, 1980b).

The study of taking consciousness (the grasp of consciousness) brings out this general tendency to internalisation very clearly, as the taking-consciousness mechanism goes from the more peripheral aspects of action to the more internal ones (Piaget, 1974/1977a). Now, this general tendency towards internalisation is linked to the process of equilibration. For Piaget, disequilibria and the process of augmentative equilibration are of prime importance in the construction of knowledge. The two main classes of disequilibria—external disequilibria (difficulty in applying or attributing schemes and operations to objects) and internal disequilibria (difficulty in composing these schemes and these operations)—account for the interaction between what is outside the subject and what is inside (Piaget, 1975/1985). This is all the more true because, for Piaget, the succession of alpha, beta, and gamma-type behaviour (behaviours that account for the type of perturbation and of compensation associated to them) shows the tendency of the construction of knowledge, which goes from the outside (empirically observed behaviour) to the inside (the same variation reconstructed on the level of the subject's operations). This tendency to go from the outside to the inside is the sign of an increasingly mobile and stable equilibrium. It should be added that the succession of these forms of compensation does not correspond to three general stages, but to recurrent phases that are found regularly according to the area studied or the problem posed.

This complex picture sketched by Piaget of the general tendency towards internalisation would be incomplete without reference to the reciprocal process of externalisation. Although this second process is just as essential in Piagetian constructivism, it has received far less attention. It is internalisation that leaves its mark on the progressive construction of internal knowledge which becomes increasingly stable, mobile, and removed from immediate perceptual data or from badly coordinated or isolated actions applied to objects. It is this process that accompanies operatory construction. Externalisation, on the other hand, enables Piaget to account for the parallel tendency of knowledge to go deeper into the properties of objects and of their relationships (causal relationships). This double tendency is clearly manifest once again in the studies on the grasp of consciousness (Piaget, 1974/1977a), where Piaget shows that this mechanism is bi-directional: internalisation, towards the more central aspects of the subject's action (the means he or she used, the properties of the coordinations such as transitivity, reciprocity, etc.), and externalisation, towards the aspects inherent in objects and in their relationships. In fact, this twofold process is specific to Piagetian interactionism which is characterised by a correlate dual construction of, on the one hand, the internal structures of thought and, on the other, of increasingly extensive knowledge about external reality.

Piaget's point of view on the connection between internal and external cannot be reduced to the "inside-out" tendency. It would be truer to say that it focuses on the passage from external knowledge (in the sense of "visible" but also of superficial, changing, because it is linked to perception or to isolated actions) to internal knowledge (in the double sense of "not visible" and of more stable knowledge, arising from the composition of actions and therefore removed from the more peripheral contact with the external world of objects). For Piaget, externalisation corresponds to the same tendency but this time applied to the knowledge of physical reality and no longer to the internal construction of knowledge.

The strong point of Piaget's conception is that he considers the subject's point of view in the construction of knowledge; he thus avoids both empiricist-type reductionism and nativist reductionism. However, the connection between internal and external is subordinated to the dynamism of the coordination of actions alone, guided by the compensatory mechanisms of equilibration. External forms of knowledge, transported by various symbolic or semiotic systems, partly constructed by the subject but forged during social interaction, play a minor role in Piaget's explanatory system. For Piaget, symbolic forms (gestures, movements, images) or semiotic ones (language, mathematical notation) are of secondary importance in the construction of knowledge and in the internalisation of thought, and are considered as simple props for operatory thinking. Semiotics, for Piaget, is subordinated to operatory thinking. It would seem necessary to analyse the role of the explicitation of knowledge in the creation of more external, more visible and more communicable forms of thought. Although Piaget recognises the fact that the differentiation of knowledge and its explicitation is a conquest of development linked to the progress of reflective abstraction (Piaget, 1977b) and of taking consciousness (Piaget, 1974/1977a), this passage from implicit knowledge to explicit knowledge plays no fundamental role as an externalisation mechanism. Finally, both the internalisation process and the externalisation process have little to do with the subject's exchanges with his or her social environment and are not affected by the subject's communicative exchanges with the people around him or her. It would thus seem necessary, within the frame of Piagetian constructivism, to give renewed importance to the effect of these external forms of knowledge on the internalisation process. Vygotsky's theses on the relationship between the inside and the outside will provide us with the occasion to reformulate Piaget's point of view in this sense.

Internalisation according to Vygotsky

Like Piaget, Vygotsky makes more allusions in his work to the internalisation process[7] than to the reciprocal one of externalisation. It is undeniable, however, that he attributes greater importance than Piaget to external functioning in the relationship between external and internal. But, as we shall see, his view cannot be reduced to a single tendency going from the outside-in.

Vygotsky tackles the problem of the relationship between external and internal functioning via the well-known "genetic law of cultural development" and, following in the steps of Spinoza and of Marxism, clearly defends the idea of a social genesis of thought: all psychological functions appear on two distinct planes, first on the social plane (interpsychological functioning) and then on the individual, psychological plane (intrapsychological functioning) (Vygotsky, 1981b). For Vygotsky, external functioning is identified with interpsychological functioning between persons (1981b, p.162):

> It is necessary that everything internal in higher forms was external, that is, for others it was what is now for oneself. Any higher mental function necessarily goes through an external stage in its development because it is initially a social function. This is the center of the whole problem of internal and external behavior ... When we speak of a

process, "external" means "social". Any higher mental
function was external because it was social at some point
before becoming an internal, truly mental function.

Thus, contrary to Piaget, Vygotsky defines the external plane as being
constituted by social interactions. In this sense, Vygotsky clearly
defends the social origin of the construction of knowledge (at least, as
far as what he calls "higher psychological functions" are concerned). But,
as Wertsch (1985) points out, this social origin of knowledge should not
be interpreted as an affirmation that a person learns through his or her
exchanges with others. For Vygotsky, there is a deep connection between
the two planes of functioning, the external plane determining the main
aspects of internal functioning. This connection is achieved through the
process of internalisation, a process that transforms social phenomena
(thought of by Vygotsky as interactions between people, especially
dyadic interactions) into psychological phenomena. These psychological
functions (internal functioning) keep some of the properties of the
functioning of social interaction.

One might think that the internal plane is created by a simple
transfer of the properties of the social processes onto the
intrapsychological plane. However, Vygotsky makes it clear that this is
not his belief and that, on the contrary, internalisation consists of an
internal reconstruction that modifies the process by changing its
structure and its function (Vygotsky, 1981b, p.151). This is
demonstrated by his analyses of internal language which show that
external language (for the others) takes on a new form when it becomes
internal (language for oneself) and possesses new properties (for
example, abbreviation) even if it keeps the dialogue structure typical of
external language (Vygotsky, 1934/1962). According to Vygotsky and
Luria (1930, quoted in Lawrence & Valsiner, 1993, p.163):

> The process here (interiorisation) undergoes alterations
> analogous to those observed in the child's transition from
> "outward" speech to "inward". As a result of the process of
> interiorisation of the higher psychological operation, we
> have a new structure, a new function of formerly applied
> methods and an entirely new composition of psychological
> processes.

Even if Vygotsky is not explicit about the exact psychological
mechanisms that might explain the passage from external functioning
to internal functioning, it is clear that the latter is not a simple copy of
external functioning. There can be no doubt either that, for Vygotsky, it

is the properties of interpersonal activities that determine the nature (essentially social) of the internal psychological processes.

But the internalisation process as described by Vygotsky cannot be fully understood without the notion of semiotic mediation. This mechanism, which is certainly the central point of Vygotsky's theory, helps us to grasp the intimate connection between the social nature of higher-order psychological functions which are, at the same time, semiotic. In fact, contrary to the elementary functions, these functions use signs. The use of signs in psychological activity (for example, language signs in memorising) does not just favour this activity but completely modifies the latter when it is mediatised by signs (Vygotsky, 1981a). It is the semiotic nature of communicative interactions between persons that makes the internalisation process possible (Vygotsky & Luria, 1930, quoted in Lawrence & Valsiner, 1993, p.163):

> ... what was an outward sign operation ... is now *transformed into a new intra-psychological layer* and gives birth to a new psychological system, incomparably superior in content, and cultural-psychological in genesis. The process of "interiorisation" of cultural forms of behaviour, which we just touched upon, is related to radical changes in the activity of the most important psychological functions, to the reconstruction of psychological activity on the basis of sign operations ...

Now, activity mediatised by signs appears first, for Vygotsky, in the context of social interaction and manifests itself by external forms, by external signs. It is the child's contact with the mediatised forms of psychological activity that appear between persons, which allows the creation of the same forms of activity, but this time on the internal plane (Vygotsky & Luria, 1930, quoted in Lawrence & Valsiner, 1993, p.163):

> We call this withdrawal of the operation within this reconstruction of the higher psychological functions related to new structural changes, the process of interiorisation, meaning mainly, the following: the fact that at their first stages, the higher psychological functions are built as outer forms of behaviour and find support in the outer is by no means accidental; on the contrary, it is determined by the very psychological nature of the higher function which, as we have mentioned above, does not appear as a direct continuation of elementary processes but is a *social method of behaviour applied by itself to itself.*

According to Vygotsky, the key to understanding the forms of semiotic mediation in the internal plane should be sought in the social and external origins of the sign. And this is in two senses. First, sign systems (language, counting systems, systems of algebraic symbols, mnemotechnic devices, etc.) are social in nature because they are the product of sociocultural evolution and are not invented by each individual in his or her relationship with nature; they become individual, internal to the functioning of each individual through the internalisation process. Second, signs are social in nature in the sense that the sign enters into the communicational dynamics of social interaction. The sign is in fact conceived by Vygotsky as a means, used at the outset for social reasons, for influencing others and, only later (thanks to internalisation), as a means for influencing oneself (Vygotsky, 1981a,b).

Vygotsky does not explain exactly how individuals become able to master and to internalise the different external sign systems offered by their culture. He indicates, nevertheless, that a first phase of this mastery consists of a control founded on a manifest act (visible, external). This is true for any psychological function and is evident, for example, in the mastery of internal language (which is preceded by a phase in which the child verbalises in a manifest way and uses the signs of language outwardly), in the mastery of counting techniques (the internalised forms of which are preceded by counting on one's fingers), or in memorising activities (first based on external signs and only later on internal signs such as words, or images). In his description of this phase of development, Vygotsky (1934/1962, p.47) adds:

> The fourth stage we call "ingrowth" stage. The external operation turns inward and undergoes a profound change in the process. The child begins to count in its head, to use "logical memory", that is, to operate with inherent relationships and inner signs. In speech development this is the final stage of inner, soundless speech. There remains a constant interaction between outer and inner operations, one form effortlessly and frequently changing into the other and back again. Inner speech may become very close in form to external speech or even become exactly like it when it serves as a preparation for external speech—for instance, in thinking over a lecture to be given. There is no sharp division between inner and external behavior, and each influences the other.

This passage is interesting for two reasons. On the one hand, Vygotsky specifies that internal functioning is preceded by a phase where the child uses signs externally (signs that exist in his or her immediate environment and are part of interpersonal activities). In some ways, this phase can be considered as the first step in the child's appropriation of the signs of his or her familiar environment. This appropriation creates a new psychological function. Thus for Vygotsky, as was the case for Piaget, the formation of an internal functioning is preceded by a phase where actions are manifest, external, and dependent on stimuli and physical indices. On the other hand, Vygotsky maintains that internal operations, once they are internalised, constantly interact with external operations; in other words, the development of the intrapsychological plane seems, in turn, to modify interpsychological activity (see also, Wertsch, 1985). Even if Vygotsky does not specify the nature of these interactions, we are far from a unilateral vision going from the "outside-in". These remarks also show that the internalisation process cannot by itself account for the interactions between the inner plane and the outer plane of functioning. Even if Vygotsky is concerned only with the passage from the outside to the inside, we can deduce the importance of a reciprocal process of externalisation which, in Vygotsky's case, is closely linked to the external manifestations of behaviour in the dynamics of communicative exchange between the child and other people.

Like Piaget, Vygotsky proposes a complex vision of the internalisation process, which far from being a unilateral movement of transfer from the outside to the inside, allows us to understand the construction of an internal, individual plane of functioning, intimately connected to the external, social functioning. Despite this position and even if it is clear for him that internal functioning is not a copy of external functioning, Vygotsky gives no details about this internal reconstruction (for example, the mechanisms that would make it possible) nor about the subject's contribution to the internalisation process. In all his research, Vygotsky considers the child as the object of social and cultural influences and he focuses unilaterally on the influence of the interpsychological functions on the intrapsychological ones (Elbers, Maier, Hoekstra, & Hoogsteder, 1992; Lawrence & Valsiner, 1993). Contrary to Piaget's position, the dynamics of the subject's actions do not play a structuring role in the internalisation process. This position raises a serious problem in a genetic perspective because Vygotsky conceives of interpsychological functioning as a given, and in some ways as atemporal. It would, however, seem just as important to explain the construction of this interpsychological functioning as to explain that of internal functioning[8]. Despite this limitation, the advantage of Vygotsky's position is that he is interested in the influence of external functioning on the construction of thought; for Piaget, on the other hand, the primacy of the external aspect of knowledge over the construction of thought is seen as a first phase, a dependency that needs to be transcended by operatory construction. Everything seems to point to the fact that whereas, for Piaget, thought is constructed to the detriment of external influences, Vygotsky believes that it is constructed thanks to their impact.

An examination of Vygotsky's thesis of semiotic mediation allows us to appreciate his position with regard to the influence of external aspects; this helps us to understand the importance he attributes, contrary to Piaget, to semiotic systems in the construction of thought. Indeed, for Vygotsky, it is the semiotic nature of activities (realised first of all in the dynamics of child–adult communication) that makes the internalisation of these activities in individual thinking possible. For Vygotsky, the importance of culturally constructed sign systems (language, mathematical systems, iconic systems, mnemotechnic systems) in the constitution of the individual's mental functioning means that the latter is closely dependent on the former. In this sense, for Vygotsky, the fact of using different semiotic systems leads to a fundamental difference in the contents and in the form of thought (Van der Veer & Valsiner, 1991). What is not explained in the Vygotskyan perspective is how these semiotic systems are constructed. By contrast, for Piaget, whose interest lay in the general aspects of knowledge, the incorporation of symbolic systems does not fundamentally change the nature of thought, although it does offer an explanation of the origin and the development of these semiotic systems. Once constructed, these signs and symbols play, for this author, a secondary role only, as a help or support to operatory activity.

TOWARDS A MEDIATIONAL CONSTRUCTIVISM

After this re-examination of Piaget's theses through Vygotskyan eyes using, in particular, the relationship between internal and external aspects, I shall now go on to discuss some of the fundamental theses of Piagetian constructivism and to elaborate on them by incorporating semiotic mediation as an essential mechanism in the development of knowledge along with the classical mechanisms proposed by Piaget. If the latter are decisive for understanding how knowledge is constructed and how it becomes increasingly autonomous, stable, and objective, we need to give a new significance to the externalisation of knowledge process and to evaluate the reciprocal influence of these external forms on internal constructions. Reference will be made to research in cognitive psychology which has shown the importance of symbolic notations for the development of knowledge in specific fields (in particular, that of mathematical knowledge).

We have already seen that, for Piaget, the externalisation process is conceived of as a deepening of our understanding of the properties and relationships of the objects of the physical world. Certain Vygotskyan theses suggest that externalisation can also be understood as a visible, explicit manifestation of knowledge that had previously remained latent. Piaget (1974/1977a) suggested the same tendency in his work on the grasp of consciousness: the construction of increasingly explicit knowledge that subjects can externalise through their gestures (when they simulate something they have just done) or through language (when they explain what they have just done). In fact, Piaget admits that taking consciousness generates conceptualisations of different degrees of explicitation, ranging from vague awareness in automatically regulated success, to manifest and clearly verbalised consciousness (Piaget, 1974/1977a). Karmiloff-Smith, despite her disagreement with some of Piaget's theoretical positions, also defends the existence of a general, recurrent mechanism—"representational redescription"— which is responsible for the passage from unconscious, implicit knowledge linked to functioning, to conscious, accessible knowledge, expressed by verbal explanations (Karmiloff-Smith, 1992a). This transformation of knowledge is due more to the stability and success of cognitive functioning than to failures or conflict, and involves at least three levels: a first level of implicit knowledge represented in a procedural way, a second level where knowledge is defined explicitly but cannot be verbalised, and a third level where knowledge can, this time, be put into words (Karmiloff-Smith, 1992b). Parallel to this recurrent mechanism, the construction of knowledge is also characterised by a progressive automatisation and encapsulement. With experience and training, certain behaviour, which was at first carried out consciously, gradually comes under the control of rapid, automatic regulations requiring little conscious attention (Brown, 1987; Kluwe, 1987). This tendency, parallel to externalisation, accounts for the progressive internalisation of knowledge.

In much the same way, Allal and Saada-Robert (1992, pp.270–271), basing their analysis partly on Piaget's typology of regulation mechanisms, have distinguished four degrees of explicitation of cognitive regulations: (1) implicit regulations, integrated into cognitive functioning, of which the subject is not aware; (2) regulations that can become conscious and be made explicit in response to an external request; (3) regulations that are explicit, conscious, and can be communicated to others; (4) implemented regulations that rely on an external support. In the latter case, which is of particular interest to us, the implementation can be based on a support produced by the subject him or herself (an outline, a diagram, a mnemotechnic notation, etc.) or on a support from another source (list of criteria supplied by a teacher, diagram provided by a computer, algebra symbols, etc.).

The point of interest of all these proposals is that they enable us to consider the externalisation process in more detail, and to give it a dynamic role in the construction of knowledge. Externalisation is not just a progressive construction of external reality (as Piaget explicitly suggests) but a reorganisation of knowledge in the sense of its gradually becoming consciously explicit. This explicitation leads to an increase in the possibilities of communication and of sharing with others. As this knowledge is constructed explicitly (and relies on signs or symbols, often concretised by external representations or specific symbolic notations) so, in turn, it modifies cognitive functioning; its communicational potential also increases. Thus, it is obvious that the externalisation process, conceived of in this way, plays an important role in the construction of knowledge; it stays closely linked to semiotic mediation and to social interaction. I shall take the example of mathematical thinking to illustrate this point.

It is interesting to note that although some mathematical developments would not have been possible without the development of a notational system, cross-cultural studies have shown that numerical notation is not a necessary condition for the development of certain arithmetical principles: cultures that do not possess numerical notation systems nevertheless use forms of counting that follow certain arithmetical principles (Karmiloff-Smith, 1992a, p.107; Tolchinksy & Karmiloff-Smith, 1993). This shows the primacy and the universality of certain principles and mathematical operations in the emergence of external, explicit, symbolic systems (Gelman & Gallistel, 1978; Resnick, 1986). Now, even without a written notational system or a list of counting words, counting often relies on external indices; this is the case in the system used by the Oksapmin people in Papua and New Guinea who base their counting procedures on a system composed of 27 parts of the body (Saxe, 1991). The use of external indices in counting activities was something Vygotsky remarked on as one of the first phases the child goes through in his or her mastery of counting operations; it has also been documented in recent observations on counting techniques (Steffe, 1990; Steffe & von Glasersfeld, 1985). It would seem that, in the case of mathematics and in keeping with Piaget's explanation, certain universal principles and procedures grow out of the activity of the action schemes[9].

It should be added, however, that these activities progress by externalisation which can lead to the construction of complex symbolic systems; these, in turn, deeply modifying mathematical thinking and its development. This return influence of sign systems on cognition has been defended by numerous authors and has been shown for different types of semiotic mediation (Martí, 1992, 1993; Papert, 1980; Pea, 1985; Salomon, 1992, for computers; Goody, 1987; Olson, 1986; Street, 1993, for writing; Greenfield, 1984; Meringoff, 1980; Salomon & Leigh, 1984, for audiovisual images). We can thus accept the idea, put forward in its general principles by Vygotsky, that the use of semiotic mediation (for example, a mathematical notation) profoundly modifies the construction of thought (in this case, mathematical thinking). But it is certain also that this mediation is, in turn, the product of a construction, characterised by a double process of internalisation and of externalisation directed by mechanisms such as taking consciousness, abstraction or regulation. One of the delicate questions that needs to be elucidated is the role of social interaction and communicational constraints in the origin of mediation.

As already shown, Piaget detached the origin of signs and of symbols from their communicative ties. He was interested in their representative function only, which he explained by the differentiation of the signifier from the significate; this arises thanks to the double assimilatory and accommodatory function of schemes. The communicative function of signs is, therefore, secondary for Piaget. Semiotic mediation emerges as a new property of individual functioning. The problem lies in explaining how other people contribute, to regulate this emergence. Now, for Vygotsky, signs are social and must be conceived of, from the beginning, as a means of influencing others. Only afterwards do they become instruments of thought, a means of representation. Semiotic mediation is present in interpsychological functioning; it is a given. The problem here is to explain how this mediation process is constructed. These two positions, which at first glance seem irreconcilable, can in my opinion be integrated if we take into account the convergent aspects of internalisation and externalisation in the construction of knowledge. As we saw before, mathematical knowledge is tied to the internalisation mechanisms inherent in the activity of the schemes; but, at the same time, it generates and leans on external, communicable (products of externalisation) symbolic forms, which in turn modify individual constructions.

Certain aspects of this double process have been revealed by historical research on the origin of notational systems and on the construction of mathematical knowledge by children in school contexts. The study of the prehistoric evolution of the first semiotic notations has shown the convergence and cohesion of internal aspects (abstraction, differentiation, taking consciousness, correspondences) with external ones (communication, social relationships) (Schmandt-Besserat, 1990). Thus, the first external traces consisting of a series of lines carved into bones (which appear at the same period as the iconic symbols representing animals) represent discrete events, probably the successive appearances of the moon or the counting of hunted animals (Schmandt-Besserat, 1990). The possibility of this sort of production is directly linked to a correspondence principle (each line represents a single event) and to an abstraction mechanism (identical geometrical signs represent, out of context, a concrete and changing piece of information). The use of such signs also shows an awareness and a differentiation between the product of knowledge (physically present) and the construction process itself. It is owing to this differentiation that notations are able to play a completely new role in the development of thought. But it would be impossible to explain the appearance of these first traces outside a precise functional context. Indeed, these traces represented the quantitative dimension of important phenomena (appearance of the moon, hunted animals) which needed to be kept in mind so that all the individuals of the community could have access to them. Moreover, the characteristics of these Palaeolithic communities of the Middle East (societies where food was not stored, egalitarian groups where all the members had access to common resources) explain some of the limitations of these first marks. On the one hand, the information carried by the traces was known only to the person who produced the marks; on the other hand, due to the fact that these marks used one type of trace only (vertical incision), they were able to represent only one type of data at a time. These notations are appropriate only for egalitarian groups who needed to register just a few obvious phenomena (Schmandt-Besserat, 1990).

The appearance in Neolithic times of a different system of numerical notation is a good illustration of this convergence between the internal and external aspects of knowledge. The novelty lay in the use of clay to make exemplars of different geometrical shapes. The form of each exemplar indicated the type of item it represented (animals, grain, etc.) and the number of exemplars indicated the number of items considered. As with the traces notched into bones, the ability to create clay exemplars supposes a mechanism for abstracting the reality represented as well as the application of the principle of establishing correspondences between objects, and a taking consciousness and a differentiation between the result of knowledge (externalised) and its process. But, contrary to the traces, the clay exemplars suppose an additional taking consciousness of the differences between qualitative information (the type of phenomenon represented) and quantitative information (the number of exemplars used); this difference is made explicit externally. In addition, contrary to the marks on the bones, the clay exemplars are artefacts, built solely to register information and to communicate it to others. These new characteristics had, in turn, repercussions on the cognitive processes. The handling of information became more flexible; this made it easier to do additions and subtractions, and to make corrections; it became possible to store a large number of various types of phenomena with a smaller risk of error than with human memory. They also made it easier to communicate information. As with the traces on bones, it would seem that clay exemplars were created in a particular social context which determined their functionality. Indeed, these more sedentary, agricultural societies had new requirements; they needed to improve the means of keeping track of products of first necessity in order to register and control them, so as to be able to distribute them in an optimal way and to plan their crop-growing (Schmandt-Besserat, 1990). These data defend neither a purely social nor a purely individual primacy of the appearance and evolution of the first mathematical notations. It would seem, on the contrary, that both the internal aspects of knowledge linked to the mechanisms responsible for the dynamics of action and the external aspects linked to communication and social constraints play an essential role in the construction of notational systems. In addition, these results show how these external sign systems profoundly modified cognition.

Research on the construction of mathematical knowledge in a school environment has also shown the importance both of individual mechanisms linked to the pupils' activity and of interpsychological mechanisms linked to communication and to semiotic mediation. Nevertheless, in this case, the child is faced with ready-constructed semiotic systems which have a long history modelled by social use. The question here is not to envisage how they were constructed in their entirety, but to see how the child re-constructs them through his or her contact with his or her social partners. Far from being a simple, unique process of internalisation of external forms of behaviour transmitted by the teacher, children build their mathematical knowledge from the dynamics of their actions, by regulatory mechanisms, abstraction, taking consciousness, and generalisation (Piaget, 1950). But this construction does not take place in isolation. It fits into a social context which reorganises it in two different ways. On the one hand, from birth and more particularly from the moment they start school, children find themselves in an environment that is rich in pre-constructed and pre-used mathematical notations, which they have to re-elaborate and re-use for their own purposes. In this sense, the child is more a "re-constructor" of mathematical knowledge and language than a simple constructor. The proof   lies in the difficulties the child has in assimilating such a language (Davis & Hersch, 1989; Gómez-Granell, 1991; Pimm, 1990; Rivière, 1990). On the other hand, other people (adults, teachers, other children), through their activities that regulate the child's behaviour, are part of this constructive process. These regulatory activities vary greatly from one situation to another and depend also on the type of relationship that grows up between the child and other people. For example, in the cooperative context between children of the same age, the fact of sharing the recall of an item of information, of comparing different points of view, or of sharing out activities in a problem-solving situation, can modify the type of strategy used (Martí, 1994b). Whatever the case, these regulations arising out of social interactions, which often use external supports (computer programs, diagrams, plans, written notations), are decisive in explicitation, in taking consciousness, and in achieving autonomous control when acquiring mathematical knowledge in a school environment (Martí, Steren, & García-Milà, 1994; Resnick, Levine, & Teasley, 1991; Saxe, 1991; Schoenfeld, 1987). As in the case of the historical research into the development of mathematical notations, the acquisition of mathematical knowledge supposes a joint process of internalisation and of externalisation, where individual mechanisms of construction and reorganisation of knowledge converge with interpsychological mechanisms linked to communication, cooperation, and semiotic mediation.

CONCLUSIONS

The concept of internalisation, which has a long tradition in European thinking (Lawrence & Valsiner, 1993) would seem essential if we wish to understand the impact of Piaget's and Vygotsky's theories. However, this is true only if: (1) we go beyond its metaphorical meaning and analyse the explanatory mechanisms underlying it (Winegar, in press) and (2) we envisage simultaneously the reciprocal process of externalisation. It is only if we take these two points into consideration that the term can account for an essential tendency in the construction of knowledge in Piaget's and Vygotsky's theories, and that it acquires a different meaning from other terms that have been proposed to replace it, such as "mastery" (Wertsch, 1993) or "appropriation" (Rogoff, 1990).

    The comparison of the Piagetian and Vygotskyan theses related to internalisation/externalisation led me to point out earlier in this chapter the importance of the mechanisms proposed by Piaget in the con-struction of knowledge (equilibration, taking consciousness, reflective abstraction); these mechanisms account for the tendency of (operatory) knowledge to become increasingly autonomous and less dependent on immediate external data (internalisation process). The absence of mechanisms accounting for a reciprocal tendency towards externalisation in Piaget's theory led me, at the same time, to stress the importance of the explicitation of knowledge as illustrated by research in cognitive psychology. The confrontation of Piaget's and Vygotsky's theses also caused me to give new significance to semiotic mediation and to regulation by other people as essential mechanisms in the construction of knowledge. A constructivism (like that of Piaget) which subordinates symbolic mediation and interpsychological regulation to the constraints of operatory activity can lead to our thinking of development as a process that is shut off from interpersonal dynamics and insensitive to the particular characteristics of the sign systems used by all acts of knowledge. The results of a wide variety of research show the limitations of such a conception. However, when the Piagetian paradigm is abandoned in favour of various Vygotskyan or neo-Vygotskyan positions, it often happens that the individual's dynamics and the mechanisms responsible for the construction of knowledge are not taken into account, and development is thought of as a process that is totally subordinated to interpsychological mechanisms and yet unconstructive from the subject's point of view. The whole tradition of Piagetian research and much contemporary research in cognitive psychology show the limits of such a view.

ACKNOWLEDGMENT

I wish to thank Ana Teberosky for her critical reading of a first version of this chapter.

REFERENCES

Allal, L., & Saada-Robert, M. (1992). La métacognition: Cadre conceptuel pour l'étude des régulations en situation scolaire [Metacognition: A conceptual frame for the study of regulations in a classroom situation]. *Archives de Psychologie, 60*,(235), 265–296.
Bidell, T. (1988). Vygotsky, Piaget and the dialectic of development. *Human Development, 31*, 329–348.
Brown, A. (1987). Metacognition, executive control, self-regulation and other mysterious mechanisms. In F.E. Weinert & R.H. Kluwe (Eds.), *Metacognition, motivation and understanding* (pp.65–116). Hillsdale, NJ: Lawrence Erlbaum Associates Inc.

Cole, M. (1992). Context, modularity, and the cultural constitution of development. In L.T. Winegar & J. Valsiner (Eds.), *Children's development within social context. Vol. 2. Research and methodology* (pp.5–31). Hillsdale, NJ: Lawrence Erlbaum Associates Inc.

Davis, P.J., & Hersh, R. (1989). *Experiencia matemática* [Mathematical experience]. Barcelona: Labor/MEC.

Elbers, E., Maier, R., Hoekstra, T., & Hoogsteder, M.A. (1992). Internalization and adult–child interaction. In R. Maier (Ed.), *Internalization: Conceptual issues and methodological problems* (pp.5–27). Utrecht: Isor.

Gelman, R., & Gallistel, C.R. (1978). *The child's understanding of number*. Harvard: Harvard University Press.

Gómez-Granell, C. (1991). Cognición, contexto y enseñanza de las matemáticas [Cognition, context and mathematics teaching]. *Comunicación, Lenguaje y Educación, 11–12*, 11–26.

Goody, J. (1987). *The interface between the written and the oral*. Cambridge, MA: Cambridge University Press.

Greenfield, P.M. (1984). *Mind and media. The effects of television, video games and computers*. Cambridge, MA: Harvard University Press.

Inhelder, B. (1976). Operational thought and symbolic imagery. In B. Inhelder, H.H. Chipman, & C. Zwingmann (Eds.), *Piaget and his school* (pp.134–149). New York: Springer-Verlag.

Inhelder, B., & Piaget, J. (1980). Procedures and structures. In D. R. Olson (Ed.), *The social foundations of language and thought: Essays in honor of Jerome Bruner* (pp.19–27). New York: W. W. Norton. [Original work published 1979.]

Karmiloff-Smith, A. (1992a). *Beyond modularity. A developmental perspective on cognitive science*. Cambridge, MA: MIT Press.

Karmiloff-Smith, A. (1992b). Auto-organización y cambio cognitivo [Self-organisation and cognitive change]. *Substratum, 1*(1), 19–43.

Kaye, K. (1982). *The mental and social life of babies*. Chicago: University of Chicago Press.

Kluwe, R.H. (1987). Executive decisions and regulation of problem solving behavior. In F.E. Weinert & R.H. Kluwe (Eds.), *Metacognition, motivation and understanding* (pp.31–64). Hillsdale, NJ: Lawrence Erlbaum Associates Inc.

Lave, J. (1988). *Cognition in practice*. Cambridge, MA: Cambridge University Press.

Lawrence, J.A., & Valsiner, J. (1993). Conceptual roots of internalization: From transmission to transformation. *Human Development, 36*, 150–167.

Martí, E. (1990). La perspectiva piagetiana de los años 70 y 80: De las estructuras al funcionamiento [The Piagetian perspective in the seventies and eighties: From structures to function]. *Anuario de Psicología, 44*, 19–45.

Martí, E. (1992). *Aprender con ordenadores en la escuela* [Learning in school with computers]. Barcelona: ICE/Horsori.

Martí, E. (1993). Aprender con ordenadores [Learning with computers]. *Substratum, 1*(3), 63–80.

Martí, E. (in 1994a). "Mediated activity". A risk of sociocultural reductionism. *Socio-cultural Research News, 1*(2), 7.

Martí, E. (1994b). Peer interaction in problem solving. A microgenetic analysis of interpsychological mechanisms. In P. del Río, A. Alvarez, & J.V. Wertsch (Eds.), *Explorations in socio-cultural studies. Vol. 3. Teaching, learning and interaction* (pp.209–216). Madrid: Aprendizaje S.L.

Martí, E., Steren, B., & García-Milà, M. (1994). *Using a computer environment in the classroom to learn the concept of proportion*. Poster presented at the Eighteenth International Conference for the Psychology of Mathematics Education, Lisbon, 29 July–3 August (Proceedings Vol. I, p.112).

Meringoff, L. (1980). A story, a story: The influence of the medium on children's apprehension of stories. *Journal of Educational Psychology, 72,* 240–249.

Mounoud, P. (1993). Piaget's concepts of equilibration and of structure in *The origins of intelligence in children* (1936) and *The construction of reality in the child* (1937). *Cahiers de la Fondation Archives Jean Piaget, 12,* 17–25. [Original French edition, 1992.]

Olson, D.R. (1986). Intelligence and literacy: The relationship between intelligence and the technologies of representation and communication. In R.J. Sternberg & R.K. Wagner (Eds.), *Practical intelligence: Nature and origins of competence in everyday world* (pp. 338–360). New York: Cambridge University Press.

Papert, S. (1980). *Mindstorms. Children, computers and powerful ideas*. New York: Basic Books.

Pea, R.D. (1985). Beyond amplification: Using the computer to reorganize mental functioning. *Educational Psychologist, 20,* 167–182.

Piaget, J. (1950). *Introduction à l'épistémologie génétique. 1. La pensée mathématique* [Introduction in genetic epistemology. 1. Mathematical thought]. Paris: Presses Universitaries de France.

Piaget, J. (1952). *The origins of intelligence in children*. [M. Cook, Trans.] New York: International Universities Press Inc. [Original work published 1936.]

Piaget, J. (1962). *Play, dreams and imitation in childhood*. [C. Gattegno & F. M. Hodgson, Trans.] New York: W.W. Norton & Company Inc. [Original work published 1945.]

Piaget, J. (1972). *The psychology of intelligence*. [M. Piercy & D.E. Berlyne, Trans.] Totowa, NJ: Littlefield, Adams & Co. [Original work published 1947.]

Piaget, J. (1977a). *The grasp of consciousness: Action and concept in the young child*. [S. Wedgwood, Trans.] London and Henley: Routledge & Kegan Paul. [Original work published 1974.]

Piaget, J. (1977b). *Recherche sur l'abstraction réfléchissante. I. L'abstraction des relations logico-mathématiques. II. L'abstraction de l'ordre des relations spatiales* [Research on reflective abstraction. I. Abstraction of logico-mathematical relationships. II. Abstraction of the order of spatial relationships]. Paris: Presses Universitaires de France.

Piaget, J. (1980a). *Les formes élémentaires de la dialectique* [The elementary forms of dialectics]. Paris: Gallimard.

Piaget, J. (1980b). *Recherches sur les correspondances* [Research on correspondences]. Paris: Presses Universitaires de France.

Piaget, J. (1980c). Recent studies in genetic epistemology. *Cahiers de la Fondation Archives Jean Piaget, 1,* 3–7.

Piaget, J. (1985). *The equilibration of cognitive structures: The central problem of intellectual development*. [T. Brown & K.J. Thampy, Trans.] Chicago and London: The University of Chicago Press. [Original work published 1975.]

Piaget, J., & Inhelder, B. (1969). *The psychology of the child*. [Helen Weaver, Trans.] New York: Basic Books, Inc. [Original work published 1966.]

Pimm, D. (1990). *El lenguaje matemático en el aula* [Mathematical language in the classroom]. Madrid: Morata.

Resnick, L. B. (1986). The development of mathematical intuition. In M. Perlmutter (Ed.), *Perspectives on intellectual development. The Minnesota Symposia in Child Development, Vol.19* (pp.159–194). Hillsdale, NJ: Lawrence Erlbaum Associates Inc.

Resnick, L.B., Levine, J.M.A., & Teasley, S.D. (1991). *Perspectives on socially shared cognition.* Washington: American Psychological Association.

Rivière, A. (1990). Problemas y dificultades en el aprendizaje de las matemàticas: Una perspectiva cognitiva [Problems and difficulties in mathematics learning: A cognitive perspective]. In A. Marchesi, C. Coll, & J. Palacios (Eds.), *Desarrollo psicológico y educación. II. Necesidades educativas especiales y aprendizaje escolar* (pp.156–182) [Psychological development and education. II. Special education necessities and school learning]. Madrid: Alianza.

Rogoff, B. (1990). *Apprenticeship in thinking. Cognitive development in social contexts.* New York: Oxford University Press.

Salomon, G. (1992). Las diversas influencias de la tecnología en el desarrollo de la mente [The various influences of technology in mental development]. *Infancia y Aprendizaje, 58,* 143–159.

Salomon, G., & Leigh, T. (1984). Predispositions about learning from print and television. *Journal of Communication, 34,* 119–135.

Saxe, G.B. (1991). *Culture and cognitive development. Studies in mathematical understanding.* Hillsdale, NJ: Lawrence Erlbaum Associates Inc.

Schoenfeld, A.H. (Ed.) (1987). *Cognitive science and mathematics education.* Hillsdale, NJ: Lawrence Erlbaum Associates Inc.

Schneuwly, B., & Bronckart, J.P. (Eds.) (1985). *Vygotsky aujourd'hui.* Paris et Neuchâtel: Delachaux et Niestlé.

Schmandt-Besserat, D. (1990). Symbols in the prehistoric Middle East: Developmental features preceding written communication. In R.L. Enos (Ed.), *Oral and written communciation. Historical appoaches* (pp.16–31). Newbury Park, CA: Sage.

Sinha, C. (1992). Vygotsky, internalization and evolution. In R. Maier (Ed.), *Internalization: Conceptual issues and methodological problems* (pp. 125–146). Utrecht: ISOR.

Steffe, L.P. (1990). Cómo construye el niño la significación de los términos aritméticos. Un modelo curricular [How the child constructs the meaning of arithmetical terms. A curriculum model]. *Cuadernos de Psicología, 4*(1), 107–162.

Steffe, L.P., & von Glasersfeld, E. (1985). Helping children to conceive of number. *Recherches en Didactique des Mathématiques, 6*(2–3), 269–303.

Street, B.V. (1993). *Cross-cultural approaches to literacy.* Cambridge, MA: Cambridge University Press.

Tolchinsky, L., & Karmiloff-Smith, A. (1993). Las restricciones del conocimiento notacional [Restrictions in notational knowledge]. *Infancia y Aprendizaje, 62–63,* 19–51.

Valsiner, J. (1994). Co-constructivism: What is (and is not) in a name? In P. Van Geert & L. Mos (Eds.), *Annals of theoretical psychology. Vol. 10.* New York: Plenum Press.

Van der Veer, R., & Valsiner, J. (1991). *Understanding Vygotsky. A quest for synthesis.* Cambridge, MA: Blackwell.

Vygotsky, L.S. (1962). *Thought and language.* Cambridge, MA: MIT Press. [Original work published 1934.]

Vygotsky, L.S. (1981a). The instrumental method in psychology. In J.V. Wertsch (Ed.), *The concept of activity in Soviet psychology*. Armonk, NY: Sharpe.

Vygotsky, L.S. (1981b). The genesis of higher mental functions. In J.V. Wertsch (Ed.), *The concept of activity in Soviet psychology*. Armonk, NY: Sharpe.

Wertsch, J.V. (1985). *Vygotsky and the social formation of mind*. Cambridge, MA: Harvard University Press.

Wertsch, J.V. (1993). Commentary (L.A. Lawrence & J. Valsiner: "Conceptual roots of internalization: From transmission to transformation"). *Human Development, 36*, 168–171.

Winegar, L.T. (in press). Can "internalization" be more than a magical phrase?: Notes toward the constructive negotiation of this process. In B. Cox & C. Lightfoot (Eds.), *Sociogenetic perspectives on internalization*. Hillsdale, NJ: Lawrence Erlbaum Associates Inc.

NOTES

1. This chapter was translated from the French by Angela Cornu-Wells.
2. In fact, Vygotsky makes explicit reference to the dialectics between the inside and the outside from the moment higher psychological functions start to arise, that is, as soon as one can talk of a "cultural line of development". This break between two moments of development (natural and cultural) has been criticised by numerous authors (Cole, 1992; Sinha, 1992; Van der Veer & Valsiner, 1991; Wertsch, 1985).
3. "Internalisation" is an important concept in 20th-century European thinking (Lawrence & Valsiner, 1993). For authors such as Freud, Janet, or Baldwin, it is a key piece of their theoretical structure. Social learning theories (Bandura, Walters, Sears) also introduce this process in their explanations but tend to interpret it in terms of the "transmission" of knowledge rather than in terms of "transformations" of actions and of external knowledge (Lawrence & Valsiner, 1993). Both Piaget and Vygotsky follow this thought tradition which gives internalisation a key place in the explanation of development; the two authors opt for a transformational model of the internalisation process.
4. A common solution in approaches that are inspired by Vygotsky's work and social anthropology consists precisely in denying this duality between the inside and the outside (either between the individual and society, or between the individual and the context) and in refusing the existence of the internalisation/externalisation processes on the basis that all activity is irremediably social and contextual and that the boundaries between people are diffuse (Lave, 1988; Rogoff, 1990). If it is true that the internal/external aspects always co-exist in an individual's actions, we still have to explain how this tension between the individual and the social is generated, otherwise we fall into a social reductionism where the opposites are amalgamated (Valsiner, 1994).
5. Translator's note: "La prise de conscience", translated here as "awareness" has also been translated as "the grasp of consciousness" (Piaget, 1974/1977a) and "taking consciousness" (Piaget, 1975/1985).
6. In Piaget's first works, we find the idea of an important structural break well before the sixth sensorimotor sub-stage, that is, well before the

appearance of the semiotic function (Mounoud, 1993). When Piaget compares the first "practical" permanencies (for example, the breast) linked to reflex behaviour with those that appear towards the third or the fourth sub-stage, which he calls "subjective", Piaget describes the former as inherent in the functioning of schemes and existing from the observer's point of view only. "Subjective" permanencies, on the other hand, start to exist for the subject him or herself when the subject becomes aware of the results of his or her actions, and this taking consciousness is the result in turn of disequilibria.The interest of such a position is that we can envisage the appearance of mental structures (of "thought" and therefore of "internal" functioning), linked to taking consciousness and to the equilibration process well before the appearance of the semiotic function. Despite Piaget's new formulation in *The grasp of consciousness* (Piaget, 1974/1977a), where he opposes sensorimotor intelligence (rebaptised "practical intelligence") to representative intelligence (strictly speaking "thought"), it is clear that Piaget's first formulation, which associated the emergence of the first forms of mental phenomena both with taking consciousness and with the equilibration process, provides a more adequate account of the appearance of this functioning which, even though it is not yet associated to differentiated symbols, clearly translates the existence of an intentionality and a point of view belonging to the subject him or herself.

7.   Translations of Vygotsky's work frequently use the term "internalisation" rather than "interiorisation". As no distinction has been made in this chapter between "internal" and "interior", I have kept a common terminology for Piaget and for Vygotsky. Even if they differ in their explanation of the process, the important thing is that both are trying to account for the construction of internal psychological functioning and to explain it in relation to external aspects of behaviour.

8.   Conceived in this way, the internalisation process can give rise to an important logical problem (Sinha, 1992, p.137): If the individual cognitive subject is envisaged as an internalised product of social life and of its organisation, what is the nature of the subject who was initially capable of internalisation acts? This difficulty can also be formulated in another way (Martí, 1994a): if the individual cognitive subject is envisaged as an internalised product of social life and of its organisation, how can we explain the creation of social life and of its organisation other than by subjects who had, in turn, to internalise what was not yet constructed?

9.   The classical Piagetian view with regard to the predominant role of the activity of schemes and their coordination in the construction of logical-mathematical principle must, however, be rectified in the light of recent research in cognitive psychology. Progress in research in different fields (language, mathematics, space, etc.) seems to indicate the presence of domain-specific constraints in the construction of each type of knowledge, for example, for the construction of mathematical thinking and its notational system (Tolchinsky & Karmiloff-Smith, 1993). In this sense, the general laws of operatory construction cannot by themselves explain the development of mathematical principles, such as those related to number. We need to add specific innate predispositions to number which constrain the processing of relevant information (Karmiloff-Smith, 1992a).

CHAPTER SIX

Units of analysis in psychology and their interpretation: Social interactionism or logical interactionism?[1]

Jean-Paul Bronckart *University of Geneva, Switzerland*

SOCIAL INTERACTIONISM

The Vygotskyan project

In a paper entitled *The historical meaning of the crisis in psychology* (1926/1982), Vygotsky studied at length the status of the discipline at the end of the first quarter of this century. He observed the existence of many "schools" (Watsonian behaviourism, Gestalt, Stern's personalism, psychoanalysis, Pavlovian reflexology, Kornilov's reactology, etc.) which, according to him, were about to make up just as many distinct sciences (or psychologies). He also emphasised the struggle that these different schools were going through in order to establish their supremacy over the whole discipline; they were all engrossed in an expanding process that led them to interpret every psychological phenomenon, some in terms of sexuality, some as a conditioned reflex, some in terms of Shape, and yet others in terms of manifestation of the Person.

From Vygotsky's complex analysis of this situation we have selected the following elements:

(a) First of all, he introduced three "analysing" concepts: the "real fact", the "primitive concept", and the "explanatory principle". The real or "crude" fact results from a discovery; it is a new event made obvious through scientific research: for instance, the salivation of the dog when

85

hearing a particular noise. The primitive concept results from the reading and the naming of this discovery, the word codifying the phenomenon necessarily being the result of a "primary abstraction" and generalisation: in our example, the term conditioned reflex applied to the salivation. The explanatory principle, for its part, is intrinsic to the process of generalisation itself: it keeps in line with the theoretical framework in which it operates; in our example, it consists in considering the reflex as conditioned, in others words, in imputing the cause of the salivation behaviour to the sound stimulus artificially associated with the natural stimulus.

(b) Vygotsky then demonstrated that each school tries to extend both the primitive concept and the explanatory principle to all new facts, first of all in its own field, then in neighbouring fields, and finally in all the fields of psychology. During this process the explanatory principles eventually break away from the facts that originated them, losing their strictly scientific nature and finally revealing their real status, that of ideological constructions (very fragile and likely henceforth to "burst as soap bubbles").

(c) Vygotsky maintained that what appeared in this case, when an explanatory idea was converted into an ideology, was in fact the philosophical options underlying, from the beginning, the subdiscipline involved. Therefore, analysing these options, he considered that the different schools could be assembled into two principal domains: on one side the supporters of a "natural" or "materialistic" psychology (reflexology, behaviourism); on the other side the supporters of a spiritual psychology (introspective psychology, psychoanalysis). The former made the presumption that no psychical phenomenon exists without a corresponding physical phenomenon and therefore adopted the explanatory procedure of natural sciences. The latter considered that because of their immateriality (their non-registration in space) psychical phenomena were irreducible to physical phenomena; they were only reachable through a subject's conscious self-examination. They henceforth adopted a methodology with introspectionist qualities, providing data (the subject's verbalisations) that could not, strictly speaking, be explained, but only "described" and/or "understood". This duality in psychology could be explained, according to Vygotsky, because the subdisciplines adhered to Cartesian *dualism*, to the radical opposition between what comes under the body (what is extended matter) and what comes under the soul (what is only mind). The former only dealt with the physical expressions of the body (the observable) and the latter only dealt with the psychical expressions of the mind (the unobservable) because both had accepted the dualism, in other words the fully immaterial status of psyche.

At the end of this process of reconsidering the status of the discipline, Vygotsky suggested a new positive procedure, a project, characterised by the resolution to approach the entire domain of psychology through a unique process, unifying both the object of psychology and the interpretative process. As humankind obviously encompasses both bodily activity (behaviour) and mental activity (thought), the purpose was to take into consideration these two aspects, and it is in this context that the importance given by the author to the problem of consciousness can be understood. It is worth pointing out that this term, especially for Vygotsky, means the objective psychical operations (the mental processes); consciousness strictly speaking (the awareness of one's own psychical functioning) being considered, as with Piaget, as a secondary or centrifugal process.

Vygotsky's purpose was mainly to put forward analysis units in which both the behavioural and the psychic aspects appeared, hence the necessity, particularly stressed later in *Thought and language* (1934/1985) not to use on "higher psychological functions" physicalist reductions that would dissolve them as such. Lastly the aim was to identify an "explanatory principle" adapted to these analysis units, in other words to seek out the causes of their appearance and their development. One wishes to emphasise that, in the Vygotskyan project, the interpretive process must be explanatory and that this explanation as such must be genetic. However in *The crisis* (1926/1982) the status itself of this genetic explanation is scarcely specified; we will come back to this point later.

The philosophical sources of the Vygotskyan project

In his wish to go beyond the dualist positions, Vygotsky was inspired by three works which, despite being remote in their historical context and their aims, are linked and which objectively extend the defence and the explanation of a monist conception of the world: Spinoza's philosophy, then Hegel's, and finally Marx' and Engels'.

It is convenient, but also not inaccurate, to oppose Spinoza to Descartes, of whom he was the disciple and from whom he took many concepts.

On the ontological side, the Cartesian "dualism" consists in stating that the world of material bodies (including the human body) and the world of the spiritual Self are of radically different essence, and that they are absolutely independent. On the gnoseological side it implies furthermore that the Self has, in full autonomy, the capacity to know itself as a regulating process of its states; that therefore the Self is, essentially, consciousness.

The Spinozistic process on the other hand is, as we just mentioned, part of the monist tradition and it is also pantheistic: Reality (or nature) is unity; God is in nature; He is Nature (*Deus sive Natura*). From the eminently complex thought of the "free thinker of Amsterdam" we will only retain the few elements that have plainly influenced the Vygotskyan process:

(a) There is only one reality, Nature, which is one and homogeneous; this nature is submitted to the rules of a universal determinism, which is coherent and perfect because it is nothing other than the manifestation of divine activity, itself unlimited and perfect. What is asserted here is that all testified phenomena in the world are "natural" in that they refer to the same and unique matter in perpetual activity.

(b) Human understanding only has access to this matter through two of its attributes; space on one side and thought on the other. First of all this means that natural matter includes extended matter and thought: therefore thought pre-exists in matter and should not be considered as referring to a purely spiritual substance; this is the thesis of "objective idealism". This also means that extended matter and thought are, ontologically speaking, active and generative processes: they define what Spinoza named *natura naturans*.

(c) However human understanding is incapable of grasping this *natura naturans* as such: the attributes of space and thought can only be perceived as "modes", in other words as finite "things" that constitute the products of the general activity of matter. These finite elements that define *natura naturae* are bodies or particular objects on the level of extended matter, and ideas, will or feelings on the level of thought. Two elements of this third theme should be emphasised. First of all the prevalence of *natura naturans* (extended matter in motion and thought in action) on *natura naturae*: The finite beings or objects under which these attributes manifest themselves to our understanding are only secondary products. Second and consequently, the affirmation according to which the "discretisation" of extended matter and thought is altogether a product of human understanding: especially concerning extended matter where the introduction of time, the use of numbers, and of measuring instruments are the results of this use of "abstract instruments" by which humans apprehend in a determined and finite manner the infinite object about which they are inquiring.

(d) Taking into account the foregoing, humankind can only be considered as a particular aspect of *natura naturae* composed of certain modes included in the two attributes of *natura naturans*: its motions (its behaviour) are only modes of the extended matter attribute, and its thoughts are only modes of the thinking attribute recognised in Nature. We wish to acknowledge here that if Spinoza accepts the *Cogito* (man thinking), he rejects its Cartesian consequence (*ergo sum*: the existence of a Self or thinking substance that is specifically human). Mankind in the Spinozistic conception is only an "accident", a secondary product of the total activity of matter, but a product within which appear nevertheless the "marks" of extended matter and the "marks" of thought in action.

(e) In addition, Spinoza attests, in the famous *VIIth proposition* of the second part of the *Ethic* (1965), that "The order and the connections of ideas are the same as the order and connections of things (bodies)". And he adds that precisely in so far as they are only two parallel aspects of a unique substance, ideas and bodies can not explain each other. Ideas are explained by other ideas; bodies by the action of other bodies. The Spinozistic parallelism is in no way a first version of the "psycho-physical parallelism" that later many clearly dualistic psychologists will sustain. Truly it is very close to the thesis defended by Piaget of an isomorphism between implication systems and causality systems.

Hegel's work explicitly takes place in the Spinozistic line of objective idealism and pantheism: the world is a product of divine idea in perpetual activity. In *The phenomenology of the mind*, Hegel (1807/1947) in particular proposes recapitulating the steps of this "self-actualisation of the world", starting with the emergence of the self, separate from the "other", and following with successive differentiations in order to end up with the set of material, social, and cultural achievements of humanity. Without going into the details (and with reason!) of this phenomenal work, let us acknowledge that Hegel, more clearly than Spinoza, states the question of the relation between the continuing infinity of *natura naturans* and the finite character of the objects of *natura naturae*, and it is this relation that is at the heart of the famous dialectic. Dialectic is first of all the process by which the mind, as an unlimited potential, meets other and limited objects that deny it, and then reorganises itself into a superior synthesis that retains the moment of the negation. But dialectic is also for Hegel a method in so far as the evolution of thought and of science can only reproduce the dialectic of reality. According to his own terms, "the concept is indivisibly motion of thing and act of understanding". Moreover it should be pointed out that Hegel, in his analysis of the genealogy of consciousness, imputes a decisive importance to the conflictual encounter of cultural objects and their reabsorption within consciousness: he therefore grants a capital importance to interaction with this part of nature constructed through work and human language.

Although he was explicitly inspired by the main philosophical theses we have just developed (albeit in dramatically simplified form), Vygotsky could not however admit their point of departure, that of objective idealism, an inescapable consequence of pantheism. In other words, he could not accept the thesis of the pre-existence, in all eternity, of idea in matter. He therefore had to find a conception of the status and origin of the psyche that was different, while remaining compatible with Spinozistic monism and Hegelian dialectic, and it was in Marx' and Engels' writings that he identified the solution to this issue. In *Theses on Feuerbach* (Marx, 1845/1951) and in *German ideology* (Marx & Engels, 1846/1972) these authors, while keeping track with the principles of Hegelian dialectic, reverse the initial postulate: It is not the dialectic of consciousness that explains material life and the history of people, but it is the material life of mankind that explains its history, and human consciousness is only a product of this material life. They also assert that the specificity of human essence, particularly the capacity for active thinking, cannot ensue directly from properties of the human body; it can only proceed, as Engels pointed out in *Dialectics of Nature* (1888/1971), from a reintegration, in mankind, of the properties of objective social life in praxis, action, and language features. By "standing Hegel on his feet", according to the famous expression, Marxism at the same time put Spinoza back on his feet, or perhaps it only revealed the deliberately hidden meaning of the Spinozistic work.

Vygotsky's track was therefore marked out: The purpose was to demonstrate how the social breaks out into the psychic and then how the psychic interacts with the corporal.

Vygotsky's psychology

If we exclude the astute attempt developed in *Consciousness as a problem for psychology of behaviour* (1925/1982), centred on the analogy between the self-releasing property (or circularity) of human reflexes and the self-releasing property of verbal dialogues, Vygotsky never returned directly or explicitly to his initial issues; owing to his short scientific life he could not elaborate a strictly theoretical synthesis of his many experimental researches. We are therefore compelled, on the basis of the last chapters in *Thought and language* to infer the status of the solution he proposed (see Schneuwly & Bronckart, 1985).

The thesis of the two roots of development is well known but worth restating. As a first stage of the ontogenesis the co-existence of two separate roots can be observed, one described as the "pre-verbal stage of intelligence" and the other as the "pre-intellectual stage of language". Testifying to the existence of the first root are the capacities of children aged less than 15 months to solve various cognitive problems without resorting to language (especially the distinction between means and ends and their recombination within practical actions). Testifying to the existence of the second root is the development of the successive patterns of interaction with social partners, monitored by vocal productions (largely semiotic: mimic and gesture playing a considerable part), but which should have "nothing in common with the development of thought" (Vygotsky, 1934/1985, p.126, our translation). In a subsequent stage, the advent of language—in other words the emergence of the capacity to produce sound units acknowledged by the human setting as "signs" of a natural language—proceeds from the fusion of these two roots. When it has arisen, language develops (in a third stage) according to two separate functional directions. The child's verbal productions fulfil, in the first place, a "social" function of communication and interaction with the setting; and, second, as they are interiorised, they fulfil a function of planning and monitoring one's own action for oneself. This interiorised language then becomes (in a fourth stage) the fundamental organiser of the psychological functioning of the child. All of the mental constructions originating from the pre-verbal root of intelligence are henceforth taken care of and controlled by the language units which the child knows are significant and on which he or she will therefore be able to operate. The psychological functioning thus becomes a conscious functioning, and thought, strictly speaking, is established as a product of the interiorisation of units and structures of the language of the social setting.

This "Y" conception of development to which we adhered for a long time, creates serious problems that we discuss elsewhere (Bronckart, in press). In particular, if the preverbal development of intelligence, defined as remote from all social and semiotic interaction, results in a form of cognisance of goal-oriented actions, then consciousness is independent from any social mediation and stems from a process of abstracting and interiorising properties of action schemata directly. At this point, Vygotsky contradicts his main thesis and comes very close to the Piagetian position that he claims to be against. Regarding the other genetic root, that of pre-intellectual language, we note that it is also characterised by the development of action structure but now of socialised and semiotic actions (interactions mediated through signs). Can we admit that there is no relation between these socialised actions and those "pure" actions that ought to develop, in parallel, within pre-verbal intelligence? As evidenced in the empirical work of Moro and Rodriguez (1989), such a conception cannot be defended.

These difficulties and contradictions result, as has often been asserted, from the absence of accuracy about what actually comprises the analysis units and the explanatory principles of Vygotskyan psychology. Two problems in particular arise. What is actually "interiorised": is it language as such (words) or general properties of communicative interaction, or even properties of "action mediated through signs"? What is, in other words, the established link between communication, action and language?

In *The crisis* Vygotsky considered that the distinction between analysis units and explanatory principles was fundamental, but circumstances compel us to observe that this distinction is not clearly established in the strictly psychological work; the three components mentioned earlier seem sometimes to play the part of analysis units and at other times of explanatory principle.

LOGICAL INTERACTIONISM

Piaget's philosophical questioning

Is the philosophical questioning to which Piaget's work is connected in line with the monist channel of thought or with the dualist channel of thought? It seems difficult to give a clear and definite answer to this question, however a few helpful elements can be introduced. We will first of all underline that even the main propositions of the monist tradition are hardly discussed by Piaget, and that there is scarcely an allusion to Spinoza or to the contributions, on this precise question, of the Hegelian or Marxist process.

During his adolescence, Piaget took an interest in the Bergsonian issue which indisputably assumes a monist and pantheist outlook and therefore leads (almost inescapably) to an objective idealistic position. For Bergson "God is life" and the scientific study of the biological facts of evolution and adaptation should enable a return to the very foundations of living beings, or even "to recapture the creative consciousness organising matter". But as Ducret (1990) noted, Piaget rapidly rejected the metaphysical and religious features of the Bergsonian issue in order to concentrate on the only problem that was scientifically approachable in his eyes, that of the development of forms of life. And Ducret, in this same work, underlines the phases of Piaget's withdrawal from "any philosophical claim" leading, in the middle of the 1940s, to exclusive attention to the issue of the growth of human knowledge.

If we can admit with Ducret this progressive retreat of Piaget regarding metaphysical issues (in particular, regarding the status of human beings) we cannot fail to note the emergence, at the same time, of the omnipresence of reference to Kant. This is a reference that can be explained easily, in so far as from now on the main issue of the Piagetian process is nothing other than the construction of the categories of understanding analysed in *The critique of pure reason*. But the Kantian process falls in clearly with the Cartesian line, from which it resumes the fundamental body–mind dualism, otherwise heightened by secondary dualism such as perception–reasoning and "pure reason"–"practical reason". We could then infer that the mature Piaget accepted the basic postulate of this philosophical trend—that of subjective idealism: the existence, at the heart of mankind itself, of the capacity of thinking *sui generis*, or in Cartesian terms, a specific psychical substance that is purely immaterial. But obviously things are not so simple. Besides the fact that his work comprises a masterly dismissal of the sensation–reasoning dualism, Piaget seems to have adopted a doubting attitude towards the question of the status of the psyche, as the following quotation (from the inaugural lesson in the Chair of Philosophy of Science he occupied at the time in Neuchâtel testifies) (Piaget, 1929, p.210, our translation):

> ... genetic analysis in psychology is impartial. It is possible (that it rehabilitates) the notion of the a priori. It is also possible that such a method leads to the idea of a radically contingent spiritual development. It is also possible that such a method enforces the notion of a sort of ideal directing reason, both an active and unachieved ideal.

As evidenced in other later positions, Piaget not only left open the issue of the ontological status of psyche but he also indicated that this question cannot in fact be solved by philosophy, because only a scientific, impartial method can settle the question once and for all.

We disclose here a first fundamental aspect of this overview of the Piagetian and the Vygotskyan processes. Vygotsky's first questioning is related to the status of psyche and it sustains a clear hypothesis: Psyche is of social origin. With Piaget the first issue is downstream: it is related to the genesis of knowledge and he leaves in abeyance the question on the status of psyche. As this quotation from the 1924 article "L'expérience humaine et la causalité physique" [The human experience and physical causality] indicates, the Piagetian programme tries to elucidate the construction of reality "not by human mind but by one given mind at a given stage of mental development" (Piaget, 1924, p.600, our translation). We emphasise here that during the 1920s Piaget firmly rejected the hypothesis of a creative role of society; for him language and social interactions were mere adjuncts, necessary indeed but secondary.

Therefore the remaining doubt about the origin and the status of psyche is often expressed in Piaget's later works by what appears strongly as a hesitation, or better still a contradiction. The most striking example is that of the issue of reductionism, in the usual meaning of the term: the reduction of the psychical to the physical or the biological. On the one hand, we record many assertions indicating that all psychical organisation actually relies on the co-ordination of the nervous system; on the other hand, we find assertions rejecting the innate character of this same psychical organisation. As an example of the first kind of assertion, Piaget (1929, p.147, our translation) writes:

> Through mathematics, the mind explains the physical reality, but through biology, physical reality reveals mind and mathematics themselves.

Later, (1972, p.177, our translation) he also stated:

> The operations of thought and the logical-mathematical structures, broadly speaking, rely on general co-ordinations of action (inclusion, order, correspondences, etc.) and not on language or on any particular social transmission, these general co-ordinations of action themselves relying on nervous and organic co-ordinations ...

As an example of the second kind of assertion, Piaget (1972, p.211, our translation) stated:

> The operatory structures of intelligence are not innate ...
> They are not preformed within the nervous system, neither are they in the physical world where they would only have to be discovered. They therefore testify a real construction
> ...

Piaget can henceforth assert that operatory structures are both "natural" and "spontaneously" constructed, and that they are none the less "non-innate".

In this context the Piagetian project is therefore to put forward a non-innate explanatory factor progressively asserting itself during the functional development of the co-ordination of actions, and we know that on the "genetic epistemology" side of his work it is the factor of equilibration (self-regulation) that was endowed with this explanatory status. But the Piagetian project nevertheless cannot dismiss the problem of the emergence of psyche, of the transformation of the co-ordinations of practical actions, biologically based, into mental, logical, and operatory co-ordinations. In other words, Piaget cannot really dismiss the matter that is at the centre of the Vygotskyan problematique: How is the physical transformed into the psychical? It is on the "psychological" side of his work, in three main books—*The origin of intelligence* (1936/1952), *The construction of reality* (1937/1968) and *Play, dreams and imitation* (1945/1962)—that a solution to this problem is actually proposed.

Piaget's developmental psychology

Contrary to Vygotsky, Piaget proposed a developmental psychology in complete harmony with the postulates of his epistemological questioning.

Everyone knows the theses presented in the three works previously mentioned, and in particular the two main locations of Piaget's demonstration. First of all, at the sensorimotor stage, the transformation of the innate interaction processes (reflex schemata), and the progressive appearance of a practical system of action co-ordination; a system that is already cognitive but which remains, in Vygotskyan terms, "unpenetrated by consciousness", or rather, unpenetrable by consciousness. Then a phase characterised by the interiorisation of this sensorimotor schematism and by its reorganisation, at the representational level under the effect of abstraction. Empirical abstraction, on one hand, that acts on the properties of the world (objects, events) and reconstructs them in ever more stable mental images. But also reflexive abstraction bearing on the properties of the sensorimotor schematism itself and contributing to transposing, onto the representational side, the objective structures of action co-ordination, transforming them by the same token into operatory structures, sketching out the logical structures of reasoning. Henceforth the subject does not only operate on the world but operates on the representations he or she has devised, and the operative system has therefore become a real "thinking system".

The process that is thus described is actually that of the "precipitation" of the physical into the psychical, and two factors were regularly invoked by Piaget as candidates for the explanation of this transformation: on one hand the role of imitation and on the other hand the role of "differentiated signifier". For us both raise problems.

In his 1935 paper (p.9, our translation), Piaget defined imitation in the following terms:

> (it) can be considered as a differentiation of assimilation, in the sense of accommodation as such, that is, a need to conserve and to reproduce one's own actions (pure assimilation), their progressive differentiations (circular

reactions or imitation of oneself), as well as their accommodation to objects themselves, considered as models to which schemata are identified.

The question here is that of the status of this "need", which actually, as Piaget indicated later in the article, is to dispose of "stable copies" of the world's objects, copies on which thought will be able to operate. At first sight this need can only proceed from functional regulations themselves in biology.

Regarding the signifier, we also know about the subdued transition Piaget proposed between the role of undifferentiated signifier (or clues), and that of differentiated and motivated signifier (or symbols) and furthermore that of differentiated and unmotivated signifier (or signs in Saussurian terms). The clues form a part, a feature, or a causal result of that which is signified; as opposed to signs and symbols specifically produced by the subject in order to invoke these. The main point here is first of all to demonstrate that the first forms of meaning are established through sensorimotor schematism, through direct (and non-mediated) interaction of the baby with the world of objects. It is then to disclose how access to verbal meanings, which Piaget accepts as decisive for the later evolution of thought, is carried out in direct continuity with this first process, and to establish that the use of differentiated signifiers proceeds from the internal and necessary evolution of the cognitive system established through mankind's solitary interaction with reality. As Piaget wrote (1972, p.344, our translation) "the initial character (of) symbols is that the subject can make them up himself". But the author nevertheless adds, in the same sentence, "despite the fact that their formation generally coincides with language". This concession is obviously not without significance, and so we can draw a few intermediary conclusions.

First of all we would like to emphasise, in concordance with Piaget, that the essential step in psychological development is the one that leads to the discretisation of psychical functioning, to the stabilisation of mental units on which to operate, and we would like to add that this same discretisation compromises the major element of differentiation between animal psyche and human psyche. We then notice, still in agreement with Piaget, that this discretisation relies on imitation and that it is achieved when the child reproduces the language of the human setting.

However the thesis of a non-social semiology, a so-called *sui generis* product of an organism's functioning, remains doubtful, and this regarding both its main aspects. First of all, referring to the sensorimotor stage, the idea that meaning proceeds directly from the individual–object interaction, without social mediation, adult's actions, and their attribution of meanings playing any part. Then the idea that the discretisation of thinking units is only linked to the emergence of language through a simple coincidence relationship.

Actually, as Piaget denies a decisive role to language and social interactions in the evolution of mental functioning, and considers them as secondary products of the general development of action co-ordinations, he can only denote the emergence of psyche through these same co-ordinations and finds himself in the *de facto* position of objective idealism from which Vygotsky was trying to escape.

Piaget and explanation in psychology

As opposed to Vygotsky yet again, Piaget often proposed a detailed analysis of what should have been for him the interpretative processes of psychological facts. In various explicitly methodological papers, Piaget considers that psychology should combine causal explanations and explanations based on abstract models.

Following the pattern of natural sciences, psychology should, first of all, try to provide an explanation for behaviour by seeking out the cause, in Humean terms, that is, by trying to identify an event, logically independent of the behaviour to be explained, whose occurrence is necessary and sufficient to provoke the appearance of this same behaviour. Whereas, for behaviourists, causes are to be searched for in the environment (reinforcement contingencies) or possibly in certain internal marks of the effect of the environment on the organism (the history of reinforcement), for Piaget, causes are internal and in fact proceed from the modalities of the central nervous system's functioning (cf the quotation given earlier from 1972, p.177). It is obvious however that this mode of interpretation is reductionist: it explains phenomena existing at a certain level of organisation (human behaviour referring to psychology) by appealing to an inferior level of organisation (the nervous system referring to biology), and so it necessarily dodges the specific properties of the phenomenon to be interpreted.

Aware of the limits of this first mode of interpretation, Piaget favoured a second one: explanation through construction of models, which involves drafting hypotheses on the structure of mental organisation underlying behaviour, then proceeding to the validation of these hypotheses. This interpretative paradigm is unfolded in three steps. First by collecting data and establishing possible "empirical laws" testifying to the generality of the dependency of a phenomenon on another and so enabling predictability ("if X, then generally Y"). Then by linking up the observed regularities and deducing new laws. As opposed to the former these "deductive laws" are not confined to the observation of the generality of certain facts; they introduce a feature of necessity, linked with the logical-mathematical properties of the activity of deduction itself. The process is completed by assembling a mathematical model (group of displacement, INCR group, etc.), and integrating the different laws according to its own norms of composition and in such a way as to enable a linking-up of transformations that characterise it and the transformations as observed in the subject's behaviour. Such a model can be validated by "going back to empirical data" and is considered as explanatory only "in so far as it enables one to attribute to the objective 'processes' themselves a structure that is isomorphic to itself." (Piaget, 1972, p.113, our translation)

Without being able to discuss here the weakening, or better still the impaired state, of this process brought about by the so-called "cognitive" sciences, we note that the interpretative schema proposed by Piaget is an interesting reformulation of the Spinozistic parallelism mentioned earlier. As the author himself indicates in the same extract (p.116, our translation), "consciousness is an implication system ... the nervous system is a causal system and psycho-physiological parallelism is only a specific case of isomorphism between implication systems and causality systems ..."

As with Spinoza the series of causes acting on the bodies and the series of connections that are established between ideas remain radically separate; an idea cannot explain a bodily behaviour, but a physical action can explain the transformation of an idea; only a general isomorphism between these two series is explanatory. But it is obvious that the assumption of this version of psycho-physical parallelism implies that the origin of ideas can only be found in ideas themselves, which pre-exist in all eternity, and so we come back to the position of objective idealism. In other extracts which do not offer explicitly meta-methodological features, Piaget also proposes, in almost identical terms to Vygotsky, another form of interpretation—that of genetic explanation. He states (1972, pp.171 & 173, our translation):

> The study of relations between individual psychology and social life ought not to be reduced to the study of mature or adult behaviour ... Genesis alone is explanatory and the source of controllable information.

Again, Piaget states (1972, p.201, our translation):

> The main future of psychology lies in comparative and psycho-genetic methods as it is only by observing the development of behaviour and its mechanisms in children

and in animals ... that we can understand its nature and its functioning in adults.

In the concluding part of this chapter, we will try to elucidate the link between this "unofficial" form of explanation and the two "official" forms mentioned earlier.

A FEW SUGGESTIONS

Analysis units and explanatory principles in psychology

Our reflection on this theme has been inspired by propositions stemming from various trends in philosophy and/or sociology, especially represented by Anscombe (1957), von Wright (1971), Ricoeur (1986) and Habermas (1987) who all develop a similar problematique, particularly as they are centred around the event–action distinction drawn up by the first author mentioned. Four propositions originating from these trends catch our attention.

We will start by reconsidering the key distinction on the grounds of the analysis of Anscombe's two famous statements:

(a) *"Two tiles fell of the roof due to the effect of the wind"*
(b) *"I arranged for two tiles to fall off the roof in order to damage my neighbour's car"*.

The statement (a) describes an event, that is, a chain of natural phenomena. In it, two phenomena are explained (*the wind blowing and the tiles falling*); they are logically distinct (or definable and identifiable independently from each other) and a relationship of determination can be established between the two: *the wind blowing* is a necessary and sufficient condition for *the tiles falling*; the first phenomenon is therefore the cause of the second. The statement (b) is more complex in so far as it refers to two different types of relationship. If we only take into consideration the tiles falling and the car's damage, it describes a simple natural event. However this statement also describes a human involvement in the world: an organism endowed with the capacity of representation triggers off the event (*I arranged for*) and this interference seems to be determined both by the representation of the (*hated*) neighbour and the representation of the effect of the event (*the car will be damaged*). This intervention in the world defines the action considered as an organised sequence of events imputable to an agent (an organism endowed with capacities of action), to which a motive (or a reason for acting: *I hate my neighbour*) and an intention (a representation of the effect) can be assigned. In Spinozistic terms the event is a chain of causes in extended matter, whereas human action is a mixture combining matter and thought.

Associated with these two units are two totally different ways of interpreting. Given the logical independence between antecedent and consequent, the event can easily be accounted for by a causal explanation. But there are two ways to interpret the action: the first one considers the agent as an exclusively natural entity that can be called the "cause" of the factual chain that is triggered off, even if, later on, the synchronic or historical phenomena that are themselves the causes of this setting-off are questioned. This is the solution adopted by Behaviourism, which only takes into account the natural observables and which only acknowledges as ultimate causes the contingencies of reinforcement and the history of reinforcement. But such an interpretation explicitly refrains from posing the question of the role that the agent's pro-active (intentions) and retro-active (motives) representations play in this setting-off; it doesn't enable, in other words, the liability of the agent to be questioned. Has he or she voluntarily triggered off the event? If so, why? When this question is tackled one can observe, with Anscombe, that neither the intentions nor the motives can be certified independently from the actual event that they are supposed to have set off; these representations of the agent can only be inferred from the event itself. The condition of the logical independence of the antecedent (the intention, for example) and the consequent (the event) not being respected, the intentions and the motives cannot be considered as causes. Consequently, human action, in so far as it summons up the conscious and active representations of the agent, cannot become the subject of a causal interpretation; according to von Wright's wording it can only be the subject of a "comprehensive" interpretation, which Ricoeur would add is hermeneutic.

As emphasised by Ricoeur, human actions can be understood from two embedded viewpoints. According to the first, sociological, viewpoint, what is certified is a stream of continuous actions in which many agents generally take part within the structural setting of one or several social formations. One of the main problems of this discipline is the analysis of the relationship of interdependency between the properties of actions and the properties of the social formations that build up the context. According to the second, psychological, viewpoint, in order to define human action one should cut the flow of social actions, to isolate an organised sequence of behaviour that can be imputable to one and only one agent. The problematique of this discipline becomes how to measure the part that these conscious representations in the agent (intentions and motives) take in the unfolding of the action thus isolated (and how to measure correlatively the part played by determinations outside of the agent). The distinction of these two viewpoints would benefit, it seems to us, from reliance on a terminological distinction (which however is not taken up by the authors to whom we refer). The phenomenon under analysis appears first of all as a "collective activity" within the context of a social formation; it is at this level that it becomes a subject of sociology. But this same phenomenon becomes a matter of psychology when questioning about the responsibility taken by an individual agent in the setting-off of an activity is introduced; it is this questioning itself that defines the part of activity under individual responsibility or even "human action".

According to Habermas, as it unfolds, every collective activity objectively exhibits claims to validity regarding the world. This means that activity, by its very production, presupposes a network of common knowledge about the world, as well as contributing to its creation and transformation (for Habermas this knowledge has three forms and defines the objective, social, and subjective worlds). This also means that this activity is permanently a subject of evaluation, that it can actually only be certified within and by the evaluations of the group; evaluations of claims to truth concerning the objective world; of claims to appropriateness concerning the social world; of claims to truthfulness concerning the subjective world. And the Habermasian thesis carries on with the affirmation that communicative activity (or language activity) is a medium through which these evaluation processes are built and developed. The evaluations expressed within language activity give to a sequence of behaviour a status of validity with respect to the knowledge constituting the three worlds, which provide, in other words, its meaning and its rationality. Further still it is the social evaluations that transform a sequence of behaviour from the form of natural event into the form of human action. Thus language activity is constitutive both of social activity and the formal worlds that build up the context. Two consequences follow: the first is that the psychological unit designated earlier as a "human action" is, to begin with, a product of social evaluations. Indeed these can apply to the group activity as a whole, but they can also concern the part played by an individual agent during its unfolding. In this case it is necessary to cut the flow of general activity, and an action is therefore demarcated and assigned to an agent. The second consequence is that the agent, because he or she takes part in the activity of the group, also takes part and contributes to the social evaluations. The interpretation that the agent gives of his or her own actions can only proceed from the appropriation and the interiorisation of this mechanism of social evaluations. The agent constructs an individual representation of the co-ordinates of the three formal worlds and applies these criteria systems to the evaluation of his or her share of responsibility, therefore building up intentions and motives. The rationality assigned by the agent to his or her own action is henceforth only a secondary product of the social rationality built within the evaluation of the collective activity.

Despite the fact that yet again they are greatly summarised here, these complex philosophical propositions seem, to us, to contribute to the clarification of certain issues in the Piaget–Vygotsky debate. First of all, they enable us to assert that the analysis unit in Piagetian psychology is of the order of event, whereas the unit of Vygotskyan psychology is of the order of action. However the two terms of this proposition must be taken *cum grano salis*.

First, for Piaget, action, either practical or mental, is explicitly proposed as the main analysis unit. But what comes under this term seems to be completely different from the human action as previously defined. To limit ourselves to the analysis of sensorimotor practical actions, if there is truly an agent acting on the environment, then it is perceived as an organism producing (or "causing") objective effects on the objects. Cognitive capacities are worked out through abstraction only of the properties of this causal chain of events to which the agent belongs. At the very heart of the agent's reason are the logical properties of the interaction between two physical entities, the organism and the environment, and not the properties of the social activity such as it is (re)defined and (re-)negotiated in language. Piagetian interactionism takes place within a solitary organism and the only objective world, free from social evaluations and their mediatory role, and it is in this sense that action according to Piaget is only in fact event.

The slight difference that should be noted concerning our second proposition is that Vygotsky, as we have previously mentioned, could not make a definite statement regarding the question of analysis units, hesitating between three candidates to this status, which Zinchenko (1985) recorded as "meaning of the word", "instrumental behaviour", or even "action mediated through signs". In the light of what comes before, it is obviously the last proposition that should be retained in as much as it corresponds potentially to the notion of human action.

These propositions enable us to go beyond the main contradiction of Vygotskyan psychology mentioned earlier: the non-distinction, in point of fact, between unit of analysis and its explanatory principle. Indeed "action mediated through signs" seems, according to Vygotsky, to be endowed with both. Referring to Ricoeur's thesis on the double status of actional phenomena, we therefore assert that collective activity, in its social context, is the explanatory principle of the unit of analysis called human action. This human action can be temporarily redefined as a modality of an agent's (or person's) participation in the socially regulated activities, or even as the setting in motion of the various potentialities of an individual agent within this same activity. This proposition leaves open the problem of the existence of other units of analysis, especially related to "lower psychological functions".

The problematique of development

At this point, we consider Habermas' and Ricoeur's theoretical contributions as decisive. We should keep in mind that, for Piaget, explanation in terms of models consists essentially in establishing an isomorphic relationship between a causality system, based on the nervous system, and an implication system, at work in thought as in the development of logic and mathematics. If we can only admit the merits of this parallelism, as we have already noted, the question of the very origin of logical-mathematical thought is left unanswered. According to Piaget, it proceeds directly (without social mediation) from an interiorisation and a reconstruction at the mental level of the causal systems as such, which is mysterious to us: How and why is this causal system transformed into a unification system?

However the propositions just mentioned assert that human activity, whether dealt with from a sociological (explanatory) or a psychological (as a unit of this discipline) viewpoint, always arises as an implication system: the relations between the constitutive ingredients of activity are never of the form of causality strictly speaking, but of the form of involving connections; and it is in this sense that the analysis of their internal structure is, as von Wright (1971) affirmed, a matter of "understanding".

Thus, it seems more reasonable to consider that the implication system within which logical-mathematical thought develops, stems from the implication system formed by human activity. This also implies that individual rationality is only a secondary consequence of the rationality at work in social interactions, which yet again implies that the rules and laws of "pure reason" are only a secondary product of the rules and laws of "practical reason".

In the light of these postulates the stages of construction of human thought can be reanalysed. Our first purpose is to demonstrate that the constitutive regularities of action schemata are constructed before the appearance of language, within and through social mediation. We can, as we are contriving to do, re-read in this perspective the corpus of Piaget's three major works. We can also—as Bruner and his school more bravely attempt to do—try to provide new empirical data, whose analysis enables us to put forward this precocious actional and semiotic mediation.

Our second purpose is then to demonstrate that after the appearance of language, the long "latency period" that separates the stage of displacement groupings from that of strictly operatory thought is fundamentally characterised by the unfolding of a double process of abstraction and generalisation out of the properties of social interaction and language—processes whose final outcome is precisely operatory logic.

We have to admit that a lot of work remains to be accomplished in order to carry out such a demonstration to the level of the Piagetian argument. But we think that this is the fundamental goal of developmental psychology: combining the richness of the empirical data and the analytic rigour of the Piagetian corpus with the exactness of the Vygotskyan questioning and positioning.

Can an explanation be genetic?

In this context how should we deal with the genetic explanation firmly claimed by Vygotsky and unofficially referred to by Piaget? As there is no space for a detailed argument, we will have to be content with answering with a few suggestions that may be considered provocative.

Piaget's work, as well as Vygotsky's, is characterised by putting into place a genetic method, which is necessitated, in both authors, by the complexity and the interpenetration of the levels of psychological functioning on one side, and by the acknowledgement of the dialectic feature of the psychological development on the other side. But a method does not constitute an explanation.

Actually when interpretation of psychological facts aims to seek causes, strictly speaking, explanation ensues, but this explanation therefore, as Piaget emphasised, discloses an inescapably reductionist feature. When interpretation of facts aims at the elucidation of the corresponding relationship between causality systems and implication systems, as Piaget also proposed, then perhaps it is an explanation, but an explanation that may have to remain synchronic, as shown by the contemporary cognitivist drifts, as well as the difficulties presently encountered by the Piagetian movement on this point; the difficulty of coming forward with an effective model of *Filiation des Structures*.

Although the ontogenetic process is, as both our authors accurately emphasised, of a capital importance, it does not allow, according to us, either a causal explanation, or an explanation through models; it can only be linked up with an interpretation of a hermeneutic or understanding type. This position will, no doubt, be contested, but we think it is the inescapable consequence of the social interactionist position: the development of mankind is inextricably linked up with the effect permanently exerted on it by social activity and language meanings already present and in perpetual evolution. In our opinion, the locus of explanatory principles to the human condition is to be found in the very construction of its social and semantic dimension. Thus, we understand literally Blonskii's statement endlessly reproduced by Vygotsky: *"behaviour can only be explained by the history of behaviour"*. Behaviour can only be explained by history, strictly speaking, that is to say through the construction and the coming into being of social organisations.

REFERENCES

Anscombe, E. (1957). *Intention*. London: Basil Blackwell.

Bronckart, J.-P. (in press). *Action, discours et rationalisation; l'hypothèse développementale de Vygotsky revisitée* [Action, discourse and rationalisation; Vygotsky's developmental hypothesis revisited]. Texte présenté au colloque de Bordeaux, décembre 1992.

Ducret, J.-J. (1990). *Jean Piaget. Biographie et parcours intellectuel* [Jean Piaget. Biography and intellectual life]. Paris: Delachaux & Niestlé.

Engels, F. (1971). *La dialectique de la nature* [The dialectics of nature]. Paris: Editions sociales. [Original work published 1888.]

Habermas, J. (1987). *Théorie de l'agir communicationnel* [Theory of communicational action]. Paris: Fayard.

Hegel, F. (1947). *Phénoménologie de l'esprit* [Phenomenology of the mind]. Paris: Aubier. [Original work published 1807.]

Marx, K. (1951). Thèses sur Feuerbach [Theses on Feuerbach]. In K. Marx & F. Engels, *Etudes philosophiques* [Philosophical studies]. Paris: Editions sociales. [Original work published 1845.]

Marx, K., & Engels, F. (1972). *L'idéologie allemande* [German ideology]. Paris: Editions sociales. [Original work published 1846.]

Moro, C., & Rodriguez, C. (1989). L'interaction triadique bébé-objet-adulte [The triadic interaction: Baby-object-adult]. *Enfance, 1–2*, 75–82.

Piaget, J. (1924). L'expérience humaine et la causalité physique de Brunschvig [Brunschvig's *Human experience and physical causality*]. *Journal de Psychologie Normale et Pathologique, 21*, 1–3, 48–101.

Piaget, J. (1929). Les deux directions de la pensée scientifique [The two directions in scientific thought]. *Archives des Sciences Physiques et Naturelles, Vol 11*, 145–162.

Piaget, J. (1935). Les théories de l'imitation [The theories of imitation]. *Cahiers de Pédagogie Expérimentale et de Psychologie de l'Enfant, 6*, 1–13.

Piaget, J. (1952). *The origin of intelligence in children*. New York: International University Press. [Original work published 1936.]

Piaget, J. (1962). *Play, dreams and imitation in childhood*. New York: W.W. Norton. [Original work published 1945.]

Piaget, J. (1968). *The construction of reality in the child*. London: Routledge & Kegan. [Original work published 1937.]

Piaget, J. (1972). *Epistémologie des sciences de l'homme* [Epistemology of human sciences]. Paris: Gallimard.

Ricoeur, P. (1986). *Du texte à l'action; essais d'herméneutique II* [From text to action; Essays on hermeneutics II]. Paris: Seuil.

Schneuwly, B., & Bronckart, J.-P. (Eds.) (1985).*Vygotsky aujourd'hui* [Vygotsky today]. Paris: Delachaux & Niestlé

Spinoza (1964). *Traité de la réforme de l'entendement* [Treatise on the reform of judgment]. Paris: Flammarion.

Spinoza (1965). *Ethique* [Ethic]. Paris: Flammarion.

Vygotsky, L.S. (1982). La conscience comme problème pour la psychologie du comportement [Consciousness as a problem for psychology of behaviour]. In *Oeuvres choisies, Tome I* [Collected works, Vol I]. Moscow: Editions pédagogiques. [Original work published 1925.]

Vygotsky, L.S. (1982). La signification historique de la crise de la psychologie. [The historical meaning of the crisis in psychology]. In *Oeuvres choisies, Tome I* [Collected works, Vol I]. Moscow: Editions pédagogiques. [Original work published 1926.]

Vygotsky, L.S. (1985). *La pensée et le langage* [Thought and language]. Paris: Editions Sociales. [Original work published 1934.]

von Wright, G.H. (1971). *Explanation and understanding*. Londres: Routledge & Kegan Paul.

Zinchenko, V. P. (1985). Vygotsky's ideas about units for the analysis of mind. In J.V. Wertsch (Ed.), *Culture, communication and cognition* (pp.94–118). New York: Cambridge University Press.

NOTE

1.   This chapter was translated from the French by Nicole Rege Collet.

CHAPTER SEVEN

The social construction of rational understanding

Leslie Smith *Lancaster University, UK*

No one seriously doubts the importance of the work of both Jean Piaget and Lev Vygotsky. Certainly, each held the work of the other in high regard (Piaget, 1977/1995, p.308; Vygotsky, 1934/1994, p.360). Difficulties, however, arise for those developmentalists who set out to provide a synthesis of their several contributions. The difficulties are apparent in the slogan "Piaget or Vygotsky". This disjunction indicates that some choice must be made, but it leaves open exactly which choice this should be. This is no easy task. Some developmentalists require an exclusive choice to be made: either Piaget or Vygotsky but not both. Other developmentalists treat this same disjunction inclusively, and it is this latter inclusive interpretation that is adopted here. Offered the choice "Port or brandy?", you may well be inclined to say "Yes please!", while also retaining the option of selecting one rather than the other on appropriate occasions. But this leads straight to the real question: which occasions are these? It is far better to move away from global claims about the relative importance of the work of Piaget and Vygotsky *en bloc* to the analysis and evaluation of specific claims. This is an essential move for those who seek an account of the social construction of rational knowledge.

My argument will have three steps. The first step is an illustration, but not a demonstration, of the overlap between the positions taken by Piaget and Vygotsky. The second step is a rebuttal of the charge that Piaget's account of the social construction of knowledge is radically deficient. The third step is a critical discussion of four issues which would have to be addressed in any minimally acceptable account of the social construction of rational knowledge. The weaker conclusion to draw from this discussion is that Piaget's social account has neglected strengths that should be attended to more than hitherto. The stronger conclusion is that Piaget's account is better than Vygotsky's account with respect to the four nominated issues.

DEMONSTRATION: ILLUSTRATION OF PIAGETIAN AND VYGOTSKYAN SIMILARITIES

The first step is an illustration of the extent of the overlap between the work of Piaget and Vygotsky. Clearly an illustration is just that—an example that does not amount to a systematic analysis. But an illustration can be useful by serving as a reminder that there is quite a lot in common in the work of Piaget and Vygotsky (cf Glassman, 1994; Smith, in press; Tudge & Rogoff, 1989; Tudge & Winterhoff, 1993).

The illustration is a self-test and is based on two recent translations (Piaget, 1977/1995; Vygotsky, 1934/1994). These translations have been used for two reasons. One is that we can read them with fewer preconceptions. The second reason is that both recent texts are collections of papers that cover good portions of the active lives of Piaget and Vygotsky.

The test is based around seven explicit themes, each of which is central to the positions taken by both Piaget and Vygotsky (see Fig. 7.1). There is, of course, no claim that these are the sole themes. The administration of the test requires you to read the 20 quotations and indicate the author of each quotation. In fact, the test should be quite easy: there is a exclusive choice; you indicate your judgment; and there are no justifications required here!

The answers are provided in the Appendix. As the self-test is offered as a *jeu d'esprit*, no technical information relevant to a formal test is to hand. If the self-test has any value, it is twofold. First, the self-test is hard even for those who are cognisant of, and even experts in, the work of Piaget and Vygotsky. Second, there are two reasons why the test is hard. One is because it is contrived. The other is more interesting: it turns out that Piaget and Vygotsky are actually committed to similar positions. This can be seen by reverting to the seven themes. Thus both do state explicitly that human development is pervasively social (Q1–2); both do state that there is a maturational element in human development, even if this is not the sole element (Q3–6); both do state that egocentric speech is a fact whose incidence is contextually variable

FIGURE 7.1
Piaget-Vygotsky Self Test

Identify the author of each quotation.
Clue: the answer is Piaget or Vygotsky.
Is social experience pervasive?
(1) Human intelligence is subject to the action of social life at all levels of development from the first to the last day of life.
(2) The entire history of the child's psychological development shows us that, from the very first days of development, its adaptation to the environment is achieved by social means.
The maturational element in developmental stages
(3) The stages of development are far from being just the manifestation of internal organic maturation.
(4) We must therefore distinguish the main lines in the development of the child's behaviour. First, there is the line of natural development of behaviour which is closely bound up with the processes of organic growth and the maturation of the child.
(5) We do in fact find, in the analysis of forms of social equilibrium, these same three structures.
(6) Development consists in three intrinsic stages.
Egocentric speech and social context
(7) What is your nationality? *I am Swiss.* Are you also Genevan? *No, that's not possible.* Why? *I'm already Swiss, I can't also be Genevan ...* Are there differences between countries that you know and the different people who live in these countries? *Yes, well, Americans are stupid. If I ask them where the rue du Mont-Blanc is, well, they can't tell me.*
(8) There is a wealth of manifestations of egocentric speech by the child. We already know that difficult situations evoke excessive egocentric speech.
(9) The simple division of statements into egocentric and socialised language varies considerably with the environment according to the degree to which the adult intervenes.
(10) Egocentric speech *per se*, for instance, is structurally lower than normal speech, but as a stage in the development of thought it is higher than social speech in the child.
Children's pseudoconcepts
(11) This pseudoconcept was thus halfway between an individual symbol and a true concept.
(12) This contradiction between the late development of concepts and the early development of verbal understanding finds its real solution in pseudoconcepts.
Psychogenesis and sociogenesis
(13) The interdependence of sociogenesis and psychogenesis is particularly marked in the field of child psychology.
(14) Between sociogenesis of higher functions and their natural history, there exists a contradiction that is not logical but genetic in character.
(15) It is also the concepts themselves, carried in language, whose roots extend into an indefinitely remote past ... while the structure of a concept may well really depend on its previous history, its value depends on its functional position within the system of which it forms a part at a given moment in time.
(16) The unity, but not the identity, of higher and lower psychological functions.
Thought-experiments
(17) Imagine a society in which almost all individuals were contemporaries, having experienced little of the family and school constraints which affected the preceding generations and exercising hardly any on the next generation.
(18) Imagine a child who will develop his concept of numbers, his arithmetical thinking, only among other children ... What do you think, will these children get far in developing their arithmetical thinking?
Who's who?
(19) Human knowledge is essentially collective, and social life constitutes an essential factor in the creation and growth of knowledge, both pre-scientific and scientific.
(20) This singularity consists of the following, namely in child development that which it is possible to achieve at the end and as a result of the developmental process is already available in the environment from the very beginning.

(Q7–10); both are committed to the presence of intermediate levels of incomplete rationality in developmental sequences (Q11–12); both accept the parallelism between psycho- and sociogenesis in normatively better developmental changes (Q13–16); both formulate a remarkably similar thought-experiment to bring out the potency of generational influences on human development (Q17–18; see Smith, in press). There is also a final similarity which masks a major difference (Q19–20). Although both Piaget and Vygotsky accept that there is a constitutively social element in the growth of knowledge, Piaget regards this element as merely one essential element, unlike Vygotsky who does regard the social element as the principal element in his account.

REBUTTAL: THE SOCIAL CRITIQUE OF PIAGET'S ACCOUNT

Some developmentalists have questioned whether Piaget has an adequate account of the social construction of knowledge, and perhaps even no account at all. My aim in this section is to offer a brief rebuttal which is elaborated elsewhere (Smith, 1982, 1989, 1992a, 1993, 1995, in press). I plan to review four criticisms which will be attributed to one developmentalist in each case, even though these four criticisms are widely accepted by others. The first three criticisms will be rejected *in toto*. The fourth criticism is another matter which awaits discussion in the next section.

Solitary knower
The first criticism is evident in the claim made by Bruner (1985, p.25) that "too often, human learning has been depicted in the paradigm of a lone organism pitted against nature ... in the Piagetian model where a lone child struggles single-handed to strike some equilibrium between assimilating the world to himself or himself to the world". The criticism is that, in Piaget's account, the social world is unimportant because any individual could acquire new knowledge alone without any social presence.

This charge has to face the fact that Piaget's position is completely different. Social experience is stated to be necessary—*but not sufficient*—for intellectual development from the cradle to the grave (cf Q1, Q9, Q17 in Fig. 7.1). Further, Piaget (1977/1995, e.g. pp. 185, 217, 240) states that social experience is as pervasive as it is necessary. It is well known that a necessary condition is not a sufficient condition (Smith, 1987). Piaget's (1977/1995, p.227) denial that social elements are the sole elements in the development of new knowledge is therefore not a reason for denying that his account has an essentially social element in the formation of rationality.

Empirical under-determination of social experience

This criticism states that although Piaget paid some attention to social factors in his theoretical writings, such attention is insufficiently specific. Social factors are bypassed in Piaget's empirical studies where children are individually interviewed about their understanding of physico-mathematical concepts (Doise & Mugny, 1984). This criticism leads to two replies, one specific and the other general.

The specific reply is that evidence is reported by Piaget (1977/1995, Ch.7) about children's ideas about the homeland and foreign relationships (for anticipations, see Piaget, 1924/1928, Ch.3, Sect.6; Piaget, 1945/1951, Obs.108). At one pole were the Swiss children who denied anyone could be both Genevan and Swiss, despite accepting that Geneva is in Switzerland. Parallel to this mistake in logical classification is a social misunderstanding: Herbert thought that Americans are stupid because they do not know where the rue du Mont-Blanc is in central Geneva (cf Q7 in Fig. 7.1). At the other pole are children whose responses were based on rational considerations: of course you can be both Swiss and Genevan because one includes the other; Switzerland is admirable because it is a free country; there are similarities and differences between people in all countries.

The general reply is an adaptation of the argument from "intellectual mutations" (Piaget, 1977/1995, p.37). The mastery of logical and scientific concepts has a social dimension, as Einstein (in Wolpert, 1992, p.48) noticed in a comment on the lag of Chinese behind Western science: "in my opinion one need not be astonished that the Chinese sages did not make these steps. The astonishing thing is that these discoveries were made at all". Science is an integral part of culture and tracking the course of "intellectual mutations" as they occur in children's rediscovery of logic and scientific method is a legitimate form of social investigation. Thus it could be said that all of the phenomena investigated in Piaget's empirical studies are social phenomena, even if the converse is not true.

Flawed epistemic norms

This criticism states that social elements are constitutive features of knowledge, which is viewed individualistically in Piaget's account. One formulation of this criticism (Hamlyn, 1978, p.58; see also Hamlyn, 1982) is that "the acquisition of knowledge, however, is in effect the initiation into a body of knowledge that others either share or might in principle share ... The concepts of knowledge, truth and objectivity are social in the sense that they imply a framework of agreement on what counts as known, true and objective ... (and Piaget's biological model) must prove inadequate for the task in hand".

The position outlined in the criticism is actually embodied in Piaget's own position, which predates the putative criticism of his work. Piaget (1977/1995) explicitly commits himself to the very position on which this criticism rests in the first paragraph of Chapter 1 (cf Q19 in Panel 7.1). Evidently Piaget's own position states that social elements are indeed essential to the formation of knowledge, whether pre-scientific or scientific and, as such, are constitutive or defining elements of the growth of knowledge. When Piaget and Szeminska (1941/1952, p.3) stated that conservation is a constitutive feature of all knowledge, they had in mind publicly available knowledge which is open to all on the basis of socially acceptable criteria. Agreement is rational not because it is generally accepted and marked by consensus in some collective group but because it is valid in relation to universally accessible norms which are accepted even in cases of disagreement as to their application to specific cases.

Available alternatives

The final criticism is that alternatives to Piaget's theory are to hand. A notable alternative is afforded in the work of Vygotsky which stands in need of worthwhile elaboration (Cole & Cole, 1989; Van der Veer & Valsiner, 1991; Wertsch & Tulviste, 1992).

Alternative theories are as welcome as they are necessary. The trouble is that it is not a one-to-one conflict in this case! There is actually no theory at all in the writings of Vygotsky, assuming standard criteria as to what counts as a scientific theory (Nagel, 1961). And Piaget has not one but several theories, assuming that a change in a model is a change in the theory (Smith, 1993, p.40). Setting this aside, Piaget's own commitment to the joint use of multiple theories in the evaluation of his own work was regularly stated up to 1987 (quoted in Smith, 1992b, pp.423–424). So this fourth criticism is both valid and important, leading straight to the question "Piaget or Vygotsky?". And this is to say that the criticism ought to be an evaluation of the relative adequacy of some specified aspect of their distinctive positions.

A comprehensive evaluation of these several aspects is not attempted here. Rather, my intention is to focus on four issues where Piaget's position has an explanatory advantage over that of Vygotsky. Or so it seems to me. This, of course, leaves quite open the conclusion to be drawn from the evaluations related to other issues.

DISCUSSION: THE SOCIAL DEVELOPMENT OF RATIONAL KNOWLEDGE

There is common ground between Piaget and Vygotsky about the end (*telos*) of development, namely the acquisition of rational knowledge. This end is explicit in Piaget's (1950) genetic epistemology which sets out to show how knowledge develops, whether in the history of science or in ontogenesis. It is also explicit in Vygotsky's (1934/1986) concern to chart the formation of scientific concepts in children's development, for example by showing how children's pseudoconcepts at one stage are replaced by valid scientific concepts at a later stage (cf Q6, Q12 in Fig. 7.1). The selection of this end is due not to serendipity but to rationality. Piaget and Vygotsky's joint aim is to identify sequences and the mechanisms so as to characterise more fully the process by which children develop rational knowledge. In this section, I now plan to review four respects in which Piaget's account could contribute to the interpretation of this process. These are: developmental zones; the learning paradox; teaching and learning; mutuality of understanding.

Developmental zones

Vygotsky (1978, 1934/1986) has made a celebrated claim about the zone of proximal development (ZPD). The main question to ask is not whether progress is always social. Certainly, for Vygotsky, you will never walk alone through the ZPD. This is equally certain for Piaget: see Q1 and Q13 in Panel 7.1. Rather, the main question to ask is how many such zones are there. According to Bidell and Fischer (1992), it is on this question that Piaget and Vygotsky part company, as the answers credited to them are "one" and "indefinitely many" respectively. Their suggestion is clarified by analogy in that intellectual development is viewed by them as a "ladder", in Piaget's account, and as a "web", in Vygotsky's account. Evidently this difference is intended to be exclusive: the implication is that the indefinitely many socio-cultural conditions of the Vygotskyan "web" make a better fit with reality than the unitary Piagetian "ladder". After all, they might say, there is ample research to show that Piagetian structures and stages are not universals as they do not generalise to fit the facts which are more diverse and heterogeneous than Piaget's account implies (Bidell & Fischer, 1992; Case, 1991; Dasen & Heron, 1981; de Ribaupierre, 1993; Feldman, 1980; Light & Butterworth, 1992; Resnick, 1990, 1992; Turiel & Davidson, 1986). There are two objections to this interpretation.

First, the fact that there are multiple developmental pathways has no bearing on their explanatory adequacy in the development of rational knowledge. In Piaget's (1977/1995) account, what is to be explained is how the autonomous creation of novel knowledge occurs despite the multiplicity, heteronomy, and orthodoxy due to social constraints. The task is to show how individuals, who all develop through a "web", succeed both in acquiring available knowledge and in creating novel knowledge. For example (cf Nunes, Schliemann, & Carraher, 1993), if a street-trading child says, in a street transaction, that $35 \times 4 = 140$ but, in a formal classroom test, $35 \times 4 = 200$, why is it that only one of these is correct, and how is it that some individuals (including the street-traders) come to know that it is the former, not the latter? Indeed, Wertsch (1990) has noted that the ability to distinguish between the differential adequacy of what he styles de-contextualised and contextualised knowledge is the central achievement in intellectual development. Changing analogies might help here: There may well be multiple pathways through a maze but there is one common property of all of the pathways that lead to the exit, namely that they—all of them— lead to the correct way out. If there is a "ladder", it is one that leads to truth in that "reason is unitary" (Piaget, 1977/1995, p.187).

Second, *universal knowledge* is ambiguous. At least two senses should be kept distinct because "it is well known that in logic 'universal' and 'general' do not mean the same thing" (Piaget, 1977/1995, p.178). My interpretation of this remark requires a distinction to be kept in mind between the transfer of knowledge and knowledge of universals (Smith, 1994, in press). The evidence shows that Piagetian structures do not generalise over tasks, contexts, domains, populations, and cultures. But this empirical finding has no bearing on the distinct question of how an individual acquires knowledge of universals. In his first book, Piaget (1918, p.46) posed the question: Can universals be known? Thus there is a clear sense in which universal knowledge is knowledge of universals qua abstract objects which are constitutive of reason. As a paradigm example of rational knowledge, consider the Kantian example $7 + 5 = 12$, which is an example of a necessary truth that is true not merely of the actual world but also across any possible world. This is because necessity is so defined (Piaget, 1986; cf Sainsbury, 1991) and any such truth is in principle exceptionless and so eternal (Quine, 1974). Notice also that we can have a priori knowledge that $7 + 5 = 12$, just because "universality and necessity ... are sure criteria of a priori knowledge" (Kant, 1787/1933, B4). To what is the origin of such a priori knowledge due? It is ironic that Piaget's rejection in the 1920s of the social reductionism of mathematical truths may have equal validity today (cf Piaget, 1977/1995, p.243).

Let us be clear: there are at least two ways of interpreting the Kantian claim. One way is to regard knowledge that $7 + 5 = 12$ as a *generalisation*: We all-and-always know that $7 + 5 = 12$. There are multiple empirical studies that show that this is false. But there is an alternative interpretation. According to Kripke (1980), a necessary truth, which is knowable a priori, may be initially learned empirically. The implication is that an understanding of the criterial properties of certain forms of knowledge is open to developmental growth. This is exactly the problem set by Piaget (1950; quoted in Smith, 1993, p.1). Questions about the initial acquisition of knowledge are distinct from questions about the rational legitimation of that knowledge. Viewed in this way, two main problems in developmental theory concern the sequence and mechanism that result in rational knowledge on the basis of the multiple forms of psycho-social experience (Smith, 1993, Sect.1). In short, the focus on the epistemological problems of universals is one of the unsuspected strengths of Piaget's account.

Learning paradox

A classical argument, which was well known to Plato and Aristotle (Smith, 1993, Sect.22), has been restated by Fodor (1976) as a severe challenge to all forms of constructivism. This challenge is called the learning paradox, stating that if hypothesis-testing is the only way in which a new predicate (concept, structure) could be acquired, then all novel acquisition is impossible. According to Fodor, there is a minimal condition that a theory of novel learning must meet, namely the extensional equivalence of the novel concept and an available concept: something is an instance of (novel) concept if and only if it is an instance of (available) concept. This condition states that the learning of a novel concept is possible only if some connection is made with a concept already at the learner's disposal. The connection is extensional equivalence in that the available and novel concepts should subsume all-and-only the same individual instances. The implication is that nativism must be accepted by default as there is currently no better alternative than hypothesis-testing.

Three comments can be made in reply to this challenge, which is elsewhere taken to be open to criticism (Smith, 1993, Sect.22).

First, the challenge is applicable to the accounts of both Piaget and Vygotsky, as both are committed to the development of rational and novel forms of knowledge. Bereiter (1991) has noted that the learning paradox is general across a family of learning theories.

Second, it is evident that Vygotsky's own account does not resolve the learning paradox: adequate resolution would require an account of internalisation, which Vygotsky (1978, p.57) denies that his own account includes. Further, Vygotskyan accounts simply postpone the problem, if they are reliant on the availability of social mediation and cultural tools in the construction of novelty. Newman, Griffin, and Cole (1989) are right to point out that, in school settings, novel concepts can always be introduced by teachers because they already have the novel knowledge at their disposal. Models of reciprocal teaching are defined through the appropriation by the learner of the expertise antecedently possessed by the teacher (Palincsar & Brown, 1984). There are two limitations here. One is that the experts are in a position to transmit novel knowledge in a construction zone but cannot thereby ensure the construction of that knowledge by the developing individual with whom they interact. If development occurs in a construction zone, the process is based neither on imitation nor on social determinism (Elbers, Hoekstra, & Hoogsteder, 1992). True enough; what exactly is it, then? The other limitation concerns how genuinely novel knowledge develops in the first place. A socially accepted authority is not always an intellectual authority. Newton said that he stood on the shoulders of giants—even so, Newtonian theory is due to his novel synthesis of available ideas. Frege was the leading logician of his day—but Russell's paradox is an effective refutation of a central tenet of Frege's logic (Smith, 1993, Sect.5.2) Feymann offered a demolition of central tenets of textbook theories in physics at his doctoral examination (Gleick, 1992). The general availability of knowledge and socio-cultural tools does not explain why novel construction occurs in only some human minds. Piaget (1977/1995, p.138) specifically requires that an account should show how any individual is in a position to think, and rethink, the system of culturally available concepts on his or her own account—not alone as a social outcast but autonomously as an intellectual equal.

Third, Piaget's account does not provide a complete resolution of the learning paradox, because his account of equilibration retains some problematic features. However that account clearly poses elements of the problem which must be resolved and so has attractive features (Smith, 1993, Sect.23). Two such elements are now discussed. The first is Piaget's (1975/1985) account of equilibration which is compatible with his social account in that both require "a general logic, at once collective and individual, that characterises the form of equilibrium common to cooperative as well as to individualized actions" (Piaget, 1977/1995, p.154). The same set of conditions is jointly applicable to the construction of knowledge within the individual's own mind and to shared construction between individuals. Notice that a neo-Vygotskyan interpretation implies social platonism whereby logic is encultured in a "social space". But any such space is analogous to a Popperian "third world". This makes realist commitments and is a form of platonism. The problem thus remains: exactly how does a developing mind gain access to the universals that are instantiated in any "social space" so as to be in a position to construct novel forms of knowledge (Smith, 1993,

Sect.21)? Let us be clear: the issue is not whether children are born, live, and die in a social world—this is common ground between Piaget and Vygotsky (see Q1–2 in Fig. 7.1). Rather, the issue concerns the form of understanding which any individual has of that social world. Social platonism and constructivism are incompatible and so an exclusive choice would have to be made between them. Evidently, Piaget (1977/1995, pp. 71, 208) denies all commitments to platonism, whereas the platonist commitments of Vygotskyan accounts have been insufficiently realised.

The second element in Piaget's contribution to a resolution of the learning paradox requires a conceptualisation of learning that depends jointly on the learner's past history and future progress (Piaget, 1978, p.238): "the construction of any one system does not depend exclusively on the bases from which it proceeds but necessarily as well on the succeeding level which provides the essential key-stone of the solidity of its predecessor". This claim does not state that unrealised future systems currently influence present construction; it does imply that current construction is effective only if aspects of the unrealised future system are instantiated in the learner's current activities.

Teaching and learning

It could be said that a Vygotskyan account implies that teaching can be an effective means to ensure good learning, but that a Piagetian account is, at best silent, and, at worst, barren in this respect. Is this so?

Consider, first, Vygotsky's own account and its suggestive but under-elaborated claim (1978, p.57) that "every function in the child's cultural development appears twice: First, on the social level and, later, on the individual level … All the higher functions originate as actual relations between human individuals". This insightful claim is elusive. Fortunately, it does not stand alone. One related claim distinguishes between the unity of and identity in social interaction (cf Q16 in Fig. 7.1). In a shared activity, a child may contribute to a successful outcome with an adult (functional unity) without using the same (non-identity) abilities and understanding. According to Vygotsky (1934/1994, p.344) this is because "one and the same event occurring at different ages of the child is reflected in his consciousness in a completely different manner and has an entirely different meaning for the child". This leads to the second comment: just how, then, does intellectual identity arise from functional unity? The short answer given by Vygotsky is by internalisation. The trouble is that Vygotsky honestly adds that "as yet the barest outline of this process is known" (1978, p.57). This is a telling admission: Vygotsky denies that his account is explanatory of one of its own central processes.

Vygotsky's account is also ambiguous in the use of the term *obuchenie* which his translators (Van der Veer & Valsiner, 1994) take to be *teaching/learning*. Note that the ambiguity is not always apparent in the standard translations of Vygotsky's (1978, 1986) two main texts. Quite simply, teaching is not learning. First, teaching is defined as the promotion of learning (Fenstermacher, 1986; Tomlinson et al., 1993). Teaching can be successful (the activity is teaching and not something else) without successful learning taking place as its intended outcome. Teaching is designed to enable learning to take place; but the quality of learning that actually occurs through teaching is quite another matter. Second, there are degrees of dependency in teaching and learning. At one pole is high dependency, marked by imitation, training, and specific guidance. At the other pole is low dependency, marked by good answers to questions that ought to be asked about the content in some knowledge domain. There is a pedagogical "ought", which learners can evade in much the way that weakness of the will occurs in the moral domain (Aristotle, 1953 edition; Macmillan & Garrison, 1988). What needs to be shown is how learners understand the pedagogical imperatives that are thrust upon them.

This is a normative matter which raises questions. First, the issue is general, as it concerns developmental progression which leads to the construction of alethic necessity, or to moral obligation, or to pedagogical imperatives. Following von Wright (1951; see Smith, 1993, Sect.25), there is a common logical structure that underlies the modalities in each of these domains. The substantive question that is unresolved is how such construction could occur on the basis of activities that are deficient in precisely the relevant respects. Although Piaget does not provide an effective account of how progress occurs, it is pretty clear that his account does address this issue squarely (cf Piaget, 1977/1995, pp. 28, 42, 53; Smith, 1995, pp.17-18). By contrast, Vygotsky's account is silent on such issues.

Mutuality of understanding

Communication has success-conditions. One key question to ask about communication is not so much whether it occurs but rather the respects in which it is successful. Successful communication does not require that two partners to an exchange accept each other's views, as there can be rational disagreement. Rather, successful communication is such that each understands what the other partner has in mind. It is Piaget's (1977/1995) central claim that ego- and sociocentrism are dual constraints on the successful exchange of views. His equilibration model of social exchange offers three conditions whose satisfaction is necessary for successful exchange (Piaget 1977/1995, ch. 2-3). These conditions require (a) a common currency or unit of exchange between two partners (which can be persons, groups, or societies) and typically manifest as shared signs and meanings; (b) conservation, in that each element in the system is used in a self-identical way through the exchange; (c) reciprocity, in that each partner uses the same elements of the same system in the same way. Piaget further claims that if these conditions are met, certain equivalences hold, notably that the actions of each partner invoke the same intellectual value (Piaget 1977/1995, ch. 1–3, p.104).

The fundamental principle that underpins Piaget's model is evident in Aristotle's (1953, p.118) discussion of proportionate equality. Two partners to an economic exchange may have different products and so a decision about their equality, or lack of equality, requires the construction of a common scale so that either product can be compared with the other. There is however a distinctive feature of intellectual exchange in that a value invoked by one partner may be the self-identical value to that invoked by the other partner. Specifically, any universal is an abstract object which could, in principle, be used in a self-identical way by either partner. For example, the actions of the two partners may be displays of one and the same concept (rule, norm, value). Leibniz (in Ishiguro, 1972) has offered a criterion of concept identity in terms of the *salve veritate* principle: *eadem sunt unum alteri substitui potest salve veritate*. One interpretation of this principle is an extension of the interpretation due to Ishiguro (1972): *Two displays are displays of the same concept if either can be substituted for the other without change in truth-value*. On this interpretation, the Leibnizean criterion requires both extensional equivalence, in that true and false displays co-vary in the actual world, but also intensional coincidence, in that true and false displays co-vary across possible worlds as well. In short, the implication is that the partners invoke the same concept (or other universal) just in case each has acquired a modal understanding of possibility and necessity (Smith, 1993, Sect.25).

Once again, the claim being made is that Piaget's account has unsuspected strengths, and even that his account has a better explanatory adequacy than Vygotsky's account with respect to the psycho-social genesis of knowledge and its rational legitimation.

REFERENCES

Aristotle (1953). *The ethics of Aristotle*. London: Allen & Unwin.
Bereiter, C. (1991). The learning paradox: Commentary. *Human Development, 34*, 294–298.

Bidell, T., & Fischer, K. (1992). Cognitive development in educational contexts: Implications of skills theory. In A. Demetriou, M. Shayer, & A. Efklides (Eds.), *Neo-Piagetian theories of cognitive development* (pp.11–30). London: Routledge.

Bruner, J. (1985). Vygotsky: A historical and conceptual perspective. In J.V. Wertsch (Ed.), *Culture, communication and cognition: Vygotskian perspectives* (pp.21–34). Cambridge: Cambridge University Press.

Case, R. (1991). *The mind's staircase*. Hillsdale, NJ: Lawrence Erlbaum Associates Inc.

Cole, M., & Cole, S. (1989). *The development of children*. New York: Freeman.

Dasen, P., & Heron, A. (1981). Cross-cultural tests of Piaget's theory. In H. Triandis & A. Heron (Eds.), *Handbook of cross-cultural psychology*. Vol. 4 (pp.295–341). Boston: Allyn & Bacon.

de Ribaupierre, A. (1993). Structural invariants and individual differences: On the difficulty of dissociating developmental and differential processes. In R. Case & W. Edelstein (Eds.), *The new structuralism in cognitive development* (pp.11–32). Basel: Karger.

Doise, W., & Mugny, G. (1984). *The social development of the intellect*. Oxford: Pergamon Press.

Elbers, E., Hoekstra, T., & Hoogsteder, M. (1992). Internalization as adult–child interaction. *Learning and Instruction, 2*, 101–118.

Feldman, D. (1980). Universal to unique—mapping the developmental terrain. In D. Feldman (Ed.), *Beyond universals* (pp.1–22). Norwood, NJ: Ablex.

Fenstermacher, G. (1986). Philosophy of research on teaching: Three aspects. In M. Wittrock (Ed.), *Handbook of research on teaching* (3rd Edn.) (pp.37–49). New York: Collier Macmillan.

Fodor, J. (1976). *The language of thought*. Brighton, UK: Harvester Press.

Glassman, M. (1994). All things being equal: The two roads of Piaget and Vygotsky. *Developmental Review, 14*, 186–214.

Gleick. J. (1992). *Genius: Richard Feynman and modern physics*. New York: Little, Brown & Co.

Hamlyn, D.W. (1978). *Experience and the growth of understanding*. London: Routledge & Kegan Paul.

Hamlyn, D.W. (1982). What exactly is social about the origin of understanding? In P. Light & G. Butterworth (Eds.), *Social cognition* (pp.17–31). Brighton, UK: Harvester Press.

Ishiguro, I. (1972) *Leibniz's philosophy of logic and language*. London: Duckworth.

Kant, I. (1933). *Critique of pure reason*. Oxford: Blackwell. [Original work published 1787.]

Kripke, S. (1980). *Naming and necessity*. Oxford: Blackwell.

Light, P., & Butterworth, G. (1992). *Context and cognition*. New York: Harvester.

Macmillan, C., & Garrison, J. (1988). *A logical theory of teaching*. Dordrecht: Kluwer Academic Publishers.

Nagel, E. (1961). *The structure of science*. New York: Routledge & Kegan Paul.

Newman, D., Griffin, P., & Cole, M. (1989). *The construction zone: Working for cognitive change in school*. Cambridge: Cambridge University Press.

Nunes, T., Schliemann, A., & Carraher, T. (1993). *Street mathematics and school mathematics*. Cambridge: Cambridge University Press.

Palincsar, A., & Brown, A. (1984). Reciprocal teaching of comprehension-fostering and comprehension-monitoring. *Cognition and Instruction, 1*, 117–175.

Piaget, J. (1918). *Recherche*. Lausanne: La Concorde.
Piaget, J. (1928). *Judgment and reasoning in the child*. London: Routledge & Kegan Paul. [Original work published 1924.]
Piaget, J. (1951). *Play, dreams and imitation in children*. London: Routledge & Kegan Paul. [Original work published 1945.]
Piaget, J. (1950). *Introduction à l'épistemologie génétique. 3 Vols* [Introduction to genetic epistemology]. Paris: Presses Universitaires de France.
Piaget, J. (1978). *Recherches sur la generalisation* [Research on generalisation]. Paris: Presses Universitaires de France.
Piaget, J. (1985). *Equilibration of cognitive structures*. Chicago: University of Chicago Press. [Original work published 1975.]
Piaget, J. (1986). Essay on necessity. *Human Development, 29*, 301–314.
Piaget, J. (1995). *Sociological studies*. London: Routledge. [Original work published 1977, expanded 2nd edn., ch. 1–9. (1st. edn., 1965, ch. 1–4 only)]
Piaget, J., & Szeminska, A. (1952). *The child's conception of number*. London: Routledge & Kegan Paul. [Original work published 1941.]
Quine, W. (1974). *The roots of reference*. Lasalle, IL: Open Court
Resnick, L. (1990). *Perspectives on socially shared cognition*. New York: American Psychological Association.
Resnick, L. (1992). From protoquantities to operators: Building mathematical competence on a foundation of everyday knowledge. In G. Leinhardt, R. Putnam, & R. Hartrup (Eds.), *Analysis of arithmetic for mathematics teaching* (pp.373–429). Hillsdale, NJ: Lawrence Erlbaum Associates Inc.
Sainsbury, M. (1991). *Logical forms*. Oxford: Blackwell.
Smith, L. (1982). Piaget and the solitary knower. *Philosophy of the Social Sciences, 12*, 173–182.
Smith, L. (1987) On Piaget on necessity. In J. Russell (Ed.), *Philosophical perspectives on developmental psychology*. Oxford: Blackwell.
Smith, L. (1989). Changing perspectives in developmental psychology. In C. Desforges (Ed.), *Early childhood education* (pp.16–32). Edinburgh: Scottish Academic Press.
Smith, L. (1992a). *Jean Piaget: Critical assessments. Vol. 3*. London: Routledge.
Smith, L. (1992b). *Jean Piaget: Critical assessments. Vol. 4*. London: Routledge.
Smith, L. (1993). *Necessary knowledge: Piagetian perspectives on constructivism*. Hove, UK: Lawrence Erlbaum Associates Ltd.
Smith, L. (1994). The Binet–Piaget connection. *Archives de Psychologie, 62*, 275–285.
Smith, L. (1995). Introduction to sociological studies. In J. Piaget, *Sociological studies*. London: Routledge.
Smith, L. (in press). With knowledge in mind. *Human development*.
Tomlinson, P., Edwards, A., Finn, G., Smith, L., & Wilkinson, E. (1993). Psychological aspects of beginning teacher competence. *Education Section Review, 17*, 1–19.
Tudge, J., & Rogoff, B. (1989). Peer influences on cognitive development: Piagetian and Vygotskian perspectives. In M. Bornstein & J. Bruner (Eds.), *Interaction in human development* (pp.17–39). Hillsdale, NJ: Lawrence Erlbaum Associates Inc.
Tudge, J., & Winterhoff, P. (1993). Vygotsky, Piaget, and Bandura: Perspectives on the relations between the social world and cognitive development. *Human Development, 36*, 61–81.

Turiel, E., & Davidson, P. (1986). Heterogeneity, inconsistency, and asynchrony in the development of cognitive structures. In I. Levin (Ed.), *Stage and structure* (pp.106–143). Norwood, NJ: Ablex.

Van der Veer, R., & Valsiner, J. (1991). *Understanding Vygotsky*. Oxford: Blackwell.

Van der Veer, R., & Valsiner, J. (1994). *The Vygotsky reader*. Oxford: Blackwell.

von Wright, G. H. (1951). *An essay in modal logic*. Amsterdam: North Holland.

Vygotsky, L. (1978). *Mind in society*. Cambridge, MA: Harvard University Press.

Vygotsky, L. (1986). *Thought and language* (2nd Edn.). Cambridge, MA: MIT Press. [Original work published 1934.]

Vygotsky, L. (1994). Academic concepts in school aged children. In R. van der Veer & J. Valsiner (Eds.), *The Vygotsky reader* (pp.111–126). Oxford: Blackwell. [Original work published 1934.]

Wertsch, J. (1990). The voice of rationality in a sociocultural approach to mind. In L. Moll (Ed.), *Vygotsky and education*. Cambridge: Cambridge University Press.

Wertsch, J., & Tulviste, P. (1992). L.S. Vygotsky and contemporary developmental psychology. *Developmental Psychology, 28*, 548–557.

Wolpert, L. (1992). *The unnatural nature of science*. London: Faber & Faber.

APPENDIX

Piaget-Vygotsky self-test

The page references are as follows:

Piaget (1977/1995)	Vygotsky (1934/1994)
1: 278	2: 116
3: 296	4: 57
5: 56	6: 216
7: 252/258	8: 118
9: 308	10: 153
11: 238	12: 231
13: 35	14: 153
15: 50	16: 163
17: 57	18: 351
19: 30	20: 347

The self-test has been completed—at conferences in Britain, Switzerland and the USA—by a small and non-random sample (n = 20) of developmentalists with known interests in the work of Piaget and/or Vygotsky. The mean correct score of this sample across the 20 items was 13 in the range 9–16. There are several possible interpretations of this finding. One is that the positions of Piaget and Vygotsky are dissimilar but this is obscured by a contrived test, its non-standardised nature, the de-contextualised manner of its presentation, and the determination of its designer actually to produce a quite hard test. Another is that the positions of Piaget and Vygotsky are similar but that this is not always appreciated. With the latter interpretation in mind, why not invoke the final page of George Orwell's *Animal Farm*, whose adapted version might have read: "they looked from Vygotsky to Piaget, and from Piaget to Vygotsky, and from Vygotsky to Piaget again; but already it was impossible to say which was which".

CHAPTER EIGHT

Construction and interpretation: Exploring a joint perspective on Piaget and Vygotsky

Jens Brockmeier *University of Innsbruck and Linacre College, Oxford*

PIAGET: THE PHILOSOPHER

Over the nearly 70 years of his intellectual life, Piaget never lost sight of the philosophical dimension of psychology. From his very beginnings as a biologist and philosopher of science until his late works, he always considered the scientific and psychological study of human development as part of a wider philosophical and anthropological project. Moreover, Piaget's well known epistemological enterprise was preceded and accompanied by a moral enterprise which gave his activities the air of a grand "existential project"—a religious (Protestant), political (socialist) and philosophical (Bergsonian) project, as Fernando Vidal (1994) has described it in his historical reconstruction of the world and *Weltanschaung* of the young man from Neuchâtel at the beginning of this century. Piaget's biological and psychological science of knowledge, his "genetic" (that is, developmental) epistemology, was essentially an experimental philosophy which sought to answer epistemological and, in the end, moral questions through the developmental study of the child.

By weaving together insights from many disciplines, Piaget hoped to create a broader understanding of how the mind works—above all how its modes of conceptualisation develop. This fundamentally philosophical stance makes him an exceptional figure in 20th-century academic psychology, leaving aside what may remain of his monumental system of genetic epistemology. Piaget's thoughts about the philosophical presuppositions and implications of psychological issues set standards—even if all too quickly ignored by most developmental psychologists thereafter.

Certainly it has always been difficult, if not impossible, to reach the standards of his sophisticated epistemological explorations in psychology. They are both challenging and encouraging, even if one does not agree with his basic convictions. So I shall deal in this chapter with some issues concerning the epistemological status of a kind of psychology that has emerged in contrast not least to Piaget's psychology. In outlining this contrast, I will examine a Piagetian line of argument presented in the current debate about culturally oriented, discursive psychology. Specifically, I shall discuss the perspective of the new developmental theory of "the child's theory of mind" which claims to have overcome some of the essential limitations of Piaget's conception of the mind.

AFTER PIAGET

Over the last two decades, the empirical and epistemological orientations of much of the research in developmental psychology has changed fundamentally. "Pragmatic turn", "narrative turn", "discursive turn" are different titles for, as well as aspects of, what has indeed been a far-reaching paradigm shift. What has shifted is not only the focus of empirical interest of many psychologists, but also their methodological procedures, conceptual models, and theoretical convictions. The emphasis has moved from the child as a monologic solo-learner, from individual cognitive operations and their mental development, to the study of social interactions and linguistic practices, to discursive and interpretive activities. Along with this, the symbolic or semiotic mediations by which all these activities take place, and finally the social and cultural contexts of development have come to the fore.

Psychologically, this shift occurred to a great extent under the sign of Vygotsky and the pragmatist and interactionalist tradition; epistemologically, it owes much to the general linguistic turn in human sciences. The influence of a particular reading of the late Wittgenstein can be noted in other disciplines, too, and may well have had even more of an impact in interdisciplinary endeavours, such as the new research fields of linguistic and psychological anthropology, cross-cultural communication studies, and cultural pragmatics. This reading has opened up new perspectives on *language in use* (which in both Wittgenstein's and Vygotsky's view means also *thinking* and *cognition in use*), and draws attention to the enormously variable discursive and other symbolic interactions of persons. It has also demonstrated the importance of these "language games"—linguistic and, in a wider sense, symbolic practices of communication that are always intermingled with physical activities—for what traditionally has been called "thought", "intellect", and "mind".

In other words, we do not need to refer to Thomas S. Kuhn's description of the course of paradigm shifts to see that Piaget's *genetic epistemology* and its Kantian approach to *Bewußtsein*—so often emphasised by Piaget himself—has tended to become a closed chapter in the history of science.

My point is not to dispute this tendency; I neither will—nor could—argue against it. However, I believe that there are still some important issues to tackle that situate the Vygotskyan, Wittgensteinian, and Piagetian views in a more productive context than the one first outlined—one might call it the *after Piaget* scenario—seems to allow. Despite the well known comments both psychologists made on the work of the other, the Vygotsky–Piaget dialogue never really started—and thus it never really finished. Consider, for example, the unsolved relation between the *constructivist* emphasis of the great Geneva scholar and the *interpretive* approach that has developed out of the ideas of the Russian psychologist, semiotician, and cultural theorist. Such "dialogical examination" of both Piaget's and Vygotsky's epistemological options may also shed light on some problems that arise in the wake of a discursive and cultural psychology of human development.

REASSESSING THE COGNITIVE REVOLUTION

Of course, not everyone would agree with the picture of the current situation that I have just sketched. Among those who would not agree are the traditional cognitive psychologists (including most Piagetians) and, at present certainly more important, the modern cognitive, that is, computational, (neuro)scientists as well as philosophers of mind, not forgetting most naturalists. In my outline, they appear rather marginalised, in all too obvious contrast to their real influence on all fields of academic psychology and philosophy—except perhaps for developmental psychology.

In October 1993, some leading representatives of cognitive psychology met with those who, admittedly, have been quite privileged in my picture: the cultural and discursive psychologists. The meeting took place at York University, Toronto, with the objective of *Reassessing the Cognitive Revolution* (and this was the title of the conference); the occasion was the re-evaluation of the cognitive turn by Jerome Bruner (1990) in his book *Acts of meaning*, a long commentary on that volume by Stuart Shanker (1992) *In search of Bruner*, and Bruner's (1992) reply *On searching for Bruner*. Bruner's point was that the cognitive revolution was originally intended to bring "mind" back into the human sciences after a long cold winter of positivist objectivism. But the cognitive movement had taken a precarious turn as it became clear that objectivism, the "dustbowl empiricism" (Allport) of behaviourism, was only replaced by a new reductionism. Information processing became the root metaphor of the mind, and in place of the concept of meaning the model of computability emerged. Instead of stimuli and responses, there was input and output, and so long as there was a computable program and a correspondent model of a computable brain, there was "mind". In fact, this conviction provides both a central motif and the systematic basis of various recent orthodoxies in cognitive psychology, artificial intelligence, semantic theory, transformational grammar, and the philosophy of mind. (A similar criticism of computational and naturalist cognitivism, albeit from an epistemologically different point of departure and with quite distinct—and ultimately Cartesian— consequences, has been developed by John Searle, 1992).

The fundamental problem of this view, Bruner (1990) argued, is that it cannot allow for a concept of mind that embraces qualities like agency and moral commitment; that is, mental states like beliefs, desires, intentions—all centred around the idea of "grasping a meaning". There is no model within the horizon of information processing that can account for what Bruner regards as the essential human characteristic of "meaning-making and meaning-using processes"—the very activities that connect people to their culture. All human constructions are "acts of meanings", deeply entrenched in the shared symbol systems that constitute, as Clifford Geertz (1973) pointed out, the semiotic fabric that we call *culture*.

Apart from Geertz's anthropological methodology of "thick descriptions" and participant interpretation of cultural sign systems, Bruner's project of a meaning-centred, culturally oriented psychology draws on insights of Vygotsky, Wittgenstein, and pragmatism, as well as on linguistic and literary theory. In examining, from an historical point of view, what philosophically links all these threads, we can locate the entire approach within the horizon of *Geisteswissenschaften*, particularly Wilhelm Dilthey's (1911/1977) idea of an historically and culturally based human science. To go one step further, we will find that this idea developed out of Hegel's dialectical philosophy of the Geist, which can be read as an early attempt at an historical theory of psychological and cultural development (Brockmeier, 1988a).

UNDERSTANDING AND EXPLANATION

The central epistemological concept that Dilthey (and Max Weber) proposed for the human sciences is *verstehen*—understanding—while natural sciences explain—*erklären*. A more or less typical definition of explanation which one encounters, for instance, in the literature on logical or scientific empiricism, states that an event is explained, in nature as in history, in so far as the assertion of its occurrence is derivable from general premises comprising descriptions of initial conditions together with, say, universal hypotheses, laws, or rules. In the ideal case a description of what is to be explained (in more restricted terms) follows deductively from general propositions of the premise material. In emphasising its two essential characteristics, this model of explanation is called deductive-nomological. It requires a special mode or form of thinking, and it is exactly the (onto)genesis of this form that Piaget sought to explain. From another vantage point, Bruner (1986) has described it as the "paradigmatic mode of thought", confronting it with a second fundamental human mode of thinking, the narrative mode. Although the explanatory or paradigmatic mode is of central importance for logico-scientific thought, the narrative form (which does not exist in the Piagetian world) is crucial for the (self)understanding of the mind as an individual and social entity: particularly, how it directs and manifests itself in language, culture, and history.

Along the lines of Dilthey's cultural-historical *Geisteswissenschaften* and Vygotsky's meaning-oriented semiotics, Bruner, thus, conceives of the psychological study of human nature as one within the hermeneutics of understanding and ("thick") description. Like history, this study cannot claim any neutral and objective viewpoint outside of, and independent from, the processes of interpretation and negotiation of meanings; these processes are themselves social and historical events. Like all human sciences, the psychological study of human nature is a way of "meaning-making" by perspectival description and narration—which is, for instance, strikingly demonstrated in Geertz's (1988) case studies of "anthropological writing".

Following Wittgenstein's idea of human activities as rule-governed and linguistically organised interactions, we also can conceive of language games at attempts at (mutual) understanding. The use of language always presupposes, as well as constitutes, a cultural system of interpretation and negotiation: a communicative web of both intentionality and the ability (as well as willingness) to understand the intentions of others. The idea of this intimate linkage between *manifested* intentions of the speaker or agent and a display of an uptake of the other is a recent innovation in socio-linguistics and social psychology, a view that has developed out of Austin's philosophy of language. It became one of the central principles of what Harré and Gillett (1994) call the "second Cognitive Revolution" which, of course, runs counter to the "first", mainstream computationalist, revolution.

It was extremely instructive to see how at the Toronto conference the representatives of the first cognitive revolution insisted on the epistemological and methodological claim of explanation: be it neurophysiological accounts or other models of cognitive action, a scientific theory of mind must be spelled out in causal terms; the principle of scientific knowledge can only be explanatory.

This view was also held by a third, non-computationalist, position that, in a certain sense, represented a Piagetian line of argument. This is one reason why I shall more closely look at this position, known in developmental psychology as "the child's theory of mind" or "children's theory of mind" (e.g. Astington, 1993; Astington, Harris, & Olson, 1988; Frye & Moore, 1991; Perner, 1991; Wellman, 1990; Whiten, 1991). A second reason is that, although there was (and is) hardly any dialogue between the two "revolutionary" cognitive movements, this third position is linked to both traditions. Its central claim is that children develop the ability to understand human activity by attributing mental states to the actors. In doing so, as Janet Wilde Astington and David Olson (1995) put it at the 1993 conference, children can be viewed as "little scientists" who, in the attempt to explain and predict their own and other's talk and action, infer such "underlying causal states" as beliefs and desires. Thus, the child is seen as an active seeker of knowledge who constructs mental models of their social world. In this sense, then, children have their "theories of mind".

According to this view, Astington, Olson, and other developmental psychologists accepted the hermeneutic-interpretive claim to understand children's activities (and their own understanding) as embedded in discourse activities ruled by the cultural conventions of "folk psychology" (for more details of this view see Astington, in press; Astington & Jenkins, 1995); but at the same time, they insisted on the principle of causal and naturalistic explanation as essential to any psychological theory of mind (for more details see Olson, 1992).

Most theory-of-mind theorists do not deny that the concrete ways and forms of children's thinking and, particularly, of their knowledge of others are culturally shaped. Rather, the new research on children's theory of mind has shown in many details that the child, from the very beginning, develops sophisticated skills for interpreting the behaviour of others in terms of underlying mental states. This kind of investigation has definitively broken with the Piagetian model of egocentrism; it has made it clear that at an early stage children acquire mental structures from semiotic encounters with adults—which certainly implies, as Fleisher Feldman (1992, p.108) remarked, "a developmental trajectory more Vygotskian than Piagetian".

In this light, it is not surprising that the theory-of-mind psychologists are sympathetic with the interpretive concept of "understanding". However, they take this stance only to a certain degree, because—as it seems to me—they are obviously bound to another and more fundamental trajectory. Accordingly, the culturally based (discursive and narrative) forms of interpretation, "can be learned only because of the availability of some essential, underlying abilities and competencies such as the ability to 'hold in mind', to 'decouple' schemata from their input-output conditions, and the ability to 'embed' schemata within other schemata" (Astington & Olson, 1995).

Evidently, this is a Piagetian argument. It is supported by a philosophical point, or more precisely, by hints and allusions to the rationalist tradition of thought which range from the mental assumption of a "Cartesian man" to the Kantian idea of investigating the intellectual conditions of the possibility of knowledge—an enterprise that the developmental theory of mind attempts to realise in its own way. In 20th-century psychology, it was up to Piaget to work out the version *par excellence* of epistemological rationalism. Now, the theory-of-mind theorists explicitly pick up again the threads of this mentalistic tradition: "Cartesian mental states cannot be had for free; their origins must be explained", as Astington and Olson state; and they refer to Dan Sperber (1986, p.1308) who holds that most cognitive psychologists are convinced that:

> ... in order to learn an ability, one has to learn an ability to learn; the more basic abilities, the linguistic ones for instance, must be, to an important extent, genetically determined; the construction of abilities from within, or the internalisation of culturally constituted abilities, can only take place on some well-developed innate foundation.

To sum up the epistemological perspective of the developmental theory of mind, one could be reminded of another rationalist *topos*, classically outlined in Leibniz's anti-empiricist argument: *"Nihil est in intellectu quod non fuerit in sensu, nisi intellectu ipse"* (there is nothing in the intellect which was not in the sense, except for the intellect itself).[1]

In the current debate in developmental psychology, the Leibnizian argument reappears as a mentalist case in point against the cultural-historical and interpretive view of the mind. Like Leibniz, the theory-of-mind psychologists clearly distinguish between *"intellectu ipse"*—the very conceptual core of cognition—and its application. Investigating them requires distinct epistemological strategies: one being concerned with cultural (that is, empirical) knowledge, the other with "the reflection of the mind upon itself". From this point of view, it appears to be a fundamental mistake "confusing" the two tasks (and modes of knowing) of explaining and interpreting: for the ontogenetic foundation of the mind must be explained in causal terms.

EMPHASISING INDIVIDUAL AGENCY

I have considerable sympathy with the anti-empiricist emphasis of this argument, carried out in the wake of Piaget's brilliant "deconstruction" of the positivist tradition in psychology. With good reasons, the new developmental theorists of the mind repudiate the assumption that cultural forms and conventions can be picked up from the social context "simply because they are there and children grow up in them". This addresses not only traditional theories of learning and cognition, but also some modern social-constructivist accounts. In examining them, one often cannot help but think that the essential difference between socio-historical *context* and socio-historical *determinism* tends to blur; as a consequence, the symbolic web of culture appears to be an iron fabric. More specifically, there is a danger that the formulae of the "cultural embeddedness or situatedness" of psychological phenomena are to be understood as implying the transformation of the individual mind into a resultant element of a large, more or less deterministic *apparatus*—whether it be one designed by Watson or Skinner, Orwell or Foucault, religious or naturalist predeterminists, socio-economical historians or psychological theorists of "interiorisation" or "socialisation", radical social constructivists or (post)modern media theorists.

Therefore I also fully agree with the strong Piagetian emphasis on the creative potentials of the individual subject. The child cannot just take over the canonical knowledge, even if the culture (parents, teachers, politicians, priests, etc.) would like them to do so—whether it be by enticing offers or severe educational practices. In Piaget's terms (1977/1995, Ch. V): "Each individual is called upon to think and to rethink—on his own account and by means of his own system of logic—the system of collective notions.". The insistence on subjective agency, and thus the focus on the decisive role of the *active* individual also sheds light on the construction of meaning-systems in their cultural contexts—even if Piaget himself did not pay much attention to this cultural dimension, either to that of the meaning-systems or to that of their semiosis (which is surprising, if we bear in mind, for example, the far-reaching claims of his study—Piaget 1945/1962—on the genesis of the symbolic function). In psychology, as Astington and Olson (1995) remind us, we know at least since Piaget that the child has to construct not just the concepts for interpreting events but also the "observables" that the concepts represent: That is to say that the child has to invent just what the culture offers; the child has to "make what he finds", as Nelson Goodman would say.

I believe this is the same emphasis that led Bruner to lay so much stress on the subjective and active aspect of *meaning-making* and *meaning-using*, an emphasis that also highlights the individual way of "world-making", to borrow another concept from Goodman. That is to say, the cultural order has to be newly re-constructed as the very personal order of each developing child, as it almost always emerges in an individually differentiated fabric of meaning (Brockmeier, 1988b).

No cultural, historical, or discursive psychology can ignore this quintessential Piagetian lesson—whatever the theoretical scenarios and empirical settings in which Piaget then may have integrated this idea. If we look closer at its individual as well as cultural background, I suppose, it can be traced back to the anti-authoritarian elements of a particular intellectual and spiritual heritage of late 19th-century *Suisse Romande*. I am especially thinking here of what Vidal (1994) calls the "Protestant context" which is linked to a sort of egalitarian social (or even socialist) commitment. This particular combination of evangelical, liberal, and social Protestantism was widespread in the Swiss-French culture at the turn of the century. One of its essential components was the replacement of external authority by an appeal to individual conscience; a consequence of this attitude is the diffusion of (Christian) dogma into a morality and theory of the "free will". Second, this Protestant individualism was supported by Kantian moral philosophy. A third component is not mentioned by Vidal (who has limited his study to the year 1918) but represents, as it seems to me, a further important part of the cultural heritage which shaped the work of the actual *psychologist* Piaget: this is the, in the end, deeply Rousseauian spirit that characterised Piaget's outlook on development and education throughout his life.

It is one thing to read Piaget's theoretical self-localisations in structuralist philosophy of science (e.g. Piaget 1968/1971), but quite another to study, above all in his earlier works, his empathetic investigation of the child's subjective *Weltanschauung* (e.g. Piaget, 1926/1951). Meyerson's dictum on positivist scientists can be applied *mutatis mutandis* to Piaget as well: even the seemingly most structuralist psychologist did not (always) act on the credo he expounded in prefaces and theoretical writings.

In sticking to this Piagetian emphasis on the subject's potential of agency, the theory of "children's theory of mind" may indeed appear as a strong candidate for representing a new paradigm for post-Piagetian developmental psychology, as Fleisher Feldman (1992) suggested. It preserves important gains of Piaget's psychology and attempts to integrate them into the new general orientation in the human sciences that I presented at the outset. According to Fleisher Feldman (1992, p.107) it:

> creates a more inclusive and powerful model of cognitive development by incorporating the … important achievements of the earlier era into a larger structure. Piaget's active, thinking, and reasonable organism was alone in a world with uninterpreted objects to be explored. The new literature on theory of mind recontextualizes Piaget's solitary thinker in a social world composed of enculturated and communicating human adults.

Despite this broad measure of agreement, there are, however, some points on which I take a different view. First and foremost, I am not convinced of the Leibnizian distinction between the mind (and its genesis), to be explained in causal terms, and its "application" in a cultural context, which allows an interpretive reading. The putative dichotomy between explanation and understanding appears all the more problematic, if we really take into account Goodman's remark that the child has to *make* what he or she finds. Why should the making of the tools follow different rules (spelled out in a causal explanation) as their use (which requires an interpretive understanding)?

FLYING CORKSCREWS AND
OTHER SEMANTIC FIELDS

Consider language as the most important symbolic tool of humans, both in communicative and cognitive contexts of use. How could the child learn to speak if not in the very process of language in use? For almost two decades, research on language development has shown that the child only learns to speak by learning to act in and by communicative and linguistic practices themselves. There is no learning to swim before entering the water. The water we are dealing with here, however, is that of the realm of human agency. To understand this realm of joint actions, one should bear in mind that it is governed not by causes (or causalities), but by rules. This is one central lesson to be learnt from Wittgenstein. If rules were causes, humans could never break them. But as we can break them (and in fact, we do so all the time), we have to renegotiate them (and indeed, we do so all the time).

As authors like Hacker (1987) and Harré (1990) have remarked on Wittgenstein's discussion of rules in the genesis of action, the apparent inexorability of rules, their necessity, is an illusion. It is not the rules that are inexorable but ourselves in the way that we use them. This is why we cannot refer to them as explanatory causal principles. They do not explain (least of all their own "application"), but are themselves a part of what has to be explained.

Nothing makes us follow this or that rule in this or that way, least of all the rule. Rather it is we, the users, who are inexorable in our use of them. In all kinds of ways they are instruments in the creation of order, but they do not lay down tramlines into the future. We mistake the grammatical force of "The rule must be followed *this* way!", for a power to constrain us in what we can do and cannot do (Harré, 1990).

If there is no hidden rule system or other cognitive machinery engendering the actions we can observe people undertaking, how then can we account for these actions? If there is no causal dynamism and, thus, no generic pattern explanation in the genesis of human action, how can we understand the processes of meaning-using and meaning-making? To put the question more precisely: How does the child learn to negotiate meanings and their rules?

Let us look at the following everyday dialogue between mother and child:

> - What are you doing?
> - This is my corb, Mom. Look: brrr … brrr … , it's up there, in the sky.
> - This is what? You mean the corkscrew? Look, darling, this is not a "corb", but a "corkscrew" [slowly]. You see, it is a corkscrew because one can screw corks out of bottles with it: like this [demonstrating]. But it is dangerous for kids. Look at this sharp point. It can hurt you.
> - No, the corbcrew doesn't hurt me. Because it's up there, in the sky.
> - Only adults use corkscrews, because only adults drink wine.
> - But sometimes kids also need corbcrews, when they wanna play with them. Look: it's my airplane, my corbplane [slowly] … , it does like that: brrrr … [demonstrating].

I want to make three comments on this short exchange. First, as Vygotsky already observed, mother and child sometimes negotiate for several months about the practical meaning and the naming of things and events. As we know, a word readily changes its meaning and sense in various contexts, and it does so even more if the contexts themselves are unstable, as it is the case in communications between children and adults. Therefore, the development of "everyday concepts" differs qualitatively from what Vygotsky called "scientific concepts". The development of scientific concepts begins—usually at school—with their verbal definition. As Vygotsky (1934/1987, p.168) states: "As part of an organised system, this verbal definition descends to the concrete; it descends to the phenomena which the concept represents. In contrast, the everyday concept tends to develop outside any definitional system; it tends to move upwards toward abstraction and generalisation".

Second, in these interactions mother and child carry out actions with textual signs and symbols—*textual actions* in the sense of modern semioticians like M. Bakhtin and Y. Lotman. In this semiotic perspective, "texts" are "generators" of new meanings, not only means of transport or containers of given meanings (see Wertsch & Bivens, 1992, for a reading of Vygotsky in the light of Bakhtin and Lotman).

There is a third interesting aspect that we can study in this little argument about what it means to be a corkscrew. It demonstrates not only how conceptual development is embedded in language development, but also how this process is fused with the interactive situations in which the child acts and negotiates the meanings as well as the rules of joint activities. So one might say that both meanings and the rules of their practical and linguistic use are discursively created, they are communicatively embedded or socially constructed and reconstructed; but they are not *caused*. Social creation is no social causation. To put it in terms of cognitive psychology: examining the development of conceptual structures (or mental or cognitive schemata) as interwoven in linguistic and interactive practices, we deal with networks of what Wittgenstein called "family resemblances".

More precisely, these semantic fields are structured on many dimensions of family resemblance *in use*. As our mother–child talk displays, both protagonists act within several semantic fields, such as the fields of what is dangerous, what can hurt, who uses (or is allowed to use) corkscrews, what adults do and what children do, what is play, what planes do and so forth. Of course, we can describe the development of these semantic fields in terms of the construction of (special) cognitive structures, too. In this sense, as Smorti (1994) points out, narratives represent differentiated cognitive schemata which embrace social events with a high degree of complication—open situations, unpredictable story lines, "breaks of canonicity", as Bruner (1991) puts it. Similarly, for Fleisher Feldmann (1991) narrative genres can take over the function of "mental models". Yet, however we define semantic fields and their practical and symbolic dimensions of use, they are neither physically given relations, nor logically ordered deductive sequences. Even if they must be understood, as I have argued, as cognitively constructed by each child in a particular way, they do not embody universal (mental or natural) causalities, but culturally defined structures of meaning.

Such semantic structures or fields are always semiotically mediated. To put it along a philosophical line of argument which, again, can be traced back to Hegel: as far as culture and history are concerned, there is no immediate or pre-semiotic meaning at all (Brockmeier, 1990). But this argument can also be put the other way round, so that it turns out to be a genuine Vygotskyan point: namely, to see semiotic action as inextricably linked to other forms of actions. As Wertsch (1991) remarked, this assumption distinguishes Vygotsky's ideas from those of many others. In contrast to analyses of language, which focus on the structure of sign systems abstracted from any context of use, Vygotsky investigated language and other sign systems in terms of how they are a part of human action and mediate social activity.

In our example, this mediation takes the form of a dialogical interpretation. This form of adult–child conversation is certainly the dominant "format" for the negotiation of meanings in early childhood—especially for the negotiation of the meaning of "the other". It constitutes a dense Vygotskyan "zone of proximal development", a zone of exploration in which the child makes sense of his or her world. Here is, as we might say, the *construction site* of interpretation.

The communicative format of dialogical interpretation does not depend on developed linguistic abilities. From the first month of their lives, as Judy Dunn (1988) pointed out, babies begin to share a communicative framework of gestures, signals, and symbols with others; for example, they wave goodbye appropriately when someone leaves, signalling their own regrets, wishes, and emotions with gestures shared by all family members. This ability to understand and to use a common interpretive framework is particularly clear in infants' attempts to make their interests and needs clear. In her investigation, Dunn has taken up Bruner's (1983) argument that the means to an end, used by children, quickly includes the actions of other people: "the infant's principal 'tool' for achieving his ends is another person". And this requires, as we might add, a particular interpretation of this person's action.

Analysing our little example more thoroughly, we note that the negotiation of the meaning of "corb" or "corkscrew" plays only a secondary role. The main function of the dialogue is not to negotiate the word meaning of a thing, but the meaning of an activity—which includes the use of this thing and, thus, its meaning.

In this process, two rhetorical strategies are crossing each other. It goes without saying that the child knows, or at least senses, that his mother does not want him to play with the corkscrew; as the theory-of-mind psychologist would put it, he attributes a mental state to her—as she does to him (i.e. she assumes that he does not *know* either that this is a corkscrew or that it is dangerous). On the basis of these reciprocal interpretations of intention and expectation, the two rhetorical strategies emerge. The mother refers to the moral order of what adults do and what children are not allowed to. She supports this by a "discourse of dangerous things", so to speak, which is presented *prima facie* as if it were information about physical properties of the corkscrew. The child, in turn, refers to the playful character of his use of the corkscrew. From his point of view, this is not a corkscrew at all. His point draws on the (clearly demonstrated) "fact" that in play things can lose their original meaning and take over another. And he knows, of course, that his mother also knows this.

Semiotically, as Vygotsky (1930/1976) emphasised, this is the very essence of play, that it transforms meanings by redefining the relation between sign and meaning. Or, as we can also say, play constructs new interpretive links between signs and meanings—new realities. But what makes play such a psychologically and semiotically fascinating phenomenon is that it remains a multilayered construction. The corbplane does not lose its underlying meaning as a corkscrew, a meaning that it will get back in the context of another semantic field.

Obviously, in both rhetorical strategies the object and the activity in question is interpreted in perspectival terms. On the one hand, it is defined as a dangerous tool that only adults are entitled to use; on the other hand, it turns out to be used as a toy airplane—a "corbplane"—to which children are certainly entitled as well. Both strategies open up particular semantic fields overlapping only in some respects; in other respects they indicate opposite structures of interests and respective interpretations.

However, it is not only the very activity of the linguistic and psychological actors themselves that proves to be a web of multilayered speech acts—and that means reciprocal acts of interpretation; it is also, on a meta-level, the psychological and linguistic investigation that necessarily takes this form. How do we, from the point of view of a linguistically and discursively oriented psychological analysis, understand what Cartesians call explanation? As Mühlhäusler and Harré (1990) showed in their inquiry of the linguistic construction of concepts of self and person in different cultures, what is traditionally called *explanans* in an account of linguistic phenomena is, in the end, to be found (p.22) "by giving a description of a collective human activity, a language game, within which this or that linguistic device has a quite definite role to play in a practical project, be it social or material" .

PSYCHOLOGICAL KNOWLEDGE

If we really are willing to overcome the central dilemma of the Piagetian paradigm in psychology—its individuocentric, mentalistic and, as I argued (Brockmeier, 1983), teleological view of human development—we need to study the language games in which the genesis of "meaning-making" takes place. That is to say, we must analyse them from the very beginning as processes of *joint* (or socially distributed) construction. In doing so, we cannot but realise that the idea of the *constructive* mind captures only one side of the coin; the other side of it is the *interpretive* mind. As soon as we conceive of construction as an essentially social enterprise, we are faced with micro-processes of mutual interpretation, of shared meaning-making and, not to be forgotten, sign-making.

I will end up by quoting a sentence from Piaget's book on structuralism published in French in 1968—in several respects a critical year in the history of structuralism. After having discussed new philosophical developments and debates—among others, Foucault's recently published *The order of things*—Piaget (1968/1971, p.143) concludes cautiously: "And since an immanent dialectic is here at work, we can be sure that the denials, devaluations, and restrictions with which certain structuralists today meet positions which they regard as incompatible with their own will one day be recognised to mark those crucial points where new syntheses overtake antitheses".

What I have been suggesting in this paper is, of course, no new synthesis. Rather, I wanted to draw attention to an issue that, however, could become a point of departure for a possible synthesis embracing the constructivist view and a discourse-oriented interpretive approach to psychological phenomena. In sum, I argue that cognitive construction always implies an interpretive dimension, as all interpretation includes a constructive aspect. To draw a clear-cut boundary between construction and interpretation is only plausible if we accept a clear-cut distinction between the principles of explanation and understanding or, more precisely, if we adopt a (causal) explanatory principle of knowledge to the study of human life. But the crux of this study is that it is itself a part of life.

This leads up to a final point already addressed at the outset concerning the epistemological status of (psychological) knowledge. I have also been trying to illustrate the idea that our knowledge about any putatively objective matter is closely intertwined with the knowledge that we have of the nature of knowledge itself. Here the interpretive and constructive nature of psychological knowledge is a strong case in point. If psychological knowledge (as, in the end, all human knowledge) is constitutively perspectival, then the question of *what* we know cannot be separated from the question of *how* we know. This insight, I believe, can be seen as the common epistemological point of departure for both Piaget and Vygotsky. Thus, the historical coordinates of both projects refer back to the very origin of the philosophical discourse sketched at the beginning: to Kant.

As has often been observed, a vital consequence of Kant's critique of the foundations of our knowledge was that it appeared to make the highest goal of traditional epistemology unattainable: there is no absolute and objective cognition of the world as it really is. There is no way of knowing reality *sub specie eternitatis* beyond the range of our forms of knowledge; and these forms or means of knowledge, as we might add, are shaped by our culture and history: they are cultural tools.

This introduced the idea that perspectivity is inescapable: that we have no way of knowing the world and ourselves independently of the structuring framework that we bring to experience—be it Piaget's cognitive structures or Vygotsky's sign systems. It is hard to conceive of any cognitive or logical construction that allows any escape from this, in the end, hermeneutic challenge of perspectivalism—particularly if we want to make sense of the constructive potentials of the human mind. However, if we want to stick to those claims that both Piaget and Vygotsky share, why should we want to escape?

REFERENCES

Astington, J.W. (1993). *The child's discovery of mind*. Cambridge, MA: Harvard University Press.

Astington, J.W. (in press). What is theoretical about the child's theory of mind? A Vygotskian view of its development. In P. Carruthers & P.K. Smith (Eds.), *Theories of theory of mind*. Cambridge: Cambridge University Press.

Astington, J.W., & Jenkins, J.M. (1995). Theory of mind development and social understanding. *Cognition and Emotion, 9*(2/3), 151–165.

Astington, J.W., & Olson, D. (1995). The cognitive revolution in children's understanding of mind. *Human Development, 4/5*, 179–189.

Astington, J.W., Harris, P., & Olson, D. (Eds.). (1988). *Developing theories of mind*. Cambridge: Cambridge University Press.

Brockmeier, J. (1983). Die Mittel der kognitiven Entwicklung. Zum Zusammenhang der individuellen mit der historischen Entwicklung des Bewußtseins bei Piaget und Wygotski. [The means of cognitive development: On the relations between individual and historical development of the mind in Piaget and Vygotsky]. *Forum Kritische Psychologie, 12*, 44–88.

Brockmeier, J. (1988a). Der dialektische Ansatz und seine Bedeutung für die Psychologie. [The dialectical approach and its significance for psychology]. In G. Jüttemann (Ed.), *Wegbereiter der historischen Psychologie* (pp.381–398). [Pioneers in historical psychology]. München & Weinheim: Beltz—Psychologie Verlags Union.

Brockmeier, J. (1988b). Was bedeutet dem Subjekt die Welt? Fragen einer psychologischen Semantik. [What does the world mean to the subject? Questions of psychological semantic]. In N. Kruse & M. Ramme (Eds.), *Hamburger Ringvorlesung Kritische Psychologie: Wissenschaftskritik, Kategorien, Anwendungsgebiete* (pp.141–184) [Hamburger courses on critical psychology: Critiques of science, categories, fields of application]. Hamburg: Ergebnisse-Verlag.

Brockmeier, J. (1990). Language, thought, and writing: Hegel after deconstruction and linguistic turn. *Bulletin of the Hegel Society of Great Britain, 20/21*, 20–54.

Bruner, J.S. (1983). *Child's talk*. New York: Norton.

Bruner, J.S. (1986). *Actual minds, possible worlds*. Cambridge, MA. & London: Harvard University Press.

Bruner, J.S. (1990). *Acts of meaning*. Cambridge, MA & London: Harvard University Press.

Bruner, J.S. (1991). The narrative construction of reality. *Critical Inquiry,* Autumn 1991, 1–21.

Bruner, J. (1992). On searching for Bruner. *Language & Communication, 1*, 75–78.

Dilthey, W. (1977). *Descriptive psychology and historical understanding* (1911). The Hague: Nijhoff. [Original work published 1911.]

Dunn, J. (1988). *The beginnings of social understanding*. Cambridge, MA: Harvard University Press.

Fleisher Feldman, C. (1991). I generi letterari come modelli mentali. [Literary genres as mental models]. In M. Ammaniti & D.N. Stern (Eds.), *Rappresentazioni e Narrazioni* (pp.113–131) [Representations and narratives]. Roma & Bari: Laterza.

Fleisher Feldman, C. (1992). The new theory of theory of mind. *Human Development, 35*, 107–117.

Frye, D., & Moore, C. (Eds.). (1991). *Children's theory of mind*. Hillsdale, NJ: Lawrence Erlbaum Associates Inc.

Geertz, C. (1973). *The interpretation of cultures*. New York: Basic Books.

Geertz, C. (1988). *Lives and works: The anthropologist as author*. Stanford, CA: Standford University Press.

Goodman, J. (1984). *On mind and other matters*. Cambridge, MA: Harvard University Press.

Hacker, P.M.S. (1987). *Insight and illusion* (2nd Edn.). Oxford: Blackwell.

Harré, R. (1990). Explanation in psychology. *Annals of Theoretical Psychology, 6*, 105–124.

Harré, R., & Gillett, G. (1994). *The discursive mind*. Thousand Oaks, CA: Sage.

Leibniz, G.W. (1896). *New essays concerning human understanding*. [Translated from Latin, French, and German by A.G. Langley.] New York & London: Macmillan.

Mühlhäusler, P., & Harré, R. (1990). *Pronouns and people: The linguistic construction of social and personal identity*. Oxford: Blackwell.

Olson, D.R. (1992). The development of representations: The origins of mental life. *Canadian Psychology / Psychologie Canadienne, 34*, 293–306.

Perner, J. (1991). *Understanding the representational mind*. Cambridge, MA: MIT Press.

Piaget, J. (1951). *The child's conception of the world*. London: Routledge & Kegan Paul. [Original work published 1926.]

Piaget, J. (1962). *Play, dreams and imitation in childhood*. New York: Norton. [Original work published 1945.]

Piaget, J. (1971). *Structuralism*. New York: Harper & Row. [Original work published 1968.]

Piaget, J. (1995). *Sociological studies*. [Edited and introduced by Leslie Smith.] London: Routledge [Original work published 1977, expanded 2nd edn. ch. 1–9. (1st edn., 1965, ch. 1–4 only)].

Searle, John R. (1992). *The rediscovery of the mind*. Cambridge, MA: MIT Press.

Shanker, S. (1992). In search of Bruner. *Language & Communication, 1*, 53–74.

Smorti, A. (1994). *Il pensiero narrativo: costruzione di storie e sviluppo della conoscenza sociale* [Narrative thought: stories' constructions and development of social knowledge]. Firenze: Giunti.

Sperber, D. (1986). The mind as a whole. *Times Literary Supplement, Nov. 21*, 1308–1309).

Vidal, F. (1994). *Piaget before Piaget*. Cambridge, MA: Harvard University Press.

Vygotsky, L.S. (1976). Play and its role in the mental development of the child. In J. Bruner, A. Jolly, & K. Sylva (Eds.), *Play—Its role in development and evolution* (pp.537-554). Harmondsworth, UK: Penguin. [Original work published 1930.]

Vygotsky, L.S. (1987). *The collected works of L.S. Vygotsky. Volume 1. Problems of general psychology. Including the volume Thinking and speech* [N. Minick Trans.]. New York: Plenum Press. [Original work published 1934.]

Wellman, H.M. (1990). *The child's theory of mind*. Cambridge, MA: MIT Press.

Wertsch, J.V. (1991). *Voices of the mind: A sociocultural approach to mediated action*. London: Harvester Wheatsheaf.

Wertsch, J.V., & Bivens, J.A. (1992). The social origins of individual mental functioning: Alternatives and perspectives. *The Quarterly Newsletter of the Laboratory of Comparive Human Cognition, 2*, 35–44.

Whiten, A. (Ed.) (1991). *Natural theories of mind: Evolution, development and simulation of everyday mindreading*. Oxford: Blackwell.

NOTE

1. Leibniz's (1896, p.81) argument, developed at the beginning of the 18th century, was that there are some abstract thoughts—necessary truths—that are qualitatively different from thoughts based on empirical knowledge—truths of experience: "The original proof of the necessary truths comes from the understanding (that is, from the intellect) alone, and the other truths come from experience or from the observation of the senses. Our mind is capable of knowing both; but it is the source of the former, and, whatever number of particular experiences we may have of a universal truth, we could not be assured of it forever by induction without knowing its necessity through reason". Thus the "intellectual ideas" of the *intellectu ipse* are prior to "external sensations"; they "must come simply and solely from internal grounds" (1896, p.38). For Leibniz these internal grounds emerge from reflection; more precisely, they "are due to the reflection of the mind upon itself" (1896, p.82).

CHAPTER NINE

Social interaction and individual understanding in a community of learners: The influence of Piaget and Vygotsky

Ann L. Brown *University of California, Berkeley, USA*

Kathleen E. Metz *University of California, Riverside, USA*

Joseph C. Campione *University of California, Berkeley, USA*

The importance of social interaction as a major force in cognitive development has become associated in America with Vygotskyan theory. In contrast, Piagetian theory has been seen as influential in mapping individual cognitive growth. However the two theorists have more in common than is usually supposed.

Vygotsky's central interest was in the evolution of cognitive processes, in growth and change rather than static state cognition. It is therefore not surprising that Vygotsky had a special interest in children's learning, where one can observe cognitive processes "undergoing change right before one's eyes."[1]

For Vygotsky, developmental analysis was central to psychological investigation in general, not just a peripheral offshoot having to do with the specialised study of children.

If Vygotsky was more interested in individual cognitive development than is usually thought, Piaget was not immune to the role of social experiences. In particular, Piaget regarded *peer* interaction as an ideal forum for helping children "decentre" their thinking from one particular egocentric view in order to consider multiple perspectives. Faced with a group of peers who not only fail to accept his or her views but hold opposing opinions, the child must compromise. In the process of compromising, the group produces a solution that is more mature than each individual effort. The conflict arising from group disagreement creates disequilibrium and the resulting adjustment to this state is a primary cause of cognitive development.

Although Piaget was especially concerned with the transitional child, one fluctuating between two levels of understanding, the parallel Vygotskyan notion of a *zone of proximal development* has been especially influential in American psychological and educational theory. As is now well known, the zone of proximal development refers to the distance between the child's "... actual developmental level as determined by independent problem solving and the level of potential development as determined through problem solving under adult guidance, or in collaboration with more capable peers."

Vygotsky argued that what children can do with the assistance of others is "even more indicative of their mental development than what they can do alone." An estimate of individual learning would be a child's performance on a task purportedly measuring a particular cognitive process. In traditional practice, the child passes or fails. But what if one does not stop here, and like Piaget in his clinical interviews, one offers leading suggestion or, like Vygotsky, one demonstrates how the problem is solved or "initiates the solution and the child completes it" — in short, what if the child "barely misses an independent solution of the problem" and is helped towards a higher level? Vygotsky described such methods of assistance as: providing prompts to a more mature solution, directing leading questions, forcing the child to defend or change a theory, and so on.

Piaget also argued that the development of logical thought is enhanced by the need to defend one's ideas to actual or imagined audiences. He lucidly describes an internalised argument (1923/1974, p.59):

> The adult, even in his most personal and private occupation, ... thinks socially, has continually in his mind's eye his collaborators or opponents, actual or eventual, at any rate members of his own profession to whom sooner or later he will announce the results of his labours. This mental picture pursues him throughout his task. The task itself is henceforth socialised at almost every stage of its

development ... the need for checking and demonstrating calls into being an inner speech addressed throughout to a hypothetical opponent whom the imagination often pictures as one of flesh and blood. When, therefore, the adult is brought face to face with his fellow beings, what he announces to them is something already socially elaborated and therefore roughly adapted to his audience.

The notion of internalisation or appropriation is central to Vygotsky's theory, as indeed are the concepts of assimilation and accommodation to Piaget. In particular, Vygotsky argued that what children can do now in social interaction becomes, in time, part of their independent repertoires. Social settings create zones of proximal development that operate initially only in these collaborative interactions. But, gradually, the newly awakened processes are internalised, they become part of the child's *independent developmental achievement*. What is the upper bound of competence today becomes the springboard of tomorrow's achievements.

The goal of our particular research program is pragmatic. We are involved in a long-term, intensive effort to design effective curricula, instruction, and assessment to improve the science education of inner city grade-school children (Brown & Campione, 1990, 1994). We refer to this work as the development of a Community of Learners. Our attempts to design new learning environments to facilitate children's learning have been concerned not only with theories regarding the social nature of learning, but also with the implications of that theorising for *what* should be taught, *when* it should be taught, and how the fruits of that teaching should be *evaluated*. In these interacting endeavours, the theories of both Piaget and Vygotsky have played pivotal roles.

Our recourse to Vygotsky and Piaget has been somewhat eclectic. We have followed the tradition of turning to Piaget to inform the design of a developmentally sensitive science curriculum and to Vygotsky to inform our design of socially supportive climates for learning. This follows a widespread stereotype of both positions, for the theories are often set in contrasts that emphasise their differences rather than their similarities. It is received wisdom that Vygotsky concentrated on the social, Piaget the individual, a misleading and seductive simplification of both theories. Maintaining these different emphases has served us as a matter of convenience rather than belief.

We begin this paper by concentrating on the design of grade-school science curricula, with particular emphasis on the problems that have followed a simplistic interpretation of Piaget's structuralist theory. We then consider the more optimistic picture of children as scientists that follows consideration of Piaget's later functionalist period, and our own curriculum development efforts. Next we turn to the design of supportive learning environments where we have been primarily influenced by a consideration of contemporary interpretations of Vygotskyan theory. Finally, we will focus our attention on assessment, where we have designed instruments influenced by both Piaget's and Vygotsky's clinical interview techniques.

PIAGET AND THE DESIGN OF GRADE-SCHOOL SCIENCE CURRICULA

The primary influence that a consideration of Piagetian theory has had on the design of science education for young students in the US has been to define constraints on what it is that children can reasonably be expected to learn and understand (for a more extensive treatment of this section, see Metz, 1995). A simplistic interpretation of Piagetian theory has led to the consistent underestimation of young students' capabilities. This slant on Piagetian theory encourages sensitivity to what children of a certain age *cannot* do because they have not yet reached a certain stage of cognitive operations.

As a result, it is received wisdom that: (a) observation, measuring, ordering, and categorising constitute appropriate science objectives, because these are core intellectual strengths of the concrete operational child; (b) science should be presented in a "hands-on" manner to primary children, who are capable of reasoning only about the concrete and manipulable; and (c) "true" scientific inquiry should be postponed until adolescence when students become hypothetical-deductive thinkers who grasp the logic of experimental design.

Here we will review the eight most common interpretations of Piaget that have led to lowered expectations of young children's capacity for scientific thought.

1. The meaning of "concrete" in concrete operations
Piaget viewed concrete operational thought as concrete in the sense that the child's mental operations are applied to some aspect of external reality, *either physically present or mentally represented*. Piaget assumed then that either tangible objects or their mental representations play a key role in the child's reasoning at the period of concrete operations. Piaget (1964/1968, p.62) argued that, "absent objects are replaced by more or less vivid representations, which are tantamount to reality". Whereas the formal operational thinker can reason on the basis of any referent—real, symbolic, or arbitrary—the

concrete thinker is restricted to operations on objects or their mental representations that are "tantamount to reality." But note the term mental representation. It is a limiting view of "concrete" to restrict its meaning to the directly touchable and manipulable, although the touchable and manipulable do, of course, have the advantage for adults and children alike.

Furthermore, although Piaget believed that childhood thought was based on concrete referents, he made no claim that the *products* of the child's thinking were concrete. Examination of Piaget's writing reveals numerous abstract constructs formulated at least implicitly by young children, including *cardinal number, speed, randomness,* and *necessity*. Each of these ideas stems from the child's interactions with the concrete and yet clearly transcends them.

2. Decontextualised skills at the expense of knowledge base factors

American science educators were primarily influenced by Piaget's structural period, where he was concerned with how an *epistemic subject* acted; Piaget's focus was not on individual psychology but rather on the general structures underlying the thought of the universal child. This interest led to a concentration on the logical operations of concrete thought: conservation, seriation, classification, etc. Children were asked to classify and seriate, but classify what? seriate what? Children's classifications in typical Piagetian-based curricula are formed apart from any purpose beyond putting together objects that are alike or belong together. But observation and classification each presume a purpose, a goal, a situation, a realm of inquiry.

The emphasis in early science on description and organisation of the directly perceptible, *decontextualised from purpose*, is problematic from the viewpoint of both developmental psychology and the philosophy of science. Scientific descriptions can only be derived and evaluated in relation to a *context of inquiry*. Young children can be asked to collect rocks and formulate their own systems of classification, but without a focus for that inquiry any internally consistent taxonomy is as good as any other, and the scientific knowledge that may result is minimal. It is because the softness-to-hardness continuum of rocks is one indicator of crystal structure that scientists choose this form of seriation.

The influence of what one knows on how one might observe and classify is a problem of knowledge and purpose, as well as logical reasoning. Children are "universal novices" (Brown & DeLoache, 1978); they know a lot less about a good many areas. If the child is not privy to the deep structure in a domain, he or she has no basis to reason with, no recourse but to fall back on surface features as the basis of classification (Brown, 1989). An example from our own work centres around classical analogy. Although Piaget believed that the ability to solve formal analogies of the form *A:B::C:D* was part of formal operational thought, studies of this ability typically confound knowledge and reasoning. When the child fully understands the basis of the analogy (e.g. simple causality: cutting, breaking, wetting), even preschool children can achieve success on such problems (Goswami & Brown, 1989, 1990).

Wellman and Gelman (1988) give many examples of preschoolers' classification in terms of nonobvious deep structure. Indeed, they argue (1988, p.116) that without knowledge, focus, and purpose, the classification task becomes absurd:

> ... when we ask children simply which objects belong together, we are neglecting the deeper question of whether the grouped objects form a motivated category, and what the consequences are of having such a category.

Many would argue that the ability to categorise is present from the first year of life (Ross, 1980): what changes with age and knowledge is the basis of that categorisation. This is also true of the development from naive to expert reasoning in adults (Chi, Feltovich, & Glaser, 1981). And there are historical precedents. For example, in his history of biological thinking, Earnst Mayr (1982) described the history of biological taxonomies from Aristotle through the medieval alchemists to Linnaeus and beyond. All entertained stable, reliable classifications that the authors could reason with and justify; what changed with time was not reasoning ability but the accumulation of scientific knowledge that forced restructuring of categories, often leading to problems of incommensurability (Kuhn, 1962) between the old and new ways of thinking.

3. Child as theorist

Children entertain theories, just as do mature scientists. Their theories may be incomplete, or just plain wrong, but they are theories. Considering work on children's theories, starting with Karmiloff-Smith and Inhelder's (1974) classic block balancing task, and including more recent work on areas as diverse as: (a) theories of mind (Gopnik, 1993; Wellman, 1990); (b) astronomy (Brewer & Samarapungavan, 1991); and (c) physics (Smith, Carey, & Wiser, 1985), we find the following claims.

Children's theories: (1) transcend the concrete and directly perceptible; (2) are internally consistent from the child's perspective; (3) involve attempts to integrate different sources of information; (4) lead to predictions; (5) reach towards a unified theory to account for all events; (6) reject nonconfirmation as due to errors of procedure; (7) are available to verbalisation, that is, the child can talk about understandings as well as act on them; and (8) support revision due to counterevidence, experimentation, and simplicity considerations. All are also hallmarks of adult theory-building.

Piaget may have underestimated the ability of children to construct theories; however, there remain obvious differences between the theorising of children and scientists. Above and beyond the massive gap in domain-specific knowledge, children have less reflective access to their theories.

4. Second-order thinking and reflection

The *sine qua non* of scientific reasoning and formal operations is second-order or reflective thought. Early on, Inhelder and Piaget (1955/1958, p.340) argued that, "... the child has no powers of reflection, no second-order thoughts which deal critically with his own thinking". Because of this inability, concrete operational children cannot think systematically. Because they cannot think systematically, they cannot construct scientific theories (ibid. pp.339–340):

> [The child's] spontaneous thinking may be more or less systematic (at first only to a small degree, later, much more so); but it is the observer who sees the system from outside, while the child is not aware of it since he never thinks about his own thought. ... No theory can be built without such reflection.

For the past 20 years or so, there has been considerable controversy concerning metacognition (Brown, Bransford, Ferrara, & Campione, 1983), some believing that it is a part of all thought processes, even in the very young, and others believing, as did early Piaget, that it is the hallmark of mature thought. Much of this controversy arises because of the use of the term metacognition to refer to at least four very different types of thoughts. We believe it is necessary to distinguish between four levels of activity that have at one point or another been called metacognition: (1) self-correction; (2) access to thought; (3) knowledge about thinking; and (4) mental experimentation.

We will discuss only mental experimentation, which is most closely associated with Piaget's concept of reflected abstraction (Piaget, 1974/1976, pp.352–353):

Finally, at the third level (from eleven to twelve years) which is that of reflected abstractions (conscious products of the reflexive abstractions), the situation is modified in that cognisance begins to be extended in a reflexion of the thought on itself. ... this means that the subject has become capable of theorising ... and no longer only of 'concrete,' although logically structured, reasoning. The reason for this is the child's new power of elaborating operations on operations ..., he thereby becomes capable of varying the factors in his experiments, of envisaging the various models that might explain a phenomenon, and of checking the latter through actual experimentation.

This argument is compelling and widely accepted, but there is the counter-argument that Piaget's theory is a theory of performance on a finite set of tasks involving combinatorial reasoning, not a model of human minds as he intended (Brown & Reeve, 1986). Johnson-Laird (1985) makes a similar point when discussing the development and use of formal logic.

5. Children lack the scientific method

When directly tested, often on arid decontextualised tasks, young children certainly evidence lacunae in their use of the traditional scientific method. Children's experiments are typically inadequately designed to enable definitive conclusions (Dunbar & Klahr, 1989; Schauble & Glaser, 1990). They ignore disconfirming evidence (Dunbar & Klahr, 1989; Kuhn, Amsel, & O'Loughlin, 1988), lose track of experimental outcomes (Schauble, 1990; Siegler & Liebert, 1975), and entertain goals that are more engineering-like than scientific (Schauble, Klopfer, & Raghavan, 1991).

These observations to some extent support the belief that scientific reasoning is a feature of formal operational thought. Prior to this stage, children lack the ability to guide their experimentation and constrain their pattern of inference rigorously because they "... lack a systematic method, notably the procedure of varying a single factor at a time while holding the others constant" (Inhelder & Piaget, 1955/1958, p.226). Without the power of combinatorial thought, propositional logic, or hypothetical-deductive reasoning, the young child's experimentation cannot be systematic, nor can his or her "experimental proof" be adequate.

But Piaget's own writings are replete with examples of children going beyond this. And at the end of his career, Piaget came to view his earlier model of the development of children's thinking, particularly formal operations, as flawed because it failed to capture the essential *role of the situation* in influencing and constraining the direction and form of children's thinking. In other words, Piaget failed to appreciate the extent to which context and semantics constrain reasoning (Metz, 1995). His last research cycle sought to replace his original model of thought based on extensional logic with one based on intensional logic (Piaget, 1980, pp.5–6, emphasis added):

> As conceived at the time, this logic of operations was too closely linked to the traditional model of extensional logic and truth tables. A better way, I now believe, of capturing the natural growth of logical thinking in the child is to pursue a kind of logic of meanings. Extensional logic is based on truth tables and leads to unacceptable paradoxes ... where p implies q whatever the relationship between p and q may be and without there being any link between their meanings .... *In a logic of meanings, the construction of extensions would be determined by the meanings and not vice versa. These extensions would thus be local and variable and not common to the set of all possible worlds.*

6. Overreliance on Piaget's middle structuralist period at the expense of later functionalist theory

If one considers conceptions of Piaget that have influenced the design of science curricula since the 1960s, it is as if Piaget as a theorist existed for only 20 years, the middle years of the structuralist period. However, very different conceptions of the child as scientist come from Piaget's early work and the functionalist period of the 1970s. Not only Piaget himself, but many other Genevan scholars of that period began considering learning in the broad sense (Inhelder, Bovet, & Sinclair, 1974) and the place of reflection and understanding (Karmiloff-Smith, 1988).

The premise that young children are not experimentalists is largely derived from *The growth of logical thinking from childhood to adolescence*, a series of studies that examines the transition from concrete to formal operational thought in the domain of scientific experimentation and inference (Inhelder & Piaget, 1955/1958). Other aspects of Piaget's work have documented young children's fruitful investigations about the physical world. Both his infancy work (Piaget, 1936/1952, 1937/1954) and late functionalist work (Piaget, 1974/1978a, 1978b) are relevant in this regard. Nevertheless, the influence of *The growth of logical thinking* continues to be felt in many science classrooms.

However, in his later, more functionalist writings, Piaget considered the changing relation between action and conceptualisation in children's thinking, interpreted in terms of *success* versus *understanding* (Piaget, 1974/1976, 1974/1978a). Here Piaget designed activities in terms of functional goals to be attained, for example, the old favourite, the Tower of Hanoi, and such tasks as constructing a bridge between two "mountains" sufficiently strong to support a toy vehicle, where the only solution with the available materials demands the use of counterweights.

Considering an array of such tasks, Piaget reports that the youngest children, from about 4 to 6 years of age, focused on *trying to succeed*. In other words, they assumed a pragmatic approach, working to attain the specified effect within the physical system. In contrast, the problem solving of the 7- and 8-year-olds reflected a balance of trying to succeed and trying to understand. Conceptualisation of why the physical system behaved as it did was as important as attaining the goal. They formed anticipations of the outcome of new design experiments, detected what went wrong, and began to grasp the relations involved in the apparatus. The characteristics that Piaget attributes to the 4–6 age group would support rudimentary learning about physical phenomena, albeit within an engineering-like frame. The characteristics that Piaget attributes to the 7- or 8-year-olds, independent design efforts and causal explorations, manifest important aspects of scientific inquiry.

7. Logical positivism as THE philosophy of science

Piaget constructed his formal operational model during an era where *logical positivism* dominated philosophy of science. Although Piaget frequently criticised logical positivism, his theory also has problems with criticisms of that form of theorising.

The first issue concerns the *objectivity of observations*. Within the logical-positivist tradition, "Observation terms were taken to raise no problems regarding their meanings, since they referred directly to experience" (Shapere, 1966, p.44). Although in later works Piaget portrays knowledge of objects and their transformations as never complete, but improving from one cycle of equilibration to the next, the problematic nature of observation was not evident in the influential work *The growth of logical thinking*. Objectivity of observation has of course been challenged. Indeed, Kuhn (1977) parodied this assumption with the phrase, "the dogma of immaculate perception". In the same vein, Popper (1972, p.46) argued that, "Observation is always selective. It needs a chosen object, a definite task, an interest, a point of view, a problem."

The second issue concerns the *connection between theory and evidence*. Within the logical-empiricist tradition, theoretical terms and observation terms were considered distinct. Scientific theories, conceptualised as axiomatic systems, were linked to experience through "rules of interpretation". Similarly, the formal operational model portrays theory and evidence as unambiguously distinct. Contemporary analyses of science contradict this perspective. For example Toulmin (1972, p.189) argues that:

> our own interest in facts is always to discover what can be made of them in light of current ideas .... In the solution of conceptual problems, the semantic and the empirical elements are not so much wantonly confused as unavoidably fused.

and Kuhn (1977, p.279) attests that:

> We [Popper and himself] do not believe that there are rules for inducing correct theories from facts, or even that theories, correct or incorrect, are induced at all. Instead we view them as imaginative posits, invented in one piece for application to nature.

Postmodernists, such as Kuhn, Medawar, and Popper, reject the logical positivism that so influenced Piaget. They argue that scientists, as human beings, do what everyday people, and indeed children, do. Scientists too confuse theory and data. They tell good stories, they create imaginary worlds. Indeed the scientific method itself (Medawar, 1982, p.111):

> like any other explanatory process is a dialogue between fact and fancy, the actual and the possible, between what could be true and what is in fact the case — it is a story of justifiable beliefs about a possible world.

8. Underestimation of the role of people and conflict in scientific discovery

Piaget has been criticised for underestimating the degree to which the development of scientific knowledge is a social activity. This point is made forcibly in Harré's (1983) description of the making of scientific experiments and Dunbar's (1995) study of the day-to-day activities of practicing scientists. Piaget did recognise the power of social interaction in the development of thought; indeed, early on in his career he argued that children's adaptation to their social environment is just as important as their adaptation to their physical environment in the development of the mind (Piaget, 1924/1928). However, the study of social adaptation was outside the scope of his already ambitious research agenda. This agenda was taken up primarily by followers of Vygotsky.

PROMISE FROM PIAGET

This pessimistic interpretation of Piagetian theory was not the only interpretation possible, even in the 1960s. Bruner (1963) is credited with the more optimistic notion that any idea could be taught in some "intellectually honest" form to children of any age. And Bruner was also influenced by the rich insights that Piaget's *qualitative descriptions* offered concerning young children's competence. He argued that it was not Piaget's formal theory of equilibrium/disequilibrium that has contributed to our understanding (Bruner, 1968, p.7, emphasis added):

> Rather, it is his brilliant formal description of the nature of the knowledge that children exhibit at each stage of development. These descriptions are couched in terms of the logical structure that informs children's solutions of problems, the logical presuppositions upon which their explanations and manipulations are based. ... There are, to be sure, faults in his formal descriptions that have been attacked by logicians and mathematicians, but this is neither here nor there. *What is overwhelmingly important is the utility and power of his descriptive work.*

A consideration of Piaget's total opus, together with subsequent research in this vein, leads to a more optimistic picture of the grade-school child as scientist. First, children of this age are able to identify variables, determine cause, and develop and refine theories. Second, when familiar situations and well developed knowledge are the domain of inquiry, children's reasoning is much more sophisticated. It is difficult to sort out deficiencies of scientific reasoning *per se* from inadequacies in domain-specific knowledge (Brown, 1990; Carey, 1985). Third, as Piaget came to realise, the hypothesis testing of children (Tschirgi, 1980) and, indeed, most adults (Johnson-Laird, 1985), does not accord well with the extensional logical model of Piaget's structural period, but rather reflects a natural inductive logic. Such logic is constructed in everyday situations where the child manipulates variables with the goal of conserving some desired effect and eliminating the undesirable. And finally, Piaget himself came to question the model of the genesis of logical-mathematical structures from which the purported limitation to young children's scientific thinking is principally derived.

GRADE-SCHOOL CURRICULA OF THE COMMUNITY OF LEARNERS

Although the grade-school curriculum we have derived looks markedly different from a traditional Piagetian model, we have been influenced by his later functional period and with the work of subsequent developmental psychologists who have based their work on Piagetian theory, even if only to refute his strong stage theory of the growth of thought. Traditional Piagetian-based curricula have been largely process models, with little emphasis on content. In contrast, our curriculum, although clearly designed as a thinking curriculum, also relies heavily on careful analysis of the scientific disciplines. We take as our starting point the types of understandings of science (in our case biology) that we know children bring to school, and we set as our goal the deep principles of the discipline in question (environmental science and ecology). It is essential to the philosophy of the community of learners that students be engaged in research in an area of inquiry that is based on deep disciplinary understanding which follows a developmental trajectory informed by contemporary research about children's understanding within a domain.

Deep disciplinary understanding

By this we mean that although it is romantic to think of young children entering the community of practice of adult academic disciplines, awareness of the deep principles of these disciplines should enable us to design academic practices for the young that are stepping stones to mature understanding, or at least are not glaringly inconsistent with the end goal. For example, in the domain of ecology and environmental science, we realise that contemporary understanding of the underlying biology would necessitate a ready familiarity with biochemistry and genetics that is not within the grasp of young students. Instead of watering down such content, we invite young students into the world of the 19th-century naturalist: scientists who also lacked modern knowledge of biochemistry and genetics. The idea is that by the time students are introduced to contemporary disciplinary knowledge, they will have developed a thirst for that knowledge, as indeed has been the case historically.

Developmentally appropriate trajectories

Following Piaget, we take seriously the fact that an understanding of the growth of children's thinking in a domain should serve as the basis for setting age-appropriate goals. For example, in our environmental science/biology curriculum we base our developmental milestones on evolving knowledge concerning children's biological understanding (Carey, 1985; Carey & R. Gelman, 1991; Hatano & Inagaki, 1987; Keil, 1992; Wellman & S. Gelman, 1988). As just one example, Piaget's interest in the animate/inanimate distinction is today reflected in interest in the concept of living thing (alive, dead, not alive, never alive, etc.). This concept is of critical interest to 6-year-olds, but it continues to be refined throughout the school years as students come to see essential similarity between plants and animals and wonder about such non-canonical cases as yeast, viruses, and so forth.

A similar developmental guideline governs our approach to reasoning within the domain. We initially permit teleological reasoning and an overreliance on causality in general (Keil, 1992), but then we press for an increasingly more sophisticated consideration of such classic Piagetian understandings as chance, probability, and necessity. Although a more optimistic picture of the child as scientist has emerged in the last part of the 20th century, it should be noted that the key issues of study—physical and biological causality, notions of chance, probability, necessity, and so forth—are all deeply Piagetian conceptions of children's thought. The primary difference is that we do not depend on notions of structural change and the concept of horizontal *décalage*; children can do a great deal more than was thought at an earlier age.

And what they know *is* influenced by instruction. We have found that as we learn more about children's knowledge and theories about the biological and physical world (Carey & Gelman, 1991), we are better able to design a spiralling curriculum such as that intended by Bruner (1963, 1968). It matters what the underlying theme is at, perhaps, kindergarten and grade two; it matters that the sixth-grade students have experienced the second-grade curriculum. Topics are not revisited willy-nilly at various ages at some unspecified level of sophistication, as is the case in many curricula that are described as spiralling, but each revisit is based on a deepening knowledge of that topic, critically dependent on past experience and on the developing knowledge base of the child. As we design learning activities that encourage reflection, thought experiments, and the development of theories coupled with supporting evidence, the level of scientific thinking habitually engaged in by young children far surpasses that which would be expected on the basis of Piaget's developmental model (for details, see Brown & Campione, 1994).

VYGOTSKY AND THE DESIGN OF
LEARNING ENVIRONMENTS

A main agenda for the Community of Learners project is devising learning environments that enable group participation and dialogic interaction, which support reflection, argumentation, and refutation. In our design of learning environments where students explore increasingly more complex and compelling issues in science, we have been influenced by Vygotskyan theory and subsequent work on discourse analysis.

Common knowledge and distributed expertise
Central to the Community of Learners classroom is the assumption of shared discourse and common knowledge (Edwards & Mercer, 1987), but individual expertise is fostered as well. Although the participants come to share a body of common knowledge, there is also a reliance on distributed expertise and individual specialisation (Brown et al., 1993). Students operate as researchers who are free to select a topic of inquiry, free to do research on whatever they like within the confines of the targeted topic for their grade. Some children become resident experts on pesticides; some specialise in disease and contagion; others become environmental activists. Within the community, these varieties of expertise are recognised and valued.

Participant structures
Knowledge sharing is then an important aspect of these learning environments. It is arranged both by design and happenstance through the use of familiar participant structures. Participation structures are few and are practised repeatedly. The ritualistic nature of these activities is an essential aspect of the classroom, for it enables children to make the transition from one participant structure (Erickson & Schultz, 1977) to another quickly and effortlessly.

In each participant structure, knowledge is gathered and shared; expertise is distributed to provide a richer knowledge base for all. A variety of thinking activities is modelled. Ideas are planted in the discourse and appropriated in the form of individual thought; the social becomes the individual. The design of the participant structures was guided by Vygotskyan theory. To illustrate, we will describe just three group activities.

Reciprocal teaching.   Reciprocal teaching seminars (Palincsar & Brown, 1984) can be led by teachers, parents, peers, or older students. Six or so participants form a group with each member taking a turn leading a discussion about an article, a video, or other materials they need to understand for research purposes. The leader begins a discussion by *asking a question* and ends by *summarising* the gist of the argument to date. Attempts to *clarify* any problems of understanding take place when needed, and a leader can ask for *predictions* about future content if this seems appropriate. These four activities were chosen because they are excellent comprehension-monitoring devices. Quite simply, if you cannot summarise what you have just read, you do not understand, and you had better do something about it.

Reciprocal teaching was designed to provoke zones of proximal development within which readers of varying abilities can find support. Group co-operation, where everyone is trying to arrive at consensus concerning meaning, relevance, and importance, helps to ensure that understanding occurs, even if some members of the group are not yet capable of full participation. Because thinking is externalised in the form of discussion, beginners can learn from the contributions of those more expert than they. Collaboratively, the group, with its variety of expertise, engagement, and goals, gets the job done; usually the text gets understood. The integrity of the task, *reading for meaning*, is maintained throughout. The task is simplified by the provision of social support through a variety of expertise, *not* via decomposition of the task into basic skills.

Jigsaw.   This idea of learning with a clear purpose in mind is a mainstay of all the components of the Community of Learners. In particular it carries over to our version of Aronson's (1978) jigsaw classroom. Students are asked to undertake independent and collaborative research. As researchers, they divide up units of study and share responsibility for learning and teaching their part of the information to each other.

Teachers, students, and domain area specialists together decide on central abiding themes visited at a developmentally sensitive level. Each theme (e.g. changing populations) is then divided into five or six subtopics (endangered species, rebounding populations, introduced species, etc.), dependent in part on student age and interest. Each group of students conducts research on one subtopic, and then shares its knowledge by teaching it to the others.

As a concrete example, recent classes of *second graders* chose to study the relationship of animals to their habitats. Some children studied how animals protect themselves from the elements or from predators. Others became experts on animal communication or reproductive strategies. Still others studied predator/prey relations. Armed with this information, design teams were configured so that each member had conducted research on one part of the knowledge (e.g. reproductive strategies). These teams designed habitats for an adopted animal or invented an animal of the future, and exhibited these products to an array of audiences. In each group someone knew about predator/prey relations and methods of defence, someone could talk wisely on the strengths and weaknesses of possible reproductive strategies or of potential methods of communication. All the pieces are needed to complete the puzzle, to design the habitat or the animal of the future, hence jigsaw.

Guided writing.   In preparation for teaching others and displaying their knowledge, research groups produce illustrated texts. These texts go through many revisions, some guided by an expert: the classroom teacher, a researcher, or an older student. Again the idea is to create zones of proximal development in which students can operate. The expert sits with each group and helps it progress to higher levels of discourse using such prompts as: "Do you think the reader will be able to understand that?", "Is this in your own words?", "What's the main point of this paragraph?", "Have you said how your animal gets food?", "Have you told us how it communicates?", "Remember that the reader hasn't read about reproductive strategies and delayed implantation, is this enough to make it clear?". Repeated exposure to these external prompts, first by a teacher and then by other children, eventually leads to internalisation in the form of self-editing procedures.

Main principles
Five main principles derived from neo-Vygotskyan work have influenced our design of instructional environments. These are: (1) classrooms invoke multiple zones of proximal development; (2) a community of academic and eventually scientific discourse is developed; (3) meaning is negotiated and refined; (4) ideas are seeded and appropriated; and (5) common knowledge and distributed expertise are both essential.

Multiple zones of proximal development.   Theoretically, we conceive of the learning community as composed of multiple zones of proximal development operating simultaneously, through which participants can navigate via different routes and at different rates (Brown & Reeve, 1987). This metaphor of a classroom supporting multiple, overlapping zones of proximal development that foster growth is the theoretical window through which we view the system of practices that constitute Community of Learners.

Community of discourse.   The learning community comes to rely on the development of a discourse genre typical of academic discourse in general and scientific discourse in particular. Such discourse features constructive discussion, questioning, and criticism as the mode rather than the exception. The core participant structures of our communities are essentially dialogic. Sometimes these activities are face-to-face; sometimes they are mediated via print or electronic mail; and at still other times they go underground and become part of the thought processes of community members (Vygotsky, 1978). Dialogues provide the format for novices to adopt the discourse structure, goals, values, and belief systems of scientific practice. Over time, the community of learners adopts a common voice and common knowledge base, a shared system of meaning, beliefs, and activity.

Meaning is negotiated.   Within this community of discourse, meaning is constantly negotiated and refined. Increasingly, scientific modes of speculation, evidence, and proof become part of the common voice. Successful enculturation into the community leads participants to relinquish everyday versions of speech activities having to do with the physical and natural world and replace them with "discipline embedded special versions of the same activities" (O'Connor, 1991).

Mutual appropriation of ideas.   Ideas and concepts migrate throughout the community via mutual appropriation (Newman, Griffin, & Cole, 1989). Within the discourse, ideas are planted by experts, teachers, and students. Ideas migrate throughout the community and are picked up (or appropriated) by its members. Some of these seeds come to fruition and others do not.

DESIGN OF ASSESSMENT: VYGOTSKY AND PIAGET

In order to assess which ideas are appropriated, what habits of mind are fostered, we use a variety of traditional measures together with tests of flexibility and generalisation (Campione, Shapiro, & Brown, 1995). Specifically, we feature dynamic assessment (Campione, 1989; Campione & Brown, 1990) of the students' developing knowledge. Our methods are similar to the clinical interviewing techniques introduced by both Vygotsky and Piaget. Dynamic assessment methods present children with problems just one step beyond their existing competence and then provide help as needed for the child to reach independent mastery. Competence is fostered in social interactions before individual mastery is expected. The degree of aid needed, both to learn new principles and to apply them, is carefully calibrated and measured. How much help is required provides a better index of students' future learning trajectories in a domain than do static tests. The ease with which students apply, or transfer, principles they have learned is regarded as an indication of student understanding of those principles; and this transfer performance is the most sensitive index of a student's readiness to proceed within a particular domain. We have worked in many domains (Brown, Campione, Webber, & McGilly, 1992), but here we will concentrate on biological knowledge.

Biological knowledge

We use the clinical interview method to assess many aspects of developing understanding in Community of Learners. To illustrate, we will describe the biological interviews here. In these interviews, a series of key questions is raised concerning central principles of the curricular themes, for example, the food chain, adaptation, etc. First, the interviewer elicits basic expository information. If the student cannot answer adequately, the interviewer provides hints and examples as necessary to test the student's readiness to learn that concept. If the student seems knowledgeable, the experimenter might question that understanding by introducing *counterexamples* to the student's beliefs, and again if appropriate, he or she might ask the student to engage in *thought experiments* that demand novel uses of the information.

For example, suppose a student has sorted pictures into herbivores and carnivores, and provided a good description of the categories. To test how robust this information is, he or she may be asked, "What would happen on the African plain if there were no gazelles or other meat for cheetahs to eat? Could they eat grain?". Students previously judged to be knowledgeable on the basis of their expository information can be surprisingly uncertain about this, suggesting that cheetahs could eat grain under certain circumstances, although they would not live happily. Some even entertain a critical period hypothesis—that cheetahs could change if they were forced to eat grain from infancy, but once they reached adolescence, they would be too set in their ways to change. Only a few invoke notions of form and function, such as properties of the digestive tract, to support the assertion that cheetahs could not change (Ash, 1991; Brown et al., 1992). These extension activities of thought experiments and counterexamples reveal the current state of students' knowledge far better than their first unchallenged answers.

Consider the following excerpts from John, an 11-year-old. Initially, John mentioned speed, body size, mouth size, and tearing teeth as functional physical characteristics of carnivores. He seemed to understand the carnivore/herbivore distinction. But when asked the cheetah thought experiment he mused:

> ... well if people are vegetarians, I think a cheetah could change.

This is a good example of a common reasoning strategy of children: personification as analogy (Carey, 1985; Hatano & Inagaki, 1987). When pressed further, John continues:

> Well ..., it would be easier for them to change to plants than it would be for me; if I had been eating meat ... because there would still be meat around for me to eat, but for them there wouldn't be any ... so if they wanted to survive, they're going to have to eat grass.

When asked if it would be easier for a baby cheetah to eat grass, he argued:

> Well, if it was a baby, it would be easier because it could eat it ... it would be right there, it would just have to walk a little bit to get it ... but then if it happens for a long time, then the animals come back [the gazelles return], then it probably would have lost its speed, because they wouldn't have to run. ... Yeah, and they'd get used to the grass and not care about the animals, because along the line they would forget.

Six months later, when asked the same question, John is able to resist countersuggestions. He makes complex analogies to the cow's intestinal system, arguing that the digestive tracts of herbivores are more complicated than those of carnivores. By knowing an animal's diet, he argues that he would be able to predict its digestive tract length and how long digestion might take, and vice versa.

This time, when confronted with a variant of the cheetah thought experiment, John responded:

> No ... no, their digestive system isn't good enough ... it's too uncomplicated to digest grasses and also their teeth wouldn't be able to chew, so then the grass would overpopulate ... and the cheetah dies.

When asked if the baby cheetah could survive by eating grass, John asserted that it would be the first to die.

These responses are in distinct contrast to those given to the same questions earlier. John has abandoned personification (Hatano & Inagaki, 1987) as an explanation ("humans can do it so cheetahs can too") and replaced it with a form–function justification. Thrown a novel twist on the old question—whether deer might be able to eat meat if there were no longer grass, the newly confident John favoured the interviewer with a broad smile and said:

> Nice try ... the digestive tract of the deer is too complicated
> and also the teeth wouldn't be able to grind meat.

These clinical interviews were modelled closely on the methods used by both Vygotsky and Piaget. Using these thought experiments, we can track the retention of knowledge, and also its fragility and applicability. The philosophy of negotiation and appropriation within a zone of proximal development is just as much apparent in our assessment procedures as in our classroom practices. Indeed, these clinical assessments are collaborative learning experiences in their own right. As such, the line between assessment and instruction becomes increasingly blurred, intentionally so (Campione, 1989).

CONCLUSION

In this chapter we have traced the influence of Piaget and Vygotsky on the design of curricula, instruction, and assessment in the domain of children's emergent knowledge of environmental science. In so doing we have concentrated on how the theories are compatible rather than concentrating on differences between them.

Two major points have guided our design efforts (Brown, 1994). First we believe that despite the enormous amount of empirical work motivated by the two theories, there is still a need for theories of learning that reflect the fruits of the cognitive revolution of the latter part of the century and guide the way to the design of complex learning environments that differ from traditional school practices (Brown & Campione, 1994). Second, the need for a *developmental* theory of learning is more pressing now than ever. A deeply embedded influence of American learning theory, particularly that of Skinner, seems to prevail, that is, that learning equals development. Curricula, instruction, and assessment are designed with little or no rationale for the differences made to accommodate younger learners: Younger learners typically receive a debased version of that provided for older students, due to putative, but often unspecified, cognitive inabilities attributed to the young.

Self-consciously linking developmental stepping stones in the growth of understanding to the design of curricula, instruction, and assessment that support and extend these developing understandings, not only situates educational practice more firmly in theoretical roots, but also promises to shed new light on the developmental stepping stones themselves. The agenda that faced Vygotsky and Piaget decades ago is still vibrantly alive for their followers today. No greater tribute can be paid to their influence on psychological and educational thought.

ACKNOWLEDGEMENTS

The preparation of this paper was supported by an NIH grant (HD-06864) to Ann Brown; Evelyn Lois Corey funds to Ann Brown; grants from the James S. McDonnell and Andrew W. Mellon Foundations to Ann Brown and Joseph Campione; and an NSF grant (#9255398) to Kathleen Metz.

REFERENCES

Aronson, E. (1978). *The jigsaw classroom*. Beverly Hills, CA: Sage.

Ash, D. (1991). *A new guided assessment of biological understanding*. Unpublished manuscript. University of California, Berkeley.

Brewer, W., & Samarapungavan, A. (1991). Children's theories versus scientific theories: Differences in reasoning or differences in knowledge? In R.R. Hoffman & D.S. Palermo (Eds.), *Cognition and the symbolic processes: Applied and ecological perspectives*. Hillsdale, NJ: Lawrence Erlbaum Associates Inc.

Brown, A.L. (1989). Analogical learning and transfer. What develops? In S. Vosniadou & A. Ortony (Eds.), *Similarity and analogical reasoning* (pp.369–412). Cambridge: Cambridge University Press.

Brown, A.L. (1990). Domain-specific principles affect learning and transfer in children. *Cognitive Science, 14*, 107–133.

Brown, A.L. (1994). The advancement of learning. *Educational Researcher, (23)*8, 4–12.

Brown, A.L., Ash, D., Rutherford, M., Nakagawa, K., Gordon, A., & Campione, J.C. (1993). Distributed expertise in the classroom. In G. Salomon (Ed.), *Distributed cognitions: Psychological and educational considerations* (pp.188–228). New York: Cambridge University Press.

Brown, A.L., Bransford, J.D., Ferrara, R.A., & Campione, J.C. (1983). Learning, remembering, and understanding. In P.H. Mussen (Series Ed.) & J.H. Flavell & E.M. Markman (Vol. Eds.), *Handbook of child psychology: Vol. 3. Cognitive development* (4th Edn., pp.77–166). New York: Wiley.

Brown, A.L., & Campione, J.C. (1990). Communities of learning and thinking, or A context by any other name. *Human Development, 21,* 108–125.

Brown, A.L., & Campione, J.C. (1994). Guided discovery in a community of learners. In K. McGilly (Ed.), *Classroom lessons: Integrating cognitive theory and classroom practice* (pp.229–270). Cambridge, MA: Bradford Books/MIT Press.

Brown, A.L., Campione, J.C., Webber, L.S., & McGilly, K. (1992). Interactive learning environments—a new look at assessment and instruction. In B.R. Gifford & M.C. O'Connor (Eds.), *Changing assessments: Alternative views of aptitude, achievement and instruction* (pp.121–211). Boston: Kluwer.

Brown, A.L., & DeLoache, J.S. (1978). Skills, plans, and self-regulation. In R.S. Siegler (Ed.), *Children's thinking: What develops?* Hillsdale, NJ: Lawrence Erlbaum Associates Inc.

Brown, A.L., & Reeve, R.A. (1986). Reflection on the growth of reflection in children. *Cognitive Development, 1,* 405–416.

Brown, A.L., & Reeve, R.A. (1987). Bandwidths of competence: The role of supportive contexts in learning and development. In L.S. Liben (Ed.), *Development and learning: Conflict or congruence?* (pp.173–223). Hillsdale, NJ: Lawrence Erlbaum Associates Inc.

Bruner, J.S. (1963). *The process of education.* Cambridge, MA: Harvard University Press.

Bruner, J.S. (1968). *Toward a theory of instruction.* New York: Norton.

Campione, J.C. (1989). Assisted assessment: A taxonomy of approaches and an outline of strengths and weaknesses. *Journal of Learning Disabilities, 22,* 151–165.

Campione, J.C., & Brown, A.L. (1990). Guided learning and transfer: Implications for approaches to assessment. In N. Frederiksen, R. Glaser, A. Lesgold, & M. Shafto (Eds.), *Diagnostic monitoring of skill and knowledge acquisition* (pp.141–172). Hillsdale, NJ: Lawrence Erlbaum Associates Inc.

Campione, J.C., Shapiro, A.M., & Brown, A.L. (1995). Forms of transfer in a community of learners: Flexible learning and understanding. In A. McKeough, J. Lupart, & A. Marini (Eds.), *Teaching for transfer: Fostering generalization in learning* (pp.35–68). Mahwah, NJ: Lawrence Erlbaum Associates Inc.

Carey, S. (1985). *Conceptual change in childhood.* Cambridge, MA: Bradford Books, MIT Press.

Carey, S., & Gelman, R. (1991). *The epigenesis of mind.* Hillsdale, NJ: Lawrence Erlbaum Associates Inc.

Chi, M.T.H., Feltovich, P.J., & Glaser, R. (1981). Categorization and representation of physics problems by experts and novices. *Cognitive Science, 5,* 121–152.

Dunbar, K. (1995). How scientists really reason: Scientific reasoning in real-world laboratories. In R. J. Sternberg & J. Davidson (Eds.), *Nature of insight* (pp.365–395). Cambridge, MA: MIT Press.

Dunbar, K., & Klahr, D. (1989). Developmental differences in scientific discovery strategies. In D. Klahr & K. Kotovsky (Eds.), *Complex information processing: The impact of Herbert A. Simon* (pp.109–144). Hillsdale, NJ: Lawrence Erlbaum Associates Inc.

Edwards, P., & Mercer, N. (1987). *Common knowledge.* London: Open University Press.

Erickson, F., & Schultz, J. (1977). When is a context? Some issues and methods on the analysis of social competence. *Quarterly Newsletter of the Institute for Comparative Human Development, 1*, 5–10.

Gopnik, A. (1993). Theories and illusions. Author's response to open peer commentary. *Behavioral and Brain Sciences, 16*, 90–100.

Goswami, U., & Brown, A.L. (1989). Melting chocolate and melting snowmen: Analogical reasoning and causal relations. *Cognition, 35*, 69–95.

Goswami, U., & Brown, A.L. (1990). Higher-order structure and relational reasoning: Contrasting analogical and thematic relations. *Cognition, 36*, 207–226.

Harré, R. (1983). *Great scientific experiments: Twenty experiments that changed our view of the world*. New York: Oxford University Press.

Hatano, G., & Inagaki, K. (1987). Everyday biology and school biology: How do they interact? *The Newsletter of the Laboratory of Comparative Human Cognition, 9*, 120–128.

Inhelder, B., Bovet, M., & Sinclair, H. (1974). *Learning and the development of cognition*. Cambridge, MA: Harvard University Press.

Inhelder, B., & Piaget, J. (1958). *The growth of logical thinking from childhood to adolescence* [A. Parsons & S. Milgram, Trans.]. London: Routledge & Kegan Paul. [Original work published 1955.]

Johnson-Laird, P. M. (1985). Logical thinking: Does it occur in daily life? Can it be taught? In S. Chipman, J. Segal, & R. Glaser (Eds.), *Thinking and learning skills: Research and open questions* (Vol. 2, pp.293–318). Hillsdale, NJ: Lawrence Erlbaum Associates Inc.

Karmiloff-Smith, A. (1988). The child is a theoretician, not an inductivist. *Mind and Language, 3*, 183–195.

Karmiloff-Smith, A., & Inhelder, B. (1974). If you want to get ahead, get a theory. *Cognition, 3*, 195–212.

Keil, F.C. (1992). The origins of autonomous biology. In M.R. Gunnan & M. Maratsos (Eds.), *Minnesota symposium on child psychology: Modularity and constraints on language and cognition*. Hillsdale, NJ: Lawrence Erlbaum Associates Inc.

Kuhn, D., Amsel, E., & O'Loughlin, M. (1988). *The development of scientific thinking skills*. Orlando: Academic Press.

Kuhn, T. S. (1962). *The structure of scientific revolutions*. Chicago: University of Chicago Press.

Kuhn, T. S. (1977). *The essential tension*. Chicago: University of Chicago Press.

Mayr, E. (1982). *The growth of biological thought: Diversity, evolution, and inheritance*. Cambridge, MA: The Belknap Press of Harvard University Press.

Medawar, P. (1982). *Plato's republic*. Oxford: Oxford University Press.

Metz, K.E. (1995). Developmental constraints on children's science. *Review of Educational Research, 65*(2), 93–127.

Newman, D., Griffin, P., & Cole, M. (1989). *The construction zone*. Cambridge: Cambridge University Press.

O'Connor, M. C. (1991). *Negotiated defining: Speech activities and mathematical literacies*. Unpublished manuscript, Boston University.

Palincsar, A.S., & Brown, A.L. (1984). Reciprocal teaching of comprehension-fostering and monitoring activities. *Cognition and Instruction, 1*(2), 117–175.

Piaget, J. (1928). *Judgment and reasoning in the child* [M. Warden, Trans.]. London: Routledge & Kegan Paul. [Original work published 1924.]

Piaget, J. (1952). *The origins of intelligence in children* [M. Cook, Trans.]. New York: Norton. [Original work published 1936.]

Piaget, J. (1954). *The construction of reality in the child* [M. Cook, Trans.]. New York: Basic Books. [Original work published 1937.]

Piaget, J. (1968). The mental development of the child. In D. Elkind (Ed.), *Six psychological studies* (pp.3–73). Brighton, UK: The Harvester Press. [Original work published 1964.]

Piaget, J. (1974). *The language and thought of the child* [M. Gabain, Trans.]. New York: The New American Library. [Original work published 1923.]

Piaget, J. (1976). *The grasp of consciousness* [S. Wedgwood, Trans.]. Cambridge, MA: Harvard University Press. [Original work published 1974.]

Piaget, J. (1978a). *Success and understanding* [A.J. Powerans, Trans.]. Cambridge, MA: Harvard University Press. [Original work published 1974.]

Piaget, J. (1978b). *Recherches sur la géneralisation*. Paris: Presses Universitaires de France.

Piaget, J. (1980). The constructivist approach. *Cahiers de la Fondation Archives Jean Piaget, 1, 3–7*. Geneva: Fondation Archives Jean Piaget.

Popper, K.S. (1972). *Conjectures and refutations: The growth of scientific knowledge* (4th Edn.). London: Routledge & Kegan Paul.

Ross, G. (1980). Categorization in 1- to 2-year-olds. *Developmental Psychology, 16*, 391–396.

Schauble, L. (1990). Belief revision in children: The role of prior knowledge and strategies for generating knowledge. *Journal of Experimental Psychology, 49*, 31–57.

Schauble, L., & Glaser, R. (1990). Scientific thinking in children and adults. *Human Development, 21*, 9–27.

Schauble, L., Klopfer, L.E., & Raghavan, K. (1991). Students' transition from an engineering model to a science model of experimentation. *Journal of Research in Science Teaching, 28*, 859–882.

Shapere, D. (1966). Meaning and scientific change. In R.G. Colodny (Ed.), *Mind and cosmos: Essays in contemporary science and philosophy*. University of Pittsburgh Series in the Philosophy of Science, Vol. 3, pp.41–85. Pittsburgh, PA: University of Pittsburgh Press.

Siegler, R.S., & Liebert, R.M. (1975). Acquisition of formal scientific reasoning by 10- and 13-year-olds. *Developmental Psychology, 11*, 401–412.

Smith, C., Carey, S., & Wiser, M. (1985). On differentiation: A case study of the development of the concepts of size, weight, and density. *Cognition, 21*, 177–233.

Toulmin, S. (1972). *Human understanding* (Vol. 1). Princeton: Princeton University Press.

Tschirgi, J. E. (1980). Sensible reasoning: A hypothesis about hypothesis. *Child Development, 51*, 1–10.

Vygotsky, L.S. (1978). *Mind in society: The development of higher psychological processes* [M. Cole, V. John-Steiner, S. Scribner, & E. Souberman, Eds., & Trans.]. Cambridge, MA: Harvard University Press.

Wellman, H.M. (1990). *The child's theory of mind*. Cambridge, MA: Harvard University Press.

Wellman, H.M., & Gelman, S. (1988). Children's understanding of the non-obvious. In R. J. Sternberg (Ed.), *Advances in the psychology of human intelligence* (Vol. 4, pp.99–135). Hillsdale, NJ: Lawrence Erlbaum Associates Inc.

NOTE

1.   All quotes from Vygotsky are taken from Vygotsky, 1978 (pp.78–86)

CHAPTER TEN

Relationships between the clinical method and the zone of proximal development in a constructivist approach to language acquisition[1]

Ioanna Berthoud-Papandropoulou
and Helga Kilcher   *University of Geneva,*
Switzerland

THE CLINICAL METHOD

In his investigations on the structural and functional aspects of intelligence Piaget devised the clinical method as a tool for assessing a subject's maximum potential in a given domain.

In Piaget's early research on children's logic and egocentrism, children's interviews did not yet have the specific characteristics of the clinical method (*The language and thought of the child* 1923/1971; *Judgement and reasoning in the child* 1924/1969). The aim was to find the form of reasoning in the child. Various means were devised to achieve this: free conversations with one child, observation of children communicating, notes about children's questions.

The clinical method, inspired by clinical psychology and psychiatry, was first used by Piaget in 1926 to probe children's beliefs. In *The child's conception of the world* (1926/1972, p.8) he describes the method in detail and discusses its benefits, compared to conventional testing methods and pure observation, for his research purposes:

The clinical examination is thus experimental in the sense that the practitioner sets himself a problem, makes hypotheses, adapts the conditions to them and finally controls each hypothesis by testing it against the reactions he stimulates in conversation. But the clinical examination is also dependent on direct observation, in the sense that the good practitioner lets himself be led, though always in control, and takes account of the whole of the mental context, instead of being the victim of "systematic error" as so often happens to the pure experimenter.

In the introduction to the book, Piaget himself indicates that children's beliefs and thoughts can only be reached by means of this new examination method. He goes on to give new specific indications about its application. The experimenter's task is to find ways in which to distinguish tales from real thought within children's utterances, tales often being suggested by the interview itself. Reaching "spontaneous thought" that is to say prior to any question by the experimenter (Piaget, 1926/1972, p.XVIII) is the goal of the author, i.e. he tries to elicit the contents of thought that pre-exist any interrogation by the adult and are uninfluenced by the very process of examination and cultural ideas.

In later years, when Piaget embarks on transversal studies of development in collaboration with A. Szeminska and B. Inhelder, the method is made more complex by including objects and materials with which the subject can interact. As Vinh Bang (1966) rightly argues, this modification was a necessary consequence of Piaget's new focus on the logic of concrete operations.

The main characteristics of the final version of the clinical method are outlined in various papers (Inhelder, Sinclair, & Bovet, 1974; Piaget, 1926/1972; Vinh Bang, 1966):

(a)   during the course of the interview the experimenter generates hypotheses about the meaning of the subject's behaviour and tests them on the spot by further questioning;
(b)   although the experimenter follows a pre-established protocol, she lets herself be guided by the subject's responses;
(c)   the experimenter does not just solicit judgements, she encourages subjects to provide arguments to justify their responses.

In relation to our focus in this paper, we propose to add a fourth general characteristic of the clinical method, namely:

d)   verbal interaction, which is an essential component of the clinical
     method. The experimenter asks questions, makes suggestions and
     counter-suggestions, the child verbalises his anticipations and
     observations, and justifies his actions and responses.

A closer analysis of the method allows us to assign various functions
to the verbal aspect. The experimenter encourages children to speak,
aiming at either gaining a better understanding of their previous
responses or testing their limits. Whether the role of verbalisation
during the clinical interview is to help subjects clarify their reactions,
or to bring them to function at the maximum of their abilities, verbal
interaction is not considered by Piagetian theory to play a constructive
part in children's cognitive development. It reveals the subject's already
constructed knowledge, it does not partake in its construction.

This theoretical point of view regarding language was not upheld by
Piaget in his earlier work (1923/1971, 1924/1969) in which he argued
that conversation facilitates awareness and thereby helps the child to
overcome his egocentrism.

THE ZONE OF PROXIMAL DEVELOPMENT

Vygotsky (1978, p.86) characterises the zone of proximal development
as the difference between a child's "actual developmental level as
determined by independent problem solving [and his] potential
development as determined through problem solving under adult
guidance or in collaboration with more capable peers."

Some authors (Wertsch & Addison-Stone, 1985) have commented that
the concept of zone of proximal development is based on a more
fundamental notion, the general law of cultural development, described
by Vygotsky (1981, p.163) as follows:

> Any function in the child's cultural development appears
> twice, or on two planes. First it appears on the social plane,
> and then on the psychological plane. First it appears
> between people as an interpsychological category, and then
> within the child as an intrapsychological category.

Both the general law of cultural development and the zone of
proximal development that is one of its instantiations, reveal the
constructive role that Vygotsky attributes to social interaction in the

child's intellectual progress. Indeed, as far as macrogenetic development is concerned, all superior psychological functions first manifest themselves in inter-individual exchanges and only later become interiorised and part of the subject's individual repertoire. As far as the *hic et nunc* of micro-development is concerned, children's improved performance during interaction with an adult reveals their ability to go beyond what they can do alone, that is, in the absence of the adult's support. What exactly the adult's support is, however, remains to be determined. For Vygotsky (1985) it involves putting appropriate questions to the child, not just giving answers.

From a practical standpoint, the zone of proximal development allows one to measure the subject's competence. Vygotsky criticised testing methods because they determine children's level of development on the basis of their performance when they solve problems by themselves. The concept of zone of proximal development leads Vygotsky to a distinction between subjects' autonomous activities and their potential developmental capacities. He thus draws our attention to the difficulties faced by psychologists when they try to evaluate a behaviour. Should they base their evaluations on subjects' autonomous activity, with the risk of underestimating their competence, or rather on their developmental potential in interactive contexts? To illustrate this issue, Vygotsky (1985) points out that two 7-year-olds with equivalent autonomous behaviour can differ in their potential developmental capacities, that is, in their performance when aided by an adult. Consequently, he subscribes wholly to the usefulness of the zone of proximal development for making psychological evaluation (1985, p.109, our translation):

> ... with this *method* [emphasis added] we can take into account not only the developmental and maturational processes that have already taken place, but also those processes that are taking form ...

Although Piaget and Vygotsky share a common aversion for testing methods, for different reasons, they uphold divergent views concerning the role of language—and social interaction in general—in cognitive development. Their theoretical points of view are irreducible to the extent that they are founded on different epistemological postulates concerning the growth of knowledge.

Nevertheless, we believe there is one domain in which the opposition between the theories weakens and yields to the possibility of reconciliation: the domain of language acquisition.

THE ACQUISITION OF COMPLEX SENTENCES:
THE GERUND

So far, we have considered language either as a tool for exploring a subject's competence or as a factor that fosters competence. In both cases, language is a means to an end. But language can be a subject matter too, and the psycholinguistic aim of the present chapter is to show the efficiency of the clinical method in this respect. We chose to examine a particular case of the acquisition of complex sentences, namely, the gerundive construction. Our study revealed some interesting phenomena which we will set in relation to the clinical method and discuss in terms of the zone of proximal development.

The gerundive construction is commonly used in French, and is frequently found in children's books. To our knowledge, however, its acquisition has not been studied yet. The gerundive construction takes the following form:

Preposition En + Gerund (invariable form of present participle), followed, or preceded, by *Noun Phrase (NP) + Verb Phrase (VP)*. A possible rendition in English is: *While/By + Gerund (-ing form)*, followed, or preceded, by *NP + VP*.

Examples:
En chantant, Marie dessine une maison (While singing, Mary draws a house).
En chantant, Marie fait plaisir à sa maman (By singing, Mary pleases her mother).

As all complex sentences, the gerundive construction contains two verbs. But its surface structure has only one subject, as the subject of the main clause is the same as that of the gerund. From a semantic point of view, the gerundive construction, although lacking connectors, can convey various meanings. It can signify, for instance, relationships of simultaneity (temporal concomitance) or causality as in our examples (see Wagner & Pinchon, 1991, and Halmoy, 1981, for a new typology).

Studying the acquisition of the gerundive construction is interesting both from a syntactic point of view (i.e. the child's understanding that the two clauses have the same subject) and from a semantic point of view (i.e. the polysemy of *En + Gerund*). We adopted a multiple task approach (Berthoud-Papandropoulou, 1994) in which the same linguistic structure was presented in the context of several different experimental situations. Some of the situations were classic ones, such as tasks involving completion and judgements of sentences. In this chapter we focus on the simplest situation, one that calls on the speaker's communicative functioning, and therefore exploits the clinical method most efficiently. The meaning of the gerundive construction that we are concerned with here is that of simultaneity. In conversing with the child, the experimenter inserts a gerundive construction in a natural, incidental manner. By incidental we mean bereft of any explicit metalinguistic formulation; in other words, the experimenter does not solicit the child's metalinguistic approach.

Procedure

The study was conducted in Geneva, Switzerland with 83 French-speaking kindergarten and primary-school children, aged 4 to 10 years. They were assigned to seven age groups of 12 subjects each (11 subjects for the 10-year-olds group). Children were interviewed individually in a classroom of the kindergarten or school. All interviews were tape-recorded and then transcribed.

First the experimenter tells the subject that she is going to talk about a boy or a girl she knows. She then uses a gerundive construction for stating something about these children's activities. Immediately after, she questions the subject about his or her personal experience concerning the activities that have been mentioned.

Here we deal with two of the test sentences:

Item 1: "I know a boy. His name is François. You know, in the evening, while eating, François watches television (*Le soir, en mangeant, François regarde la télévision*: test sentence 1). Does that sometimes happen to you too?"

Whether the subject replies "yes" or "no" the experimenter continues by asking: "What happens (doesn't happen) to you? Tell me about it."

If the subjects' verbal responses show that they have understood the meaning of the gerundive construction, in particular the concomitance of the two events expressed by the sentence, the experimenter moves on to the next item.

If they do not evidence an understanding of the gerundive construction—for instance, if they relate their personal practice by referring to only one of the contents of the test sentence, the experimenter engages a clinical type of conversation to see whether the subjects can proceed further. Here are some examples of questions that the subjects' responses might lead to: "Oh, you also watch television! Like François?", "What does he do?", "Do you do something else at the same time?", "When does he watch television?".

Item 2. "I know a girl called Sophie. You know, in the afternoon, while drawing, Sophie talks to herself (*L'après-midi, en dessinant, Sophie parle toute seule*: test sentence 2) Does that sometimes happen to you too?"

The experimenter then asks questions analogous to those in item 1. For the subjects, the task involves the following three aspects:

(i) Comparison between *Ego* and *Alter*. The subjects have to compare their own practice to that of someone else, as presented in the test sentence, and recognise whether there is a convergence or divergence between them (e.g. Oh yes, me too ...; No, I never do that.)

(ii) Comprehension of the gerundive construction. To be able to talk about their own practices, the subjects have to understand the test sentence in one way or another. "Correct comprehension" implies understanding the temporal concomitance of the events expressed.

(iii) The production of utterances. The subjects are required to express themselves verbally about the practices mentioned in the test sentence, basing themselves on examples from their everyday life. Answering the question whether something "happens to you too" is a familiar activity even for young children.

Hence, this situation explores both subjects' linguistic comprehension and production, simulating as closely as possible a natural conversation in which the child is alternatively listener and speaker.

Results

Initial responses
We first analysed children's initial responses about their own activities. Out of a total of 166 initial responses, 54 utterances (32%) evidenced a correct understanding of the test sentences. As shown in Table 10.1, the frequency of correct comprehension increased with age, especially after age 7. Some of the responses contained a gerundive construction (reproduction of the test sentence's structure), but in most cases children's utterances were paraphrases of the test sentence:

GRE 9;10. Test sentence 1. Does that happen to you too?—*No*—What doesn't happen to you?—*To watch TV at the same time as I eat (De regarder la TV en même temps que je mange)*.

CRE 10;5. Test sentence 1. Does that happen to you too?—*Yes*—What happens to you?—*While eating, I watch TV (En mangeant, je regarde la TV)*.

TABLE 10.1
Comprehension of the Gerundive Construction (G.C.)

Age		Incorrect comprehension of G.C.	Correct comprehension of G.C. expressed by		
			Gerunds	Paraphrases	Total
4 years	(n = 24)	23	0	1	1
5 years	(n = 24)	21	2	1	3
6 years	(n = 24)	18	1	5	6
7 years	(n = 24)	12	4	8	12
8 years	(n = 24)	14	2	8	10
9 years	(n = 24)	16	3	5	8
10 years	(n = 22)	8	7	7	14
Total		112	19	35	54

Distribution of initial responses by age group, items 1 and 2 combined

FAB 7;5. Test sentence 2. Does that happen to you too?—*Yes*—What happens to you?—*Sometimes when I draw, I say to myself I want to draw that (Des fois, quand je dessine, je me dis ah je vais dessiner ça).*

If such correct responses were obtained initially, the experimenter passed on to the next item. When a child reproduced the test sentence structure very closely, the experimenter verified the child's understanding by asking "What does that mean?".

The remaining 112 initial responses (68%) indicated an incorrect, partial or unclear understanding of the test sentence; they divided into four categories, as shown in Table 10.2:

(a)   Silences;
(b)   mention of practices not contained in the test sentence (Invented contents);
(c)   mention of only one of the test sentence's components (One propositional content); and
(d)   uncertain comprehension of the temporal concomitance (Unclear responses).

Examples:
Invented content. KEV 4;0. Test sentence 1. Does that happen to you too?—*Yes*—What happens to you?—*I play games in the living room (Je fais des jeux dans le salon).*

One propositional content. SEB 7;6. Test sentence 1. Does that happen to you too?—*Yes*—What happens to you?—*I watch a movie and then a cartoon (Je regarde un film puis un dessin animé).*

TABLE 10.2
Incorrect comprehension of the Gerundive Construction (G.C.):
Response Categories

Age	Response categories				
	Silence	Invented contents	One content	Unclear responses	Total
4 years	11	4	7	1	23
5 years	4	0	10	7	21
6 years	4	0	10	4	18
7 years	1	0	9	2	12
8 years	1	0	11	2	14
9 years	2	0	11	3	16
10 years	1	0	5	2	8
Total	24	4	63	21	112

Reactions such as these initiated a clinical interview in which the experimenter pursued the following goals: (a) encouraging comparison between the other's and the subject's own practices (Do you remember what François does? Do you do the same?); (b) encouraging a focus on the propositional content not mentioned by the subject (François watches TV. What else does he do? Or: You watch TV. Do you also do something else?); (c) encouraging the child to take into account the simultaneity expressed in the test sentence (François watches TV. Does he do something else at the same time? Or: Do you do something else at the same time?).

It should be noted that these interventions are not equally suggestive. Furthermore, the experimenter sometimes reused the test sentence once or twice during this questioning.

Final responses

We now examine the outcomes of the clinical interviews following the child's initial response. As shown in Table 10.3, the interview had multiple effects. Globally we noticed a clear change towards higher-level responses (83 out of 112 responses, 74%). The proportions of regressions (6%) and stable responses (20%) were much smaller. A significant proportion of the positive changes resulted in success: 33 final responses (29%) indicated an understanding of the temporal concomitance that was absent in the initial responses.

TABLE 10.3
Distribution of subjects according to the categories of their initial and final responses, age groups and items combined

Final responses	Initial responses				
	S	I.C.	One C.	N.C.	Total
S	1	0	1	0	2
I.C	0	3	2	0	5
One C.	10	1	18	3	32
N.C.	1	0	0	1	2
Two C.	8	0	22	8	38
Sim.	4	0	20	9	33
Total	24	4	63	21	112

S = Silence; I.C. = Invented contents; One C = One content; N.C. = Non clear; Two C. = Two contents; Sim = Simultaneity.

Example:
SEB 7;6. Test sentence 1. Does that happen to you too?—*Yes*—What happens to you?—*I watch a movie and then a cartoon*—Do you do something else at the same time?—*I think (Je réfléchis)*—[Repetition of test sentence 1.] Does that happen to you too?—*No, not often (Non, pas souvent)*—What doesn't happen to you often?—*To eat in front of the TV (De manger devant la TV)*.

In contrast, other positive changes did not reach this level of comprehension. They consisted in successive mention of the two propositional contents during the interview without expression of a temporal relationship. This was the case for 34% of the answers.

Example:
THI 6;4. Test sentence 1. Does that happen to you too?—*Yes*—What happens to you?—*I also watch TV sometimes (Moi aussi des fois je regarde la TV)* — Do you do something else at the same time?—*I sometimes play cards (Je joue aux cartes des fois)*—[Repetition of test sentence 1.] What does François do?—*He watches TV in the evening (Il regarde la TV le soir)*—[Repetition of test sentence 1.] You too?—*Yes*—What do you do?—*I eat (Je mange)*.

Finally, here is an example of an unchanged response in spite of the clinical interview:

SOP 4;11. Test sentence 1. Does that happen to you too?—*Yes, my mom watched the Ninja Turtles (Oui, ma maman elle a regardé les tortues Ninja)*—And you do like François?—*Yes*—Do you remember, [repetition of test sentence 1]: Does that happen to you?—*Yes, my brother played cars and me too (Oui, mon frère il a joué aux voitures et puis moi aussi)*—What does he do, François?—*He watches TV (Il regarde la TV)*—Does he do something else?—*He has the remote control and he turns on the TV (Il a la commande et puis il allume la TV).*

Analysis and interpretation of observed changes

Comparison of initial and final responses for a given item (Table 10.3) showed that the initial performance of a subject did not predict the changes that occurred during the clinical interview. Initial silences gave place to either "One propositional content" or "Two propositional contents" and in some rare cases to correct responses. Although "One propositional content" initial responses usually remained stable, they occasionally led to "Two propositional content" responses or even correct responses. Shifts from low-level responses (for example, from "Invented contents") to correct understanding of temporal concomitance did not occur.

How can such signs of progress be interpreted? Are they the outcome of the interaction with the adult who "places the child" in the zone of proximal development, as Vygotsky would argue? In this case, the subjects can be said to have constructed something that they could not have produced on their own. Or should we side with Piaget and consider that the clinical interview simply revealed the subjects' competence? From this point of view, we can understand why the same questioning leads to more advanced responses in 8–10-year-olds than 6–8-year-olds.

To distinguish between the outcome of a subject's inherent potential and the contribution provided by interaction with the adult, two types of analysis were performed: an intra-individual analysis, in which the same subject's responses to the two items were examined, and an analysis of the mere form of the child's utterances (use of the gerundive construction or of a paraphrase).

Intra-individual analysis

Let us imagine that a subject's initial and final responses for the first item indicate progress; will he be able to transfer this progress during the second item—which contains a sentence with the same structure—or will the interaction with the adult have only a local, short-lived effect? The analysis of individual patterns of responses for both items allowed us to distinguish three groups of subjects characterised by three different patterns: The first group (*Integrated change*) showed a capacity to integrate into the second item the change made during the first one; the second group (*Repeated change*) did not show such an integration, but repeated in the second item the path followed in the first one. The third group (*Apparent regression*) regressed between the first and the second item.

Integrated change.   One group of 12 children, most of whom were 9 and 10 years old, evidenced a rapid change. In the first item these children arrived at the correct response (comprehension of simultaneity) during the clinical interview; in the second item, they immediately gave correct responses, without the help of the adult's questioning. Did these children rapidly integrate the complex linguistic structure via the interaction with the experimenter, or had they already understood the structure during the first item? In the latter interpretation, which seems to us to be the most probable one, the clinical interview merely served to familiarise subjects with the task.

Repeated change.   Another group of 10 subjects, drawn from different age groups, also benefited from the clinical interview during the first item. However, contrary to the previous group, these subjects had to go through the same steps during the second item. In other words, they provided similar initial and final responses in both items. These children presented different levels of understanding: the younger ones progressed mainly from *One content responses* to *Two content responses* (for both items); the older ones from *One content responses* to *Correct responses* (for both items). Such patterns of change could indicate a gradual learning where interaction is necessary each time. In Vygotskyan terms we might say that we have touched on the difference between the actual level of development (indicated by the initial responses) and the potential level of development (indicated by the final responses).

Apparent regression.   A third group comprising 12 subjects from age 7 to 10 presented a more surprising pattern than the preceding groups. For the first item these children immediately arrived at the correct response; they were not submitted to a clinical interview. However, in the second item they started off by giving less-evolved responses; they needed interaction with the experimenter to reach the level of performance that they had achieved on their own during the first item. How do we interpret such regressions? There are two possible explanations. The first one involves semantics: Test sentence 2 is probably more difficult. Indeed, the activities evoked by the first item (eating and watching television) can be more easily represented, whereas those evoked by item 2 seem more complex (drawing and talking to oneself), especially the activity of "talking to oneself", which refers to a mental and metalinguistic content. Such *décalages* (developmental disparities) in behaviours for sentences that have the same syntactic structure but different semantic contents are well documented (see for example, Sinclair & Ferreiro, 1970). The second explanation involves pragmatics: if the subject does not partake in one of the activities evoked by the test sentence (which is more frequent for test sentence 2 than for test sentence 1), it is then quite relevant to focus on only one of the propositional contents (the non-shared activity) when conversing. Subjects need not express the relationship between the two contents, even if they could do so. For example, they say: "No, I don't talk to myself" without adding "when I draw". The aim of the clinical interview would then be to determine whether subjects have in fact understood the relation of simultaneity expressed by the test sentence, but have failed to express this relationship in their initial response due to pragmatic reasons.

Use of the Gerundive construction
This analysis concerns subjects' use of the construction produced by the experimenter. Let us recall that subjects do not need to use the gerund to show that they have understood the relation of simultaneity it conveys. Indeed, various paraphrases exist (using *when, at the same time as*, etc.).

The results presented earlier show that most correct initial responses took the form of various paraphrases rather than the structure of the test phrase. However, it might be interesting to see whether the group of children who provided correct final responses as a result of the clinical interview were more likely to imitate the form of the test sentence than the group who responded correctly immediately. If this were the case, we would be informed about the nature of the benefit obtained from the interaction, namely the presentation of the grammatical form itself in addition to the semantic relation it establishes. Table 10.4 shows that the frequency of utterances containing the gerundive construction varied according to the two groups.

Imitative use of the gerundive construction might be due in part to repetition of this form by the experimenter during her interaction with the child. We believe that complete comprehension of a linguistic construction is more likely to be expressed by a paraphrase than a repetition of the construction used by the interlocutor, a paraphrase being an indicator of a process of interiorisation, in a Vygotskyan sense. Similarly, imitative use of a complex linguistic form seems to reveal a process of co-construction (reminiscent of the "inter-" phase described by Vygostsky). Paradoxically, therefore, correct use of a complex

TABLE 10.4
Simultaneity of the Gerundive Construction understood:
Distribution of gerunds and paraphrases in initial and final responses

	Paraphrases	*Gerunds*	*Total*
Initial response	35 (65%)	19 (35%)	54
Final response	15 (45%)	18 (55%)	33
Total	50	37	87

linguistic construction by the child is not necessarily a sign of full (autonomous) understanding. This view gains support from the fact that even children who did not achieve comprehension of the temporal simultaneity expressed by the test sentence during the interaction nevertheless used the gerundive construction occasionally.

Other psycholinguistic studies on early stages of language development, such as Veneziano (1988), show the importance of imitative repetition during mother–child interaction for the acquisition of new words. Imitative repetitions, which are very frequent at a given stage of development, give way later on to exchanges in which the semantic aspect takes precedence (see also Berthoud-Papandropoulou & Veneziano, 1989).

CONCLUDING REMARKS

The dialogue set up between child and adult in the present study permitted most subjects to develop behaviours that were more evolved than those initially provided. Namely, some children showed that they could arrive at an understanding of the simultaneity conveyed by the gerundive construction, or at least at verbalising this understanding. This suggests that it is important, from a methodological point of view, not to limit oneself to subjects' single and local responses when one's aim is to determine their linguistic competence. Both Piaget and Vygotsky stressed the importance of using methods for evaluating competence that go beyond *hic et nunc* performance.

In the dialogue between an adult experimenter and a child, language intervenes on two levels, which are theoretically distinct from the experimenter's point of view. The first level consists in presenting to the child the linguistic construction that one aims to study, the second consists in the natural conversing with the child about the contents that are likely to concern him. As to the first level, the incidental insertion of a complex sentence during the dialogue turns the sentence into an utterance that becomes an object of interaction for the child. The child as interlocutor receives the utterance, and even if its structure slightly exceeds his competence, he will handle the utterance in one way or another. As to the second level, the conversation is composed of the experimenter's questions and the child's answers. Let us recall that in appearance the experimenter's questions bear only on the comparison between the child's own experience and that which he has heard. In reality, however, the questions are designed to explore the subject's understanding of the test sentence and to allow him, should the occasion arise, to take into account the relevant aspects of the linguistic construction being studied.

Of course, from the point of view of the child—and probably also of a naive external observer, or "overhearer" (Clark, 1992)—the two levels merge into one, that is, a natural conversation. According to us, it is precisely this aspect that makes the clinical method interesting for studying language development. The clinical method is efficient because it simulates modes of linguistic functioning that are familiar to the child. Indeed, the experimental situation resembles everyday life situations: children are familiar with complex linguistic structures heard during their interactions with adults and older children.

The constructive role of interaction in the early phases of language acquisition has often been stressed, and numerous observational studies employ interactive settings as a means for obtaining data on young children's speech as well as that of their mothers. It is therefore surprising that very few studies have attempted to reap the benefits of interaction for studying the acquisition of complex linguistic structures in older children. The present study shows that the clinical method, far from being an "interview", as it has been qualified by some researchers (e.g. Berko Gleason & Bernstein Ratner, 1993), can be a source of inspiration for designing interactive methods adapted to the study of language development. Such methods are also appropriate for exploring language production. Currently language production is rarely studied in experimental settings, undoubtedly because existing methods come up against the problem of having to give directives to subjects so that they produce utterances. In our opinion, the interactive method enables us to study the subject's production by relocating him or her in the position of an interlocutor.

But such a method doesn't only provide an efficient means for obtaining verbal interactions. As our results show, it is also an instrument that helps subjects go beyond their initial responses. Here we are faced with a theoretical issue. The clinical method was not intended to be a way of producing developmental progress, nor did it lead to such results, except when it was adapted to the investigation of learning (Inhelder et al., 1974), which is not the focus of our work. Is it possible, then, that the clinical method leads to a different type of change when it is applied to language than when it is applied to other cognitive domains? We suggest that it does. And we have referred to the zone of proximal development to account for the observed changes. Indeed, language is a domain in which the subject finds the opportunity, through interaction with more advanced speakers, to produce terms and linguistic constructions that he or she cannot yet fully master. Hence, interaction constitutes a fruitful terrain for the co-construction of meaning, as well as of form. Other authors have recognised the relevance of the concept of the zone of proximal development for psycholinguistic research. For example, in her book on speech acts in children, Bernicot states that "the idea of the zone of proximal development can certainly be used very fruitfully in studying language acquisition" (1992, p.91, our translation).

However, our results show that the zone of proximal development has ill-defined boundaries and that it depends on various factors, such as the particular content of the problem, the age of the subject, his or her initial level, and also the type of interaction. All these variables determine whether or not a subject will enter the zone of proximal development. Some of these factors relate to the subject, others to the interaction. To account for the former we might invoke Piaget's concept of *assimilability* which allows us to specify the limits of the zone of proximal development for a given subject faced with a particular problem. In contrast to the general mechanism of assimilation, assimilability refers to the subject's potential ability—at a given point in his or her development—to integrate new objects by slightly readapting existing schemata. Here we find a theoretical complementarity between Piaget and Vygotsky: both lend a developmental potential to the subject, *hic et nunc*. However, in so far as interaction is concerned, there remains the problem of characterising interaction in terms that go beyond simply describing the relative contributions of the interactants and that will permit us to understand the role of interaction in the zone of proximal development and cognitive development in general.

REFERENCES

Berko Gleason, J., & Bernstein Ratner, N. (1993). *Psycholinguistics*. Fort Worth: Harcourt Brace.
Bernicot, J. (1992). *Les actes de langage chez l'enfant* [The child's acts of language]. Paris: PUF.

Berthoud-Papandropoulou, I. (1994). Quelques réflexions théoriques et méthodologiques sur les multiples acquisitions d'une phrase chez l'enfant [Some theoretical and methodological considerations about the acquisitions of a complex sentence by the child]. *Paroles d'Or* (Revue de l'association romande des logo pédistes diplômés), *No. 14*, 5–8.

Berthoud-Papandropoulou, I., & Veneziano, E. (1989). La signification énonciative dans les débuts du langage [Enunciative meaning in early language]. *Archives de Psychologie, 57*, 271–281.

Clark, H.H. (1992). *Arenas of language use*. Chicago: University of Chicago Press.

Halmoy, J.O. (1981). *Le gérondif. Elements pour une description syntaxique et sémantique* [The Gerundive. Elements for a syntactic and semantic description]. Doctoral Dissertation, University of Trondheim, Norway.

Inhelder, B., Sinclair, H., & Bovet, M. (1974). *Apprentissage et structures de la connaissance* [Learning and the development of cognition]. Paris: PUF.

Piaget, J. (1969). *Judgement and reasoning in the child*. Totowa NJ: Littlefield Adams. [Original work published 1924.]

Piaget, J. (1971). *The language and thought of the child*. London: Routledge & Kegan Paul. [Original work published 1923.]

Piaget, J. (1972). *The child's conception of the world*. Totowa NJ: Littlefield Adams. [Original work published 1926.]

Sinclair, H., & Ferreiro, E. (1970). Etude génétique de la compréhension, production et répétition des phrases au mode passif [A genetic study in understanding, production and repetition of passive sentences]. *Archives de Psychologie, 40*, 1–42.

Veneziano, E. (1988). Vocal–verbal interaction and the construction of early lexical knowledge. In M. Smith & J. Locke (Eds.), *The emergent lexicon: The child's development of a linguistic vocabulary* (pp.109–147). New York: Academic Press.

Vinh Bang (1966). La méthode clinique et la recherche en psychologie de l'enfant [Clinical method and research in child psychology]. In *Psychologie et épistémologie génétique. Thèmes piagétiens* (pp.67–81) Paris: Dunod.

Vygotsky, L.S. (1978). *Mind in society. The development of higher psychological processes*. Cambridge: Harvard University Press.

Vygotsky, L.S. (1981). The genesis of higher mental functions. In J.V. Wertsch (Ed.), *The concept of activity in Soviet psychology* (pp.144–188). Armonk: Scharpe.

Vygotsky, L.S. (1985). Le problème de l'enseignement et du développement mental à l'âge scolaire [The problem of teaching and mental development in school age]. In B. Schneuwly & J.-P. Bronckart (Eds.), *Vygotsky aujourd'hui* (pp. 95–117). Neuchâtel: Delachaux et Niestlé.

Wagner, R. L., & Pinchon, J. (1991). *Grammaire du français classique et moderne* [Grammar of classical and modern French]. Paris: Hachette.

Wertsch, J.V., & Addison-Stone, C. (1985). The concept of internalization in Vygotsky's account of the genesis of higher mental functions. In J.V. Wertsch (Ed.) *Culture, Communication and Cognition: Vygotskian perspectives* (pp. 162–179). New York: Cambridge University Press.

NOTE

1. This chapter was translated from the French by Emiel Reith.

CHAPTER ELEVEN

Intentionality, communication, and language

Ignasi Vila *University of Girona, Spain*

INTRODUCTION

Many researchers have emphasised the importance of the study of pre-linguistic communication in order to understand the genesis of language. This research, which began during the 1970s, grew largely out of the popularisation of the theoretical postulates of Piaget and Vygotsky. In fact, it responded largely to the exhaustion of most of the proposals made in the 1960s, stimulated by Noam Chomsky. Up to the 1980s, the discussions dealt with several questions such as the appearance of communicative intention, the existence or not of continuities throughout development, the role of adults and social interaction in the genesis of communication, etc. Some aspects of these discussions, especially those related to the genesis of communicative intention and the role of social interaction, have recently been taken up again on the basis of conceptions inspired directly by the proposals derived from the "theories of mind" model.

In this chapter I would like to contribute my point of view about these questions by revising the hidden theoretical proposals and by presenting new data about pre-linguistic development. In the first part I review the most important aspects of Piaget's and Vygotsky's respective theories. In the second, I approach the theoretical and methodological problems involved in the notion of communicative intentionality directly and, in conclusion, I describe the genesis of pre-linguistic communication.

PIAGET, VYGOTSKY, AND
THE GENESIS OF LANGUAGE

Piaget's and Vygotsky's theses on the genesis of language are both widely known. Therefore, I will limit myself to discussing their most important ideas. Piaget asserted the primacy of cognition over language: language, understood as representation, appears together with other symbolic types of behaviour. Piaget believed that, at the end of the sensorimotor stage, the child, by coordinating and differentiating sensorimotor schemata, constructs the capacities to represent objects, events, people, etc., and to act in a different way from that of practical intelligence in relation to internal reality itself, which appears in the form of symbols. This conception opened up the way to the study of what is prior to language and of the cognitive prerequisites that make language possible. Consequently, notions such as causality, means–ends relationships, etc. were incorporated into the terminology of communicative development, with the aim of explaining the genesis of communicative intention.

By contrast, Vygotsky approached the genesis of language in a completely different way. In fact, he relied on Sapir, and along with him asserted the unity of communicative and representative functions in language: language is as much an instrument of knowledge as a means of influencing the behaviour of others. Thus, Vygotsky believed that language has a specific development which has its roots in pre-linguistic communication and does not necessarily depend on cognitive development. In this perspective, a number of studies were initiated to study the first routines of social interchange between the baby and its care-takers.

THE GENESIS OF COMMUNICATIVE INTENTION

One of the points on which both views diverged was that of the genesis of communicative intention, although everyone agreed that its appearance constituted one of the most important touchstones for the development of communication. In fact, discussion of the origins of communicative intention is difficult because of methodological and theoretical difficulties involved in it; it is probably unnecessary in any case, because, as Bruner (1975) points out, the adult treats the child's behaviour as intentional from birth. Furthermore, as Newson (1974, 1979) says, the adult treats the newborn child as a fully equipped human being with intentions, desires, and feelings. In any event, it is interesting to reflect on this question because the way in which we approach it determines, at least in some respects, our expectations about what is prior to language.

Discussions about the appearance of communicative intention have also led to various controversies: in the first place, to the origin of intentional activity itself; second, to the definition of communicative intention; and last, to the mechanisms that explain its appearance (cognitive development or socio-cultural practices involved in the first social relations between the baby and its care-takers).

The origins of intentional activity are discussed by Piaget (1937) and Bruner (1973, 1984), who share some views, but differ considerably on others. Piaget sees the beginnings of intentional activity in sensorimotor stage III, in relation with secondary circular reactions (when the child is capable of coordinating behaviour in sequences directed towards an end). Certainly, Piaget is reluctant to consider these first types of behaviour as authentically intentional because, from his point of view, continued action and its subsequent effects are probably not yet completely distinguished in the baby's experience. However, these same types of behaviour are considered as clearly intentional in sensorimotor stage IV, because, in this stage, there is a clear coordination of ends and means. Thus, for Piaget intentional activity is a construction made by the baby throughout the sensorimotor stage, thanks to the elaboration and differentiation of sensorimotor schemata which are revealed in the use of sequenced and ordered means to achieve a goal and in a first level of causality.

Bruner, for his part, does not dispute the notion of intentional activity involved in Piaget's theory and agrees that intentional activity is composed of the following elements: "the goal, the choice of means, persistence and correction and a final instruction of ending" (Bruner, 1984, p.101). However, Bruner's explanation is very different. He considers that before the baby is capable of identifying the means that lead to an end, depending on the situation, it is able to display a general activation which shows a diffuse intentionality. Bruner points to babies' preference for certain stimuli and the display of appropriate types of behaviour. Therefore, the development of intentional activity must be understood as the "learning process" in the use of adequate means to reach the desired end. In this sense, Bruner (1984, p.103) evokes the immaturity of the human species, in that babies "cannot act in order to achieve their aims (understand them, if that is what it is about) by means of trial and error behaviour, and lack a sufficient repertoire of routines of innate trials which could guide them in this process of trial and error". Bruner favours the existence of a tutoring process carried out by adults who allow babies to learn how to perform their intentional actions. Adults act as if the child had intentions in his or her mind, as if the child were trying to use the necessary means to perform them, in short, as if the idea of the already finished task were in the child's head, but he or she did not have the capacity for adequate coordination to satisfy his or her intentions and those of the interlocutors. Following Vygotsky, Bruner considers that the evolutionary process has led the human species to handle instruments and symbols; therefore, human behaviour is organised and controlled as much by real intentions as by those attributed to others. "Folk Psychology"—to use his own term—within which children are brought up to participate in culture, reflects such an organisation.

Both points of view gave rise to opposing positions on the genesis of communicative intention. Piaget's view was widely adopted by different authors (Camaioni, Volterra, & Bates, 1976; Harding, 1982; Harding & Golinkoff, 1979; Sugarman, 1978) in order to justify its appearance at the end of the first year of life, when the child is able to use the adult as a means of obtaining an object and, at the same time, to use an object as a means of attracting the attention of the adult. The first type of behaviour is called proto-imperative, and the second one proto-declarative.

In the area of communication, the use of an adult as an agent of a particular action and the use of an object to attract the attention of the adult are considered to be clear signs of the existence of communicative intention, which, as already mentioned, is explained according to one and the same cognitive mechanism. Authors who defend socio-cultural practice and social interaction as privileged mechanisms for explaining the appearance of communicative intention do not question either the moment of its appearance or the type of signs through which it appears. In other words, they accept that, up to the end of the first year of life, the child uses procedures that are clearly directed at influencing the behaviour of others with the aim of either obtaining some benefit, or contemplating reality together. However, the explanation for the appearance of these modes of behaviour is completely different to that presented previously. For Vygotsky (1966, p.42), at first "the pointing gesture is merely an unsuccessful grasping movement". Independent of the child's subjective consciousness when it performs these types of movements, objectively, the whole of its activity signals the object.

It is precisely the objective character of this set of movements that allows the adults around the child to act. Thus, according to Vygotsky (1966, p.43): "the child's unsuccessful grasping movement gives rise to a reaction not from the objects, but from another person. The original meaning to this grasping movement is thus imparted by others". The adults bring the object nearer to the child so that it can reach it, making comments, at the same time, about the wishes of the child to obtain it, etc. In this way, (ibid. p.43) "on the basis of the fact that the child associates the unsuccessful grasping movement with the entire objective situation, does the child himself begin to treat this movement as a pointing gesture" or, in other words, when the child becomes aware that the object is too far away and, for this reason, he or she cannot reach it, the child uses the same gesture with a completely distinct function from the one intended at the beginning. The child stretches out towards the object and, at the same time, alternates his or her glance between the object and the adult. At this moment (ibid. p.43) "from a movement directed toward the object, it becomes a movement directed toward another person, a means of communication: the grasping is transformed into pointing". From then on, the gesture becomes stylised: shorter and simpler and, at the same time, more efficient.

I would like to emphasise two points in this explanation. First, Vygotsky considers that the child's movements to get hold of the object possess, objectively, all the functions involved in the indication and, for this reason can be "comprehended as a pointing by the surroundings of the child" (ibid. p.43). Second, "the pointing gesture first begins to indicate by movement that which is understood by others and only afterwards becomes a pointing gesture for the child himself" (ibid. p.43). Certainly, this is a good example of the Vygotskyan concept of *Zone of Proximal Development*, by means of which he explains the relationships between learning and development. Thus, this explanation, taken up again mainly by Bruner through his concept of format, emphasises the existence of a functional continuity between the child's first acts of behaviour and a series of more or less sophisticated gestures, facial expressions, etc., which have a clear cultural meaning in the context of communication. Therefore, for Vygotsky's followers, pre-linguistic communication is not derived from the construction of cognitive mechanisms throughout sensorimotor development, but from learning how to use a cultural object. In this learning process two aspects turn out to be decisive: first, the objective meaning of many of the child's acts of behaviour in a cultural context and, second, the contingent treatment given by the adult. In this context, Wallon's claim that human beings are genetically social, acquires its full meaning, in that there is no survival independent of others. Thus, from birth on, babies are included in social routines, building up an "intersubjectivity" by adjusting their rudiments of awareness and intentionality to the subjectivity of others. This is made possible by a set of proto-social kinds of behaviour and by socio-cultural practices performed by the adult in which these kinds of behaviour are inscribed.

COMMUNICATIVE INTENTION AND
JOINT ATTENTION

As we have seen, both views coincide, to a great extent, in their description of babies' pre-linguistic types of behaviour, but differ widely in their explanation. Recent empirical research, bringing up new data on pre-linguistic communication, allows us to evaluate the earlier propositions with greater precision.

In the first place, data from observations of chimpanzees and gorillas as well as from studies of autistic children cast doubts on the existence of an association, from the point of view of development, between proto-imperative productions and proto-declarative ones. Gómez (1990) showed that a gorilla, raised in a human environment, is capable of both using a human being as an object to obtain another object and requesting his care-takers to perform an action so that he can obtain some benefit. Gómez distinguishes the two cases as "acts of intentional manipulation" and "acts of intentional communication" and shows that, between them, there is a period of 10 months. This time separation between the instrumental use of the adult and the appearance of a proto-imperative in the strict sense casts doubts on the fact that both types of behaviour can stem from the same cognitive mechanism. Moreover, proto-declarative productions have never been observed in the case of this gorilla. This confirms, according to Gómez, the dissociation of these types of behaviour and makes a new explanation necessary. Similarly, numerous investigations with autistic children, have shown a wide dissociation between proto-imperative and proto-declarative types of behaviour. For example, Baron-Cohen (1989) carried out a study on the proto-imperative and proto-declarative gestures of indication in autistic children and showed that these children have no difficulties in understanding and using the proto-imperative gesture whereas they fail to understand and use the proto-declarative gesture.

Second, some authors (Baron-Cohen, 1989; Camaioni, 1993; Gómez, 1991) have emphasised the existence of functional differences (in addition to structural ones) between proto-imperative and proto-declarative productions, which is manifest in the types of communicative intention: proto-imperatives influence someone's conduct; proto-declaratives influence someone's mental state. Camaioni (1993) distinguishes the two kinds of conduct on the basis that the requirements of object or action ("I want X") modify the state of the world and the requirements of attention ("look at X") influence the internal state of the adult. In her opinion, proto-imperatives require, from the child, a practical understanding of the relationships between action and attention, whereas proto-delaratives presuppose a representational level. Camaioni considers that proto-imperative productions require three skills: to coordinate the orientation towards an object or event with that towards the other person; to perceive human beings as autonomous agents and, at the same time, anticipate the actions that they can perform in relation to certain objects; and to use distal modes of interaction (vocalisations, signalling, etc.) in order to influence the others' behaviour. None of these conditions, nor their combination, evidences the existence of communicative intentions, as they do not involve a representation of others as capable of intentions and of understanding others' intentions. Communicative intention, in the strictest sense of the word, requires a new skill: that of being able to construct a concept of the human being as a person capable of paying selective attention and of possessing independent psychological states such as, for example, showing interest in objects or events. This is precisely the skill that is present in proto-declarative productions.

Because of structural and functional differences between proto-imperative and proto-declarative productions and their dissociation throughout development, these authors deny the cognitive hypothesis derived from Piagetian theses. Instead, they place the origin of communicative intention in the field of joint attention and recognise its first signs in proto-declarative productions.

Most of these studies have been carried out within the theoretical framework that stems from the "theory of mind "model. Baron-Cohen (1994), for example, proposes the existence of a Joint Attention Mechanism (JAM), a modular component of the neurocognitive system, whose function is "to read the mind" of others. The role of this mechanism is to decide whether the subject and other agents are paying attention to the same object or event at the same time. In addition, it is supposed to be innate and to satisfy some of the other conditions proposed by Fodor for the modular organisation of the mind and the brain. Some authors (e.g. Baron-Cohen, 1994) affirm that this mechanism does not exist in autistic children, which implies that in this group of children the "theory of mind" mechanism proposed by Leslie is not activated. In this way, communicative intention would appear to be independent of the instrumental use of the adult in order to obtain an object or perform an action, and its explanation would lie in innate mechanisms that make joint attention towards objects or events possible.

However, as Bronckart (1992) indicates in his proposal for a psychology of pure reason, in order to explain the step from protolanguage to language, it is not necessary to call on an innate theory of mind; rather it would be more productive to study the modalities through which adults guide children in their communicative habits.

Thus Bronckart takes a socio-cultural perspective similar to that of Vygotsky and Bruner, as discussed earlier.

Naturally, this does not mean that babies are "blank pages" on which the environment gradually writes its behavioural repertoire. On the contrary, today we know that a newborn child possesses a repertoire of behaviour that enables it to establish a primary relationship with another human being, to look for it, to initiate it and, at the same time, to regulate the level of social stimulation.

In this sense, the latest contributions to babies' pre-linguistic development do not question Vygotsky's point of view on the appearance and development of communicative intention. For example, one of the arguments used by defenders of the existence of an innate mechanism that makes joint attention possible, lies in its ontogenetic characteristics. Thus, towards 9–12 months of life, children are capable of following an adult's gaze and, at the same time, use proto-declarative gestures; these capacities are preceded, also ontogenetically, by the baby's early ability to search out and sustain the adult's gaze. However, even if they accept that the baby is particularly sensitive to the eyes of a human face, those who see development as the result of the maturation of innate mechanisms forget how adults treat this behaviour.

Right away, adults adjust their behaviour to the innate models of the child and synchronise their movements, gestures, and vocalisations in a sort of "give and take", which Bateson (1971) calls "protoconversation". More specifically, in the area of attention, Fogel (1977) indicates that, during the first three months of life, the baby and the adult are often linked together in affective situations looking at each other in a continuous way. But the baby is unable to sustain the gaze interchange with the mother indefinitely for biological reasons, which force it to turn its face away, while the mother spends nearly the whole time of the interaction looking at the child and performing a series of behavioural actions (facial exaggeration, vocalisations, etc.) which successfully prolong the period of sustained attention. Thus, it is not preposterous to think of adults as the principal agents responsible for the mutual adjustment, in that they constantly try to coordinate their behaviour with that of the child. At around 4 months, the child begins to be interested both in people and objects (Beebe & Stern, 1977). In situations described as "face-to-face" it begins to reject the maternal gaze and direct its own towards its surroundings. It is the period when games begin, first with adults and, later on, with both adults and objects. Between 4 and 6 months, babies like to touch mother's face, eyes, mouth, or hands. Beebe (1982) describes the interaction between the mother and a 4-month-old baby characterised by the childish attitude of "avoiding" the maternal gaze whereas the adult continued to gaze at the child. For nearly 20 fruitless minutes the mother took hold of the baby's hand and made it move backwards and forwards on a horizontal plane. The interaction changed radically and the positive affective levels were restored (continuous and mutual gaze). Beebe indicates that the mother obtained the most positive result when the swinging movement of her child's hand was formed by kinesic and temporarily regular sequences, so much so that, at this age, rhythm and repetition can be considered as involving positive implications between baby and care-takers.

These games begin to diversify the attention of the mother–baby dyad, a necessary condition for the progress of communication. The focus of attention is no longer the mother's eyes, but certain parts of her body and, later on, something external to the dyad. At first, these games are very simple, they are well adapted to the child's capabilities (hiding one's face and then making it reappear, moving the adult's hand in a rhythmical way while singing a song, etc.) and include variations whose goal is to satisfy the baby's interest. These variations are usually made in a predictable way taking the form of "routines". Kaye (1977) considers that this is probably one of the most important aspects of the adult's activity, because of the imbalance created between the participants leading to further negotiations.

As already mentioned, at about 6 months of age, the child reduces the moments of face-to-face contact with the adult: it looks at objects or at the mother, but never looks at the adult when it wants to get hold of an object. I believe that the world of physical objects and the world of people are considered by the child as mutually exclusive, which keeps it from embodying them into the same conscious activity. However, adults do not accept this and, as Vygotsky noticed, almost inevitably help the child to reach the objects, while saying things like "What do you want?", "Do you want X?" etc. Thanks to this behaviour, the child integrates both worlds in a few months, and thus becomes capable of calling for the adult's help in reaching out for an object as well as attracting her attention to an interesting aspect of the physical world. Both types of behaviour probably depend on different mechanisms, but I believe that they are the result of socio-cultural practices in which the behavioural repertoire of the newborn child is inscribed.

Finally, throughout the first six months of life, adults treat the baby's skills in a particular way and attribute a cultural meaning to them. Therefore, it is not surprising that, throughout the third trimester of life, the interchanges that take place between the adult and the child are preceded by visual contact, by means of which both indicate that they share a subject-matter.

Later, as Bruner (1982) demonstrated with his concept of format, the child and the adult maintain situations of joint attention and action, in which the child progresses in the conventionalisation of the procedures to "announce attention", "regulate the deixis", and maintain "presuppositional control". So the child enters the field of linguistic communication.

CONCLUSIONS

In this chapter, I first discussed Piaget's and Vygotsky's theories used for the study of pre-linguistic communication mechanisms, and showed how these positions have brought about research with very different purposes. On the one hand, we have seen that studies stemming from Piaget's model, which presupposes a single cognitive mechanism constructed through elaboration and differentiation of sensorimotor schemes, seem inconsistent with the set of empirical data now available. On the other hand, I have described the arguments of those who, relying on these data, favour the existence of innate mechanisms which permit joint attention and, as a result, communicative intention. However, although to a large extent I accept the criticisms of the neo-Piagetian positions made by these authors, I believe that, beyond the existence of innate types of behaviour used in the area of joint attention, their social and cultural use responds to a learning period guaranteed by the adult through socio-cultural practices which have a clear "instructive" character.

Thus, I have adopted Vygotsky's viewpoint, according to which language is as much an instrument for influencing others' behaviour as it is knowledge about the physical and social world. Therefore, I disagree with Werner and Kaplan's (1963) conception of language as only a tool of knowledge. On the contrary, I think that both functions, influencing others' actions and knowledge, are inseparably linked in language, although corresponding to different cognitive mechanisms. The point is that, for a better understanding of the emergence of these two functions, one must remember that they both come about within social interaction, that is, within cultural meanings adopted by the partners in a communicative situation.

ACKNOWLEDGEMENT

This research has been possible thanks to a grant from the DGICYT of the Ministry of Education and Science.

REFERENCES

Baron-Cohen, S. (1989). Perceptual role-taking and protodeclarative pointing in autism. *British Journal of Developmental Psychology, 7*, 113–27.

Baron-Cohen, S. (1994). How to build a baby that can read minds: Cognitive mechanisms in mindreading. *Cahiers de Psychologie Cognitive, 13*, 1–40.

Bateson, M.C. (1971). The interpersonal context of infant vocalization. *Quarterly Progress Report of the Research Laboratory of Electronics*, MIT, N. 100, 170–176.

Beebe, B. (1982). Micro-timing in mother–infant communication. In M.R. Key (Ed.), *Nonverbal communication today. Current research* (pp.169–195). Berlin: Mouton.

Beebe, B., & Stern, D. (1977). Engagement–disengagement and early object experiences. In N. Freedman & S. Grand (Eds.), *Communicative structures and psychic structures* (pp.35–55). New York: Plenum Press.

Bronckart, J.P. (1992, September). *Théories de l'action, langage, langues naturelles et discours* [Theories of action, language, natural languages and discourse]. Paper presented at the first Conference for Socio-Cultural Research, Madrid.

Bruner, J.S. (1973). Organization of early skilled action. *Child Development, 44*, 1–11.

Bruner, J.S. (1975). From communication to language. A psychological perspective. *Cognition, 3*, 255–287.

Bruner, J.S. (1982) The formats of language acquisition. *American Journal of Semiotics, 1*, 1–16.

Bruner, J.S. (1984). La intención en la estructura de la acción y de la interacción [Intention and the structure of action and interaction]. In J. Linaza (Ed.) *Jerome Bruner. Acción, pensamiento y lenguaje* (pp.101–115) [Jerome Bruner. Action, thinking and language]. Madrid: Alianza.

Camaioni, L. (1993). The development of intentional communication. A re-analysis. In J. Nadel & L. Camaioni (Eds.), *New perspectives in early communication development* (pp.82–96). London: Routledge.

Camaioni, L., Volterra, V., & Bates, E. (1976). *La comunicazione nel primo anno di vita* [Communication in the first year of life]. Torino: Boringhieri.

Fogel, A. (1977). Temporal organization in mother–infant face-to-face interaction. In H.R. Schaffer (Ed.), *Studies in mother–infant interaction* (pp.119–151). London: Academic Press.

Gómez, J.C. (1990). The emergence of intentional communication as a problem-solving strategy in the gorilla. In S.T. Parker & K.R. Gibson (Eds.), *Language and intelligence in monkeys and apes* (pp.333–355). Cambridge: Cambridge University Press.

Gómez, J.C. (1991). Visual behaviour as a window for reading the mind of others in primates. In A. Whiten (Ed.), *Natural theories of mind* (pp.195–207). Oxford: Basil Blackwell.

Harding, C.G. (1982). The development of intention to communicate. *Human Development, 25*, 140–151.

Harding, C.G., & Golinkoff, R.M. (1979). The origins of intentional vocalisations in prelinguistic infants. *Child Development, 50*, 33–40.

Kaye, K. (1977). Toward the origins of dialogue. In H.R. Schaffer (Ed.), *Studies in mother–infant interaction* (pp.89–117). London: Academic Press.

Newson, J. (1974). Towards a theory of infant understanding. *Bulletin of the British Psychological Society, 27,* 251–257.

Newson, J. (1979). The growth of shared understandings between infant and caregiver. In M. Bullowa (Ed.), *The beginning of interpersonal communication* (pp.207–222). Cambridge: Cambridge University Press.

Piaget, J. (1937). *La construction du réel chez l'enfant* [The child's construction of reality]. Neuchâtel: Delachaux et Niestlé.

Sugarman, S. (1978). Some organizational aspects of preverbal communication. In I. Markova (Ed.), *The social context of language* (pp.49–66). New York: Wiley & Sons.

Werner, H., & Kaplan, B. (1963). *Symbol formation.* New York: Wiley & Sons.

Vygotsky, L.S. (1966). Development of the higher mental functions. In A. Leontiev, A. Luria, & A. Smirnov (Eds.), *Psychological research in the USSR, Vol I* (pp.11–45). Moscow: Progress Publishers.

CHAPTER TWELVE

Some impressions of a visit to Soviet psychologists[1]

Jean Piaget *University of Geneva, Switzerland*

After the excellent contact made at the Montreal Congress with Soviet psychologists, particularly with Leontiev and Teplov, four Parisian psychologists (or rather four who are teaching in Paris!) were invited to visit their colleagues and institutions of psychological research in Moscow and Leningrad. These four were Piéron, Fraisse, Zazzo and myself. Besides my personal desire for information, I thought that it was the duty of the President of the International Union of Scientific Psychology to accept gratefully every occasion for scientific liaison. At the last moment Piéron was unfortunately unable to go for reasons of ill health, and we three others spent about ten days together in April, 1955, in Moscow, with two days in Leningrad (notably at Pavlov's famous institute about half an hour's drive out in the country).

Without emphasising the very cordial and truly friendly welcome of our hosts (we were received most charmingly at home, not only in excellent hotels), I shall first mention three general impressions which struck us with increasing force.

The first is the importance enjoyed in Moscow by men (and women) of science, independently of their position in the party. In this connection we were very much impressed to find a certain number of our colleagues in important posts and in full scientific activity; before our trip we had been wondering what their present situation would be.

The second is the diversity of individual opinions on a great number of essential questions, such as, for example, the point of psychology. We were all aware, for instance, before our departure, of the controversy that had opposed Teplov to Leontiev in this matter, but we intended to avoid any indiscreet allusion to it. Now, one day while discussing with those whom we called the "great five" (Leontiev, Teplov, Rubinstein, Luria and Smirnov) the question of the aims of psychology, Teplov declared, turning with a smile to Leontiev, who also was smiling, that he stuck to his position, according to which the states of consciousness (images, intellectual operations, language, etc., in so far as conscious) constituted the most important aspect of these aims. When we asked them whether they believed in animal psychology, all five burst into laughter, replying that they held five different opinions on that point! And nevertheless they made up an excellent team ...

Our third general impression relates to the objectivity and frankness of our colleagues on the questions we submitted to them for discussion. At the end of our stay, for instance, we had a frank discussion of a certain number of questions which remained in our minds, especially concerning the real implications of reflexological explanations in psychology: now, we found not only a full comprehension of our questions, but in addition a critical position more highly nuanced than we would have thought from some of the publications on the subject of these essential problems. We learned *inter alia* that the publications of Ivanov-Smolenski by no means carry authority in Moscow, as was supposed outside the country. A fine example of objectivity was provided to us by Professor F.P. Maiorov at the Pavlov Institute, where we were shown some experiments on the "dynamic stereotypes" of chimpanzees. Be it because of excitement due to our presence or to some quite different cause, two of the three chimpanzees examined in our presence (after about 200 previous daily sessions) failed to react according to expectations. For the first time they pushed a key through the opening of an apparatus until then ignored (as a consequence of their stereotype). Now, instead of cutting short this situation, which many laboratory directors would have found unpleasant, Maiorov kept us there for about two hours so that we could get a complete idea of the phenomenon that had just occurred!

In quite another field as well, I noted the same effort at objectivity shown by my Soviet colleagues at the Moscow Academy of Science, in connection with an epistemological discussion, a brief résumé of which follows. The philosopher Kedrov opened the debate: "For us the object exists before our knowledge of it. Are you of the same opinion?". I replied: "As a psychologist, I think that the subject knows an object only in acting upon it and transforming it somewhat. Thus I do not know what the object is before knowledge of it." Rubinstein then proposed this conciliatory formula: "The object is a part of the world, which could doubtless be divided up into objects in different ways. Do you agree then that the world exists before knowledge?". I replied: "As a psychologist, I think that knowledge supposes an activity of the brain; now the brain is a part of the organism, which is itself a part of the world ... so, I agree." After this followed a little discussion in Russian of which I unfortunately understood only two words: "Piaget" and "idealism". When I asked the connection between these two words, they answered: "Piaget is not an idealist." I do not think our amiable colleagues will be bound forever by this conclusion, but I warmly appreciate this attitude of reciprocity and search for agreement in a field where dissention is much more common.

I come now to some more specific impressions. But here I would need about fifty pages to mention them all, so rich and varied were the research projects that we were shown.

First, I must mention the large number of Moscow psychologists. In my ignorance I had expected to find a lot of physiologists and few psychologists at Moscow. Now, although there are a great many physiologists, the psychologists are no less numerous; those of the University, those of the institutes dependent on the Academy of Sciences, those of the psychological institute connected with the Academy of Pedagogic Sciences (director, Smirnov), those of the Institute of Defectology, etc. I dare not give a number, but in a general closing session where I had the honour of giving a lecture before the Moscow psychologists—and when Fraisse and Zazzo also spoke of their work—a large amphitheatre was filled without the inclusion of any students except a few advanced postgraduates. In connection with the discussion that followed the lecture, I should like to mention that these psychologists read everything that appears abroad, particularly in French and English. I was particularly amazed to find Russian colleagues who had read brief articles whose contents I had partially forgotten. If I may be permitted a critical reflection, the only one that occurred to me in the course of my visit or in analysing some studies like those of Kostiouk on the psychology of number in children—I am under the impression that certain writers quote non-Russians less than they read them.

If we turn now to the experiments or important research that interested us, they are quite innumerable.

In the purely reflexological field, the work of Asratyan on the diverse combinations between the tonic and phasic reflexes made a great impression on us. This research was already presented at the Montreal Congress, but we were struck by the elegance of the experiments showing the difference in reaction of animals according to attitude, and by the lively realisation on the part of this author of the problems still to be resolved in the explanation of the central notions of reflexology (beginning with the notion of excitation!).

In the field of the psychology of intelligence and of thought we saw a large number of research projects on intellectual operations, especially on the solution of problems on the basis of acquired experience, on the assimilation of classroom information (Mentchinskaja), etc.; but I would mention particularly the hypothesis that absolute lack of knowledge does not exist, and that new information is always grafted on previous information.

In connection with intelligence, we know that the Soviet psychologists are supposed to be distrustful of tests and statistics and to prefer direct observation or clinical observation in a natural environment. However, although they do not want "blind tests" or those made haphazardly, they have no objection whatsoever to standardised tests when there is exact verification, and they make use of correlations, etc., when necessary. "What we cannot admit, however," they told us, "is that mathematical treatment can give psychological meaning to facts which do not have such meaning."

In child psychology, great attention is given to the difference in reactions in play context and in other contexts; for instance, visual acuity is not the same in play and in the laboratory, and perceptual constants are better on real objects with motivation than on neutral figures.

The role of language is studied in the classification and perception of colours, in perceptive organisation, in the regulation of motricity (Luria) and the formation of mental images (Chemjakin) in conjunction with the action of motricity. From the point of view of the role of motricity in the constitution of images, an interesting experiment of Mrs. Zemtsova shows that drawings of the blind are much better when their eyes are open than when closed (with electromyographic control), the situation being naturally quite different with those born blind.

In the realm of drawing I could mention numerous research projects, for instance those of Ignatiev on drawing in stages (with carbon papers changed at fixed intervals), to judge the degree of synthesis and the progressive differentiation of the parts in relation to the whole.

A great amount of energy is expended at the Institute of Defectology on the study of oligophrenia, notably by means of the EEG techniques. True oligophrenes seem to have a different rhythm from those with organic brain defects from the very first month. In this connection, we were impressed by the excellence of the electric equipment of the laboratories, with apparatus of local manufacture.

I could add indefinitely to this list. From the point of view of the practical and immediate conclusions to be drawn from our visit, I would like to insist on two points. First, we made an effort to persuade our Soviet colleagues to admit how useful it would be for the psychologists of the whole world if their reviews, scientific journals and monographs contained summaries or résumés in English, French or German, so that we could see at a glance the subject discussed, and then make use of translators and more extensive analyses in the case of important results. Second, I reminded those of our colleagues who were at Montreal, and our new friends whom we met in the course of our visit, how anxious the International Union of Scientific Psychology is to be universal; we hope with all our heart that the contacts initiated at the last international congress of psychology, and renewed in such an encouraging manner in the course of visits like ours, would result in permanent relationship and fruitful exchanges for the greater good of psychology.

NOTE

1. Jean Piaget (1956). "Quelques impressions d'une visite aux psychologues soviétiques", published in *Bulletin International des Sciences Humaines*, Vol. VIII, No. 2, pp.393–397. English version published in *American Psychologist*, 1956, Vol. 11, pp.343–345. © UNESCO, 1956. Reprinted by kind permission of UNESCO.

Author index

Subject index